ALLAH vs JESUS

ALLAH vs JESUS

which is the true God?

by Moses Ilyas

Dayspring Publisher, LLC

ALLAH vs JESUS: which is the true God?

by Moses Ilyas

Published by: Dayspring Publisher, LLC

ISBN print ed. 978-0-9779996-0-6

Muslims are mentally enslaved by fear of each other, and in countries where Islam rules they are physically enslaved also, and everywhere they are taught to love being enslaved, and to despise freedom of religion, freedom of assembly, and freedom of speech. Dedicated Muslims who truly understand and believe the Quran and Hadiths consider freedom a very bad thing. But, in truth, freedom is not bad, but exceedingly good. Without freedom life is very grievous and painful. This book invites Muslims to the joy of freedom in Christ. On Oct. 16, 2009, angry Muslims carrying anti-freedom signs gathered outside Dutch politician Geert Wilder's press conference in central London to protest his being allowed into the United Kingdom. They even threatened Wilder's life because he said he loves Muslims but hates Islam, and made a film exposing the evil intentions of Islam. [To see a video of that event go to: http://www.youtube.com/watch?v=det7TUsLy8U]

Contents

Figure 1: *Ka'abah surrounded by Masjid al-Haram (also called The Grand Mosque) in Mecca, Saudi Arabia,*
The Masjid al-Haram is the largest mosque in the world, and is said to be able to hold four million people!
[Photo ©Mardetanha; licensed under the Creative Commons Attribution-Share Alike 3.0 Unported license.
`http://en.wikipedia.org/wiki/File:Masjidalharam.JPG]`

Chapter 1

An Invitation

[Note: All **boldface** emphasis found in Bible or Quran verses or other sources I quote is my own emphasis unless otherwise noted.]

This book is an invitation:

⇨ To non-Muslims to learn the truth about Islam and Muhammad.

⇨ To Muslims to learn the truth about Jesus Christ—as opposed to what Muslim teachers claim.

1.1 Does truth matter?

The question of the hour is: does the truth matter to you? Consider carefully this easy to understand fact from the Bible: "...**no lie is of the truth**" (1 John 2:21). A religion that lies to achieve its goals is not of the truth. In an effort to convert weak Christians to Islam, Muslim teachers lie about what the Bible teaches concerning Jesus Christ and many other important issues. If you are a Muslim, and the truth matters to you, then you will find life-changing facts in this book.

All religions are forced to deal with Jesus— He cannot be ignored.

> Matthew 16:13 When **Jesus** came into the coasts of Caesarea Philippi, he asked his disciples, saying, **Whom do men say that I the Son of man am?** 14 And they said, Some say that thou art John the Baptist: some, Elias; and others, Jeremias, or one of the prophets. 15 He saith unto them, **But whom say ye that I am**? 16 And Simon Peter answered and said, **Thou art the Christ, the Son of the living God.** 17 And Jesus answered and said unto him, Blessed art thou, Simon Barjona: for flesh and blood hath not revealed it unto thee, but **my Father** which is in heaven.

Everyone **will** make a decision concerning Jesus, and that decision will determine whether he or she spends eternity in Heaven or Hell. **You** will make a decision concerning Jesus, and that decision will determine whether **you** spend eternity in Heaven or Hell.

1.2 Are you afraid?

The wise Muslim will make an informed decision, rather than a foolish decision based on fear of Muslim friends or relatives. The wise Christian will also not fear Muslims.

> Revelation 21:8 But the **fearful**, and unbelieving, and the abominable, and murderers, and whoremongers, and sorcerers, and idolaters, and all liars, **shall have their part in the lake which burneth with fire and brimstone: which is the second death.**

The word "fearful" in the above verse means cowardly. It refers to the fear of man. Most Muslims live in constant fear of other Muslims. They are literally afraid to think. They can neither think nor make decisions on their own, and cannot resist peer pressure. They care more about what other Muslims think, then they do about what God thinks. The Bible clearly declares such fear to be a grave sin, which—unless repented of—will result in that fearful person spending eternity in Hell with the most wicked of sinners for his or her punishment

> Proverbs 29:25 The **fear of man** bringeth a snare: **but whoso putteth his trust in the LORD shall be safe**.
>
> Matthew 10:28 And **fear not** them which kill the body, but are not able to kill the soul: **but rather fear him which is able to destroy both soul and body in hell**.

You are eventually going to die physically no matter what. It is far better to believe in Christ, and thus risk being murdered by Muslims—in which case you will get to Heaven quicker—, than to reject Christ to prevent being murdered by Muslims, and thus eventually ending up in the Lake of Fire to be tormented forever in the flames.

1.3   This book's purpose

One purpose of this book is to prove that the Jesus Christ of Islam, called Isa Almasih, is not the true Jesus. The Bible warns us of false prophets preaching "another" Jesus, "another" spirit, and "another" gospel by which these false preachers would corrupt people's minds.

> 2 Cor. 11:2 For I am jealous over you with godly jealousy: for I have espoused you to one husband, that I may present you as a chaste virgin to Christ. 3 But I fear, lest by any means, as the serpent beguiled Eve through his subtilty, **so your minds should be corrupted** from the simplicity that is in Christ. 4 For if he that

cometh preacheth **another Jesus**, whom we have not preached, or if ye receive **another spirit**, which ye have not received, or **another gospel**, which ye have not accepted, ye might well bear with him.

Gal. 1:8 But though we, or an angel from heaven, preach **any other gospel** unto you than that which we have preached unto you, **let him be accursed**. 9 As we said before, so say I now again, If any man preach **any other gospel** unto you than that ye have received, **let him be accursed.**

Muhammad and all the Muslim teachers teaching Muhammad's doctrines are under the curse just mentioned. As will be clearly shown in this book, Islam has a false Jesus, a false spirit, and a false gospel, and it has indeed corrupted millions of people's minds so that they are unable to receive the "simplicity" that is in the true Christ.

This book is a tool you can give to your Muslim friends so that they can see for themselves that the Jesus (Isa) of Islam is not the true Jesus. In fact the Jesus of Islam never existed except in the vain imagination of Muhammad or whoever actually authored the Quran.[1]

This book is very useful for Christians who are desiring to learn how to minister to Muslims.

Most of all, this book is for the sincere Muslim who is genuinely seeking the truth. He or she will find this book to be very enlightening. In contrast to Muhammad, Jesus did not use the sword to force people to follow him against their will, but by love and mercy persuaded people to follow him with their whole heart. There is no death threat for leaving Christianity. But no true believer ever wants to leave.

---

[1]For an in-depth analysis of who actually authored the Quran read: http://www.islam-watch.org/AbulKasem/WhoAuthoredQuran/who_authored_the_quran3.htm

Chapter 2

Islam 101

It is needful to understand some of the basic terms and history of Islam in order to be able to understand the chapters following this one.

2.1 Definition of Islam

The word "Islam" means submission. Islam is a political system which uses religion to attempt to force the whole world to submit to a system of religious law set forth in the Quran and in the teachings and example of Muhammad. This law is called "shariah." Shariah law covers all aspects of life, including: crime, politics, economics, sexuality, hygiene, diet, prayer, and fasting. A person who submits is called a Muslim. In theory the submission is to Allah, but in practice the submission is to Muslim leaders.

The www.freedomhouse.org website lists Saudi Arabia, along with 9 other Muslim countries, among the 20 most repressive (not free) countries in the world. Concerning Saudi Arabia—the center of Islam—, they point out that

> Religious freedom does not exist in Saudi Arabia. All Saudis are required by law to be Muslims, and the government prohibits the public practice of any religions other than Islam.... Women are not treated as equal members of society, and many laws discriminate

> against them. They may not legally drive cars, their use of public facilities is restricted when men are present, and they cannot travel within or outside of the country without a male relative. Daughters generally receive half the inheritance awarded to their brothers, and the court testimony of one man is equal to that of two women.[1]

Since Islam seeks to rule the whole world, **a Quran-believing Muslim cannot in good conscience support any form of government except Islam. Therefore, dedicated Muslims living in countries not yet ruled by shariah law are seditious and subversive.** The so-called "Muslim Spring" is a good example of this sedition. Even though the leaders of those Middle Eastern countries where the "Muslim Spring" is happening are all Muslims themselves, that isn't enough for dedicated Muslims—who demand shariah law. So, they are traitors to their own Muslim-led governments. For the same reason, the truly dedicated Muslims in the USA, who know the Quran well, are also treasonous.

> "The Department of Defense considers the U.S. homeland the most dangerous place for a G.I. outside of foreign war zones — and the top threat they face here is from violent Islamist

---

[1]www.freedomhouse.org/uploads/special_report/101.pdf

Figure 2.1: *The duty of every Muslim is to fight non-Muslims until Islam rules over the whole world. The signs above were held by angry Muslims protesting Dutch politician Geert Wilders being allowed into the United Kingdom to promote a film exposing Islam's plan to dominate the world. Their protest proved him right! Can they make their intentions any clearer than this? [Another sign read, "SHARIAH IS INEVITABLE— ISLAM WILL CONQUER EUROPE." See:* `http://talcohen.photoshelter.com/gallery-image/161009-Geert-Wilders-in-London/G0000qEbv4JG39qU/I0000X3laav0Y9ps` *And you can watch a video of Sheik Ali Al-Faqir, former Jordanian Minister of Religious Endowment, revealing that Islamic leaders intend for Islam to conquer the USA and the whole world also:* `http://www.youtube.com/watch?v=aYDfACr-y4s]`

extremists," Rep. Peter T. King, chairman of the House Homeland Security Committee, said during a special joint House-Senate hearing.

Military officials testified about the **home-grown** terrorist threat at U.S. military bases in the wake of several attacks, including the November 2009 shooting rampage at Fort Hood, Texas. Army Maj. Nidal Malik Hasan, 41, has been charged in the killing of 13 people and wounding of 29 others in the worst shootings ever to take place on an American military base.

"The Fort Hood attack was not an anomaly," said Mr. King, New York Republican. "It was part of al Qaeda's two-decade success at infiltrating the U.S. military for terrorism — an effort that is increasing in scope and threat."

The Congressional Research Service has identified 54 **homegrown** terrorism plots and attacks since Sept. 11, 2001. Of those, 33 were directed against the U.S. military, said Sen. Joe Lieberman, chairman of the Senate Governmental Affairs and Homeland Security Committee.[2]

Note the word "homegrown" in the quotation above. That means these were terrorism plots and attacks by USA citizens. Paul N. Stockton, assistant secretary of defense for homeland defense, was "asked repeatedly by Rep. Daniel E. Lungren, California Republican, about his refusal to use the word 'Islamic' or 'Islamist' when describing al Qaeda." His response was,

> Sir, with great respect, I don't believe it's helpful to frame our adversary as 'Islamic' with any set of qualifiers that we might add, because we are not at war with Islam.[3]

Perhaps the USA is not at war with Islam, but Islam is at war with the USA. The USA not facing that fact makes her look very foolish in the eyes of Muslims, and also places her in a very weak position. Know your enemy is one of the major rules of war. If you don't even know who your enemy is, and much less understand him, you are very likely to be defeated by him.

2.2   A brief history of Islam

When first trying to study the history of Islam, it is easy to get so involved with details that you miss the most important events. It is much easier to understand the details once

[2]`http://www.washingtontimes.com/news/2011/dec/7/terrorists-said-to-be-infiltrating-military/`
[3]Ibid.

Figure 2.2: *US Major Nidal Malik Hasan, who murdered 13 US soldiers and wounded 29 others is a US citizen and a devote Muslim. He is also obviously a traitor.*

the order of major events are known. We will divide the history of Islam into two sections. First, from the beginning of Islam until Muhammad's death. Then, from Muhammad's death to the present.

It is important to realize that the Quran sets Muhammad as the pattern of conduct for Muslims.

> YUSUFALI surah 33:21: Ye have indeed in the Messenger of Allah a beautiful pattern (of conduct) for any one whose hope is in Allah and the Final Day, and who engages much in the Praise of Allah.

Because of this verse, most Muslims believe that if Muhammad did something it cannot possibly be sin. Therein lies the extreme danger of Islam.

2.2.1 During Muhammad's life

Islamic history during Muhammad's life can be divided into three time periods: (1) its beginning and early years in the city of Mecca; (2) its rapid growth in the city of Medina; and (3) its return to Mecca and the waging of all out offensive war to force people into submission to Allah and Muhammad.

2.2.1.1 Beginning in Mecca

Muhammad was born in 570 A.D. In 610 A.D. he claimed that while meditating in a cave on Mt. Hira near Mecca, the angel Gabriel appeared and he was given and recited the first surah of the Quran, and began to teach his new religion. He and his new religion were not well received by the leaders of Mecca, who rightly viewed him as a threat. He and his followers were mocked and persecuted. As they were vastly outnumbered, during this period Muhammad issued surahs to his followers to be tolerant and not to retaliate.

2.2.1.2 Hijra (migration) to Medina

In 622 A.D. Muhammad accepted an invitation to go to the the city of Medina, approximately 300 miles to the north of Mecca, to resolve conflicts between opposing communities there. He soon became the head of Medina, and in that position of power rapidly began to gain converts to Islam. In 624 A.D. Muslims began robbing Meccan camel caravans. In response, the Meccans sent an army of 950 men against the Muslims, but were defeated by an army of only 324 Muslims at the Battle of Badr. Later that same year the Meccans routed the Muslims at the Battle of Uhud. In 627 A.D., at the Battle of Ahjab, the Meccans attacked the city of Medina, but the Muslims repelled the Meccans. In 628 A.D. Muhammad signed the Treaty of Hudaibiyah with the Meccans, promising not to wage war against them for 10 years, in exchange for being allowed to make the pilgrimage to the Ka'abah[4] in Mecca the next year.

In addition to robbing camel caravans, during this period Muhammad also raided neighboring towns and villages, killing all the men who would not either convert to Islam, or else

---

[4]Ka'abah is also spelled Kaabah, or Kaaba by various authors.

pay him a tax, taking all their wealth as booty, and taking their wives and children as slaves.

> Abu Said al-Khudri said: "The apostle of Allah sent a military expedition to Awtas on the occasion of the battle of Hunain. They met their enemy and fought with them. They defeated them and took them captives. Some of the Companions of the apostle of Allah were reluctant to have intercourse with the female captives in the presence of their husbands who were unbelievers. So Allah, the Exalted, sent down the Quranic verse [Sura 4:24], "And all married women (are forbidden) unto you save those (captives) whom your right hands possess". That is to say, they are lawful for them when they complete their waiting period."[5]

Note that Allah supposedly sent down the above Quranic verse allowing Muslim men to rape married women captured in war whose husbands were still alive—and with no thought whatsoever of marrying them first or ever! How can such a god as that be called righteous?

In 629 A.D. Muhammed's army successfully attacked Khaibar, a fortified district where Jews lived. After the battle, Muhammed ordered that the treasurer of Khaibar, Kinana al-Rabi, be tortured to force him to reveal where the treasure was stored, after which he was beheaded. Muhammed then took Kinana al-Rabi's beautiful 17 year old wife, Safiyya, whose father and many of her people had also just been murdered by Muhammed's men, and immediately forced her into a sham marriage, without even waiting for her to observe the four months plus ten days waiting period required of widows by Surah 2:234-235 of the Quran. Any sane person will recognize that this was pure and simple rape by Muhammad himself.[6]

---

[5]http://www.muslimhope.com/RightHand.htm

[6]For full documentation of this, read: http://www.answering-islam.org/Muhammad/Inconsistent/idda_safiyyah.html

In volume 8, part 11, p. 196 of his book *"The Sweetened" Al Mohalla*, Muslim scholar Ibn Hazm wrote:

> It was truly related to us that Muhammad used to force the Arab pagans to embrace the faith. He used to give them the option either to accept Islam or death. That is forcing people to accept Islam.

Figure 2.3: *Spread of Islam by forced conversion with the sword in the days of Muhammad.*

2.2.1.3 Return to Mecca

In 629 A.D. Muhammad broke the Treaty of Hudaibiyah,[7] and returned to Mecca with an army of 10,000 men. Seeing they were vastly outnumbered, the Meccans submitted to Islam out of fear for their lives. Muhammad then supposedly destroyed the idols in the Ka'abah. However, it is certain that he didn't destroy the Black Stone, and he later

---

[7]To learn more about this treaty, read: http://answering-islam.org/Silas/hudaybiyya.htm

knelt down and kissed it. He then returned to Medina. For the rest of his life he spread Islam with the sword and terror. In 632 A.D. Muhammad died in Medina at the age of 63 as a result of being poisoned by a Jewish woman whose father, uncle, and brother had been killed by Muhammad.

2.2.2 After Muhammad's death

The period immediately after Muhammad's death was extremely bloody, as his successor used extreme cruelty to keep Islam from immediately dying.

2.2.2.1 The first caliph—Abu Bakr

With Muhammad dead, someone had to become the leader of Islam. Some Muslims wanted Ali son of Abu Talib, Muhammad's cousin and son-in-law, to be the caliph (leader of the Muslim nation, who must be an Arab of the Quraish tribe), but a larger number wanted Abu Bahr, the father of Muhammad's child bride, Aisha. So, Abu Bakr became the first caliph.[8] Later, Ali became the fourth caliph. However, this popularity contest immediately after the death of Muhammad eventually resulted in a major split in Islam, with the followers of Ali being called Shiites, and the followers of Abu Bakr being called Sunnis.

2.2.2.1.1 Mass murder of apostates.
After Muhammad died, multiplied thousands of people whom Muhammad had forced into Islam were greatly relieved, and immediately left Islam. Abu Bakr waged the "Wars of Apostasy" against them, killing tens of thousands of people who refused to return to Islam. Abu Bakr said,

> Call them to re-embrace Islam; **if they refuse, do not spare any one of them. Burn them**

> **with fire and kill them with force and take the women and children as prisoners of war**. (Chronicles of the Tabari (part 2, pp. 258, 272)[9]

Dr. Abu Zayd Shalabi, professor of Islamic civilization at the College of Arabic Language wrote in his book The khulafa' al-Rashidun, on pages 41-60:

> Abu Bakr sent eleven Muslim generals against eleven cities to fight the apostates. Many were **forced** to re-embrace Islam. Among those countries were Bahrin which was invaded by al-'Ala' Ibn al-Hadrami, and Yemen which was attacked by Suwayd Ibn Maqrin. Kalid Ibn al-Walid went to fight against Tulayha, the tribe of Bany Asad and its neighboring Arab tribes.... **The victories gained by Muslims in the wars of apostasy had one very significant result: These victories deterred anyone who intended to apostatize from Islam.**[10]

2.2.2.1.2 The penalty for leaving Islam.
Indeed, the Quran demanded—and still demands—that Muslims who leave Islam must be killed.

> YUSUFALI surah 4:89: They but wish that ye should **reject Faith, as they do**, and thus be on the same footing (as they): But take not friends from their ranks until they flee in the way of Allah (From what is forbidden). **But if they turn renegades, seize them and slay them wherever ye find them**; and (in any case) take no friends or helpers from their ranks;-

The fact to recognize is that it is easy to get into Islam, but very difficult to get out. **Important question: if Islam is so great, then why did so many people want to leave Islam the moment they thought they safely could?**

---

[8]A caliph is the head of a caliphate, which is an ummah (Islamic community) ruled by shariah law.

[9]http://www.answering-islam.org/ BehindVeil/btv1.html

[10]Ibid.

2.2.2.2 Rapid expansion of Islam under the caliphs' direction

What is the most amazing about this period is how far Islam expanded in its first 128 years, and that the Muslim armies met so little resistance. So widespread was corruption in the Catholic areas being attacked that the political leaders would conspire with the invading Muslim armies against their local political opponents, thus betraying their own cities or countries into Muslim hands to achieve their personal agendas—similar to what is happening in the West today.

Muslim armies would slaughter everyone in a town that they thought might oppose them, then return home with the town's wealth and the women and children as booty. The children became slaves, and the women became sex-slaves.

This barbaric behavior continued up to and through the Crusades, and in fact has never completely stopped.

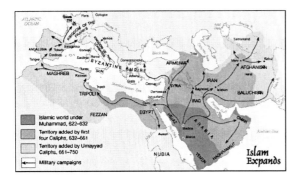

Figure 2.4: *The vast spread of Islam with the sword in its first 128 years.*

2.2.2.3 Dhimmitude

Dhimmitude is the state of subjection and humiliation imposed upon non-Muslims living under Islamic rule. If when the Muslim armies approach a Jewish or Christian town the inhabitants decide not to fight, they are given a choice of becoming Muslims with full rights under Islamic rule, or to become *dhimmi*, which means "protected people." They are "protected" **from Muslim violence** provided they pay the *jizya* (protection tax). *Dhimmi* permanently dwelling under Muslim rule are also called *Zimmis*. If later the *Zimmis* are unable to pay the *jizya* tax, they are made slaves. This law was given in the Quran, and still applies today.

> YUSUFALI 9:29: Fight those who believe not in Allah nor the Last Day, nor hold that forbidden which hath been forbidden by Allah and His Messenger, nor acknowledge the religion of Truth, (even if they are) of the People of the Book, **until they pay the Jizya with willing submission, and feel themselves subdued.**

If Muslim's gain control of Europe and America, what treatment should Christians and Jews (called "People of the Book" in the above verse) expect from them beside having to pay the protection tax? Samuel Shahid sums it up well:

> According to Muslim jurists, the following legal ordinances must be enforced on Zimmis (Christians and Jews alike) who reside among Muslims:
>
> ⇨ Zimmis are not allowed to build new churches, temples, or synagogues. They are allowed to renovate old churches or houses of worship provided they do not allow to add any new construction. "Old churches" are those which existed prior to Islamic conquests and are included in a peace accord by Muslims. Construction of any church, temple, or synagogue in the Arab Peninsula (Saudi Arabia) is prohibited. It is the land of the Prophet and only Islam should prevail there. Yet, Muslims, if they wish, are permitted to demolish all non-Muslim houses of worship in any land they conquer.
>
> ⇨ Zimmis are not allowed to pray or read their sacred books out loud at home or in churches, lest Muslims hear their prayers.

⇨ Zimmis are not allowed to print their religious books or sell them in public places and markets. They are allowed to publish and sell them among their own people, in their churches and temples.

⇨ Zimmis are not allowed to install the cross on their houses or churches since it is a symbol of infidelity.

⇨ Zimmis are not permitted to broadcast or display their ceremonial religious rituals on radio or television or to use the media or to publish any picture of their religious ceremonies in newspaper and magazines.

⇨ Zimmis are not allowed to congregate in the streets during their religious festivals; rather, each must quietly make his way to his church or temple.

⇨ Zimmis are not allowed to join the army unless there is indispensable need for them in which case they are not allowed to assume leadership positions but are considered mercenaries.[11]

Such humiliating treatment as this is what Muslims mean when they say Islam is "tolerant" of other religions, and "protects" them.

2.2.2.4   The Golden Ages of Islam

Muslim writers make big boasts about the Golden Ages of Islam, but historian Arbulan makes an important observation concerning these so-called Golden Ages:

One thing about the historical record is noteworthy; the various golden ages of Islamic civilization always occur early in the first few centuries in which a new territory is occupied. Wherever the various Muslim vanguards invaded, the vast majority of the population was non-Muslim. It would take many years for this population to be converted and assimilated. These non-Muslims or recent converts are the

ones who carried on the work which many historians are prone to attribute to "Islamic" civilization. Thus, a distinction must be drawn between the so-called high Islamic civilization and the religion of Islam. Eventually as the process of Islamization proceeds the non-Islamic component of the population becomes a small minority and stagnation sets in. This process is evident in the first centuries of the Arab conquests where the process of Arabization and conversion to Islam took a few centuries to complete; this was the "Arab" golden age, a product of unconverted or recently converted Christians, Jews and Zoroastrians. In Spain the golden age lasted longer, perhaps because the process of Islamization was never as complete in Moorish Spain as in the Arab East.

It is remarkable how closely this pattern was repeated in the subsequent expansions of Islam as a consequence of the Turkish and Mogul conquests. The initial splendors of the Seljuk and Ottoman empires were the result of unconverted or recently converted subjects. When the Islamization of the newly conquered territories was complete intellectual stagnation once again set in. Similarly, an initial flowering as an extension of the ancient Hindu culture followed the Mogul conquest of India.[12]

The sad fact is that even in the Muslim lands which have been unbelievably enriched by oil money the Muslims are several hundred years behind the West in technological achievements. Islam destroys people's ability to think rationally, and destroys incentive.

2.2.2.5   The Crusades (1095-1291)

Muslims conquered Jerusalem in 638, but allowed Christian pilgrims into the city until 1071 when the Muslim Seljuk Turks conquered Jerusalem from the Egyptian Fatimid Muslims. The Turk Muslims were more hostile to Christian pilgrims, and would not let

[11]http://answering-islam.org/ NonMuslims/rights.htm

[12]http://islamicexpansionanddecline. blogspot.com/2007/04/chapter-11-parasitic-civilization.html

9

them into the city. The Crusades were a series of European Catholic military campaigns against Muslims in response to the pope's pleas to re-capture the Holy Land from Islamic oppression. The behavior of the Crusaders was bad toward Muslims just as it was bad toward other Christian groups and Jews. However, it was no worse than the Muslims had behaved toward Christians. It is important to remember that it was merely the retaking of lands viciously stolen from the West by Muslims. These were lands Muslims had no right to conquer in the first place, and the suffering Muslims endured from the Crusaders was nothing compared to what the people of the West had endured from Muslims. Had the Muslims not stolen these lands the Crusades would not have happened. If the Muslims had just allowed Christians into the Holy Land the Crusades probably wouldn't have happened even though Muslims controlled Jerusalem. The Muslims brought the crusades on themselves by their own cruelty.

Furthermore, the Crusades failed to stop vicious Muslim aggression. For the next four centuries, Muslim armies kept advancing, conquering, murdering, plundering, raping, and taking slaves. To the Muslim mind this is righteous behavior, but when their victims retaliate Muslims become whiny babies and complain of the unfair and wicked treatment.

2.2.2.6   The decline of Islam

The historian Arbulan lists the following reasons for the decline of Islam:

⇨ The increasingly repressive political despotism sapped the energy and destroyed the initiative of both Muslims and dhimmis.

⇨ The slave mentality inherent in Muslim theology became more ingrained.

⇨ The fatalism of Islam eventually undermined intellectual curiosity.

⇨ The continuing dependence on vast numbers of slaves destroyed the incentive for invention and innovation.

⇨ The Muslim system of sexual slavery working at the highest levels of the governing class created a chronic condition of harem intrigue which weakened the administration of the state.[13]

To Arbulan's list I will add:

⇨ As Islam expanded further and further away from its home base, communication became difficult and fragmented leadership.

⇨ The Muslims' inclination to fight with one another over even minor details divided and weakened them.

⇨ In an effort to curb violence, heads of states with large Muslim populations began appointing leaders in mosques, choosing only preachers who would agree not to teach the jihad verses in the Quran.

2.2.2.7   The rise again of Islam

Islam has risen again in its power to prey on others due to several factors:

⇨ **The invention of the automobile in the West, and the discovery of oil on Arab lands.** Selling oil to fuel automobiles has literally put trillions of dollars into the hands of Muslims to use to promote and spread Islam. By refusing to develop oil fields at home, and by refusing to use atomic energy, corrupt Western politicians have betrayed their countries into the hands of Islam. Is is hard to believe that they did not accept huge bribes to do this.

---

[13]http://islamicexpansionanddecline.
blogspot.com/

⇨ **The use of birth control by Christians around the world (especially by Americans and Europeans), but far less so by Muslims.**[14] The harsh fact is that people cannot vote if they aren't born, and if there are not enough voters on your side you lose elections and power. Also, soldiers cannot protect you if they aren't born. And without soldiers wars are lost. Birth control is materialism in its purest, most destructive form.

⇨ **The revival of true jihadist Islam due to the writings of Egyptian Muslim scholars.** Due to the writings of Muslim scholars such as Hasan al-Banna, founder of the Muslim Brothehood, many Muslims have returned to the true teachings of the Quran. **Said Hasan al-Banna:** "[Islamic scholars] agree unanimously that jihad is a communal defensive obligation imposed upon the Islamic ummah in order to broadcast the summons (to embrace Islam), and that it is an individual obligation to repulse the attack of unbelievers upon it.... It has become an individual obligation, which there is no evading, on every Muslim to prepare his equipment, to make up his mind to engage in jihad, and to get ready for it until the opportunity is ripe and God decrees a matter which is sure to be accomplished."[15]

⇨ **The decline of the West due to rejection of God and Bible-based morality.** This is easily seen by the sensual dress, use of alcohol and drugs, open sexual

depravity, self-centeredness, and brasen atheism of many Westerners. Sadly, Hollywood movies have shaped modern Western culture far more than has Christianity.

⇨ **The betrayal of the USA and European countries by left wing politicians.** Communists and humanists have conspired with Muslims to destroy the Judeo-Christian culture which they view as the main obstacle to them establishing a one-world atheist government.

⇨ **The encouragement that the Al-Qaeda attack on the World Trade Center gave to Muslim jihadists worldwide.** And then, after such a huge loss of life, the US president at the time calls Islam a "peaceful religion," and then the American people voted into office a pro-Islam president. Muslims worldwide now think Americans are too stupid and foolish to defend themselves, and they are coming in for the kill.

2.2.2.8 Islam today

American Thinker published an article titled "Islam's Global War against Christianity" which correctly describes what Islam is doing to Christians today.

> From Nigeria to Indonesia, Christians are under siege in virtually every single country in the Muslim world, the victims of countless acts of discrimination, depredation, brutality, and murder that are so widespread and systematic that it can rightfully be called the new Holocaust. This time, however, the perpetrators of this Holocaust aren't wearing swastikas, but kufi skull caps and hijabs.
>
> Some of the oldest Christian communities in the world are subject to relentless attack and teeter on the brink of extinction at the hands of the "Religion of Peace": Palestinian Christians in Gaza and the West Bank; Assyrian, Syriac

---

[14] According to data from the World Bank, the fertility rate in the USA is presently 2.05, which is below the replacement rate of 2.1, yet the U.S. population growth is among the highest of industrialized countries due to a high rate of immigration—including many immigrants who are Muslims.

[15] http://en.wikipedia.org/wiki/Hassan_al-Banna

and Chaldean Christians in Iraq; Coptic Christians in Egypt; Evangelical and Orthodox Christians in Eastern Ethiopia and Eritrea; Armenian Orthodox Christians in Turkey; and Maronite Christians in Lebanon....

The global war on Christianity by Islam is so massive in size and scope that it is virtually impossible to describe without trivializing it. Inspired by Muslim Brotherhood ideology and fueled by billions of Wahhabi petrodollars, the religious cleansing of Christians from the Muslim world is continuing at a break-neck pace.

I personally have had Muslims enter my home, and try to jerk the Bible out of my hands. They have scraped my car with knives, so that it had to be repainted. They have thrown vegetables at me, and threatened to murder me unless I quit telling others about Christ. Muslim soldiers entered the home of a friend of mine, and ushered him at gunpoint to a Muslim judge, where he was forced to sign a letter stating that he would cease having Christian worship services in his home. I have numerous friends who have had family members murdered by Muslims in surprise jihad attacks on their villages.

Muslim violence against the Jews is in the news every day. This news is impossible to miss unless a person is blind and deaf. Just today there was the following news:

Iran is warning Israel that its citizens should flee the Middle East or face annihilation.

The chief commander of Iran's Basiji forces, Brig. Gen. Mohammad-Reza Naghdi, recently stated that Iran has no option but to destroy Israel. Ratcheting up the war of words, Naghdi is now threatening Israelis in the "occupied lands" that they are surrounded by mujahedeen of Islam bent on their destruction.

"I quote our supreme leader, Imam Khamenei, who clearly stated during the recent gathering of the leadership's elite that Zionists are now encircled by those who are willing to wage jihad for Islam, and that those concerned for their safety and well-being should quickly go back to the countries they left behind," Naghdi told

the Fars News agency, the media outlet for the Revolutionary Guards.[16]

In light of all this evidence, only a fool would believe that Islam is a religion of peace.

2.2.2.9   The future of Islam

Anyone who has lived among Muslims and has studied the history of Islam knows that jihad terrorists are not going to stop attacking until either they win or they are somehow persuaded that the Quran is not true. There are too many of them to defeat by conventional warfare, so the only choices America has are:

1. Encourage and protect Christian missionaries so that they can evangelize Muslim nations.

2. Submit to Islam.

3. Use nuclear weapons to annihilate as many Muslims as possible.

Choice number two is not an option for anyone concerned about the truth. As I will prove in this book, Islam is a political system based on lying, deception, and the abolition of all freedom. No true Christian would ever submit to it; it would be better to die resisting it. So, that leaves only two choices: (1) encourage and protect Christian missionaries so that they can evangelize Muslim nations; or (2) use nuclear weapons to annihilate as many Muslims as possible. Which will it be?

Note carefully: I advocate choice number one: encourage and protect Christian missionaries so that they can evangelize Muslim nations. I want to see Muslims repent of their false religion, and believe in Christ, so that they will go to Heaven. I don't want to see them go to Hell, which is where they are headed in their present unbelief. The

---

[16]http://www.wnd.com/?pageId=333941# ixzz1VDVP30Ts

present war against Islamic terrorism is a war of clashing ideas. True Muslims get their idea of terrorism from their Quran. They are going to continue to use terrorism as long as they believe the Quran is true. They will not be persuaded otherwise if Christians are denied freedom of speech to witness to them. If our own government is going to continue to prevent Christian soldiers from witnessing to Muslims in Afghanistan and Iraq, then the USA is doomed to lose those two wars. Bullets don't win wars—ideas do.

By denying freedom of speech and freedom of religion to our own soldiers so that they cannot witness to Muslims, and by sending monetary and military aid to countries which deny freedom of speech and freedom of religion to Christians, our government has us on a road to certain destruction and defeat. If we allow this to continue, then eventually we are going to find ourshelves being forced to either submit to Islam, or else use nuclear weapons to keep from being destroyed by Muslim jihad armies which we ourselves equipted and funded.

There is a time to use the military. When Muslims are using violence to deprive us of the vital freedoms of speech, assembly, and religion, then the military must be used to protect American citizens. When an advocate of evil ideas tries to force those ideas upon us against our will by force, then the military must be used to stop the attack. Immediately after the destruction of our Twin Towers— symbols of the success of our ideas—the USA government should have immediately bombed the Ka'abah in Mecca—the symbol of the Muslim idea, to convince Muslims worldwide that Allah is a false god. Had this been done, Islamic jihad would be a thing of the past, and no more American lives would have been lost. As it is, we have already lost many more soldiers than we lost citizens in the World Trade Center. And if we continue on this path we are obviously going to lose the wars in Afghanistan and Iraq—with all

our soldier's lives lost in vain. And the Muslim jihad armies are going to keep up their terrorism until eventually the West wakes up to the fact that it is either them or us.

I'm **not** advocating that churches take up arms to kill Muslims. It is the duty of **civil governments** to protect their citizens by terrorizing evil doers with the sword.

> Romans 13:3 **For rulers are not a terror to good works, but to the evil.** Wilt thou then not be afraid of the power? do that which is good, and thou shalt have praise of the same: 4 For he is the minister of God to thee for good. But if thou do that which is evil, be afraid; for he beareth not the **sword** in vain: for he is the minister of God, **a revenger to execute wrath upon him that doeth evil.**

It is wrong for a president to send soldiers to potential death when more potent weapons (such as nuclear bombs) can do the job faster and more effectively without loss of the lives of our young men and women in uniform. Had we not dropped atomic bombs on Japan, we would still be fighting World War II, and the loss of both American and Japanese lives would have been much, much greater. But those two bombs convinced them that their emperor was not God, and so ended the war.

2.3 Allah—a god of Islam

The main things to remember about Allah are:

⇨ Allah is a mono-person god, in contrast to JEHOVAH who has three Persons.

⇨ Allah is impotent (can't father children) and is therefore barren—childless, in contrast to JEHOVAH who is omnipotent and has a Son.

⇨ Allah is a personal name, and does not mean God. Allah and JEHOVAH are

Figure 2.5: *Muslims in Malaysia protesting the use of the word Allah by Christians. They burned several churches to make sure Christians understood that they weren't joking.*

not the same. Allah is not the same God that is worshiped by Christians. "Allahu Akbar!" does not mean, **God** is great. It means, **Allah** is great.

Why Allah is "a" god of Islam, instead of "the" god of Islam, will be explained in a later chapter of this book.

2.4 The Sunnah of Muhammad

Muslims are taught to pattern their lives after the life of Muhammad, which is called his sunnah. The sunnah includes all of Muhammad's words, practices, habits, and way of life as recorded in the Quran and Hadiths.

2.4.1 The Quran

The Quran is also called the Al-Quran or Koran. Muhammad claimed that the surah (books) making up the Quran were given to him by Allah. Some of the surah were supposedly given to him in a cave, and others while he was in bed with Aisha, his youngest

wife, who he married when she was only six years old, and he was fifty-three.

2.4.1.1 How it is divided

Explanation for non-Muslims: the Quran is not divided like the Bible into books, chapters, and verses. Instead the Quran is divided into 114 surahs (books), with each surah being divided into ayahs (verses). Surah is often spelled sura. Each surah has a name and a number. In this book we will only use the numbers to refer to them. The ayahs also are numbered, but not named. So surah 1:1 refers to surah 1 verse 1.

2.4.1.2 Translations

In this book, we will quote from three popular translations of the Quran into English: (1) Yusuf Ali's translation (shown as YUSUFALI), Shakir's translation (shown as SHAKIR), and Pickthal's translation (shown as PICKTHAL). In quoting a verse (ayah) from the Quran, the translators name will be given first, then the surah-ayah reference number, then the verse.

When you use the Quran to disprove Islam, one of the tricks of Muslim teachers is to say that the Quran can't be understood if translated, and so the verse you quote doesn't actually mean that in Arabic—even if every translation says the same thing!

2.4.1.3 Chronology of the surahs

The surahs are not presented in chronological order. Therefore, the Quran is a very confusing book if the surahs are read in the order presented in the Quran.

2.4.1.3.1 The correct chronology. Muslim scholars say that the surahs were given to Muhammad in the chronological order listed in Appendix A on page 173.

2.4.1.3.2   The four stages of jihad. If the surahs are read in chronological order, it becomes clear that Muhammad's teachings concerning peace and war changed in four stages, as shown below:

1. **Command to be peaceful and tolerant.** In Mecca when Muhammad started Islam in 610 A.D., he had few followers, and they were very much at the mercy of the other people of Mecca. So, none of the 90 surahs given during the first 12 years of Islam in Mecca taught jihad. Rather, they taught Muslims not to retaliate to persecution (it would have been self-defeating), and to be peaceful and tolerant. These are the surahs Muslims still show non-Muslims today in areas where Muslims are a minority and therefore weak. These are the surahs that are used to deceive people into believing that Islam is "a religion of peace."

2. **Permission to wage war in self defence.** Eventually, Muhammad was invited to the city of Medina. He fled to Medina with his followers in 622 A.D., and was made the head of the city. At this point, Muhammad began to attract followers much faster. Soon, Muhammad and his men were robbing Meccan camel caravans in the name of Allah. For this the city of Mecca sent an army against Muhammad. A surah was immediately issued contradicting the peace, tolerance, and "don't retaliate" surahs by allowing Muslims to wage war and kill in self defence.

3. **Command to wage war in self defence.** When some of Muhammad's followers didn't want to go to war, surahs were issued changing the permission into a command—thus even more forcefully contradicting the peace, tolerance, and "don't retaliate" surahs. Unfortunately for the whole world, the Muslims won these wars with the Meccans, and rapidly increased in numbers and strength.

4. **Command to wage offensive war to spread Islam.** Eventually, more surahs were issued declaring all out offensive war against non-Muslims to convert them to Islam with the sword. All teachings commanding peacefulness, tolerance, and not retaliating were replaced with commands to wage cruel and violent war.

2.4.1.4   The law of abrogation

When a non-Muslim—especially if he be a Westerner—tries to read the Quran, he wonders how anyone can follow a book with so many contradictions, especially contradictions concerning jihad. **THE LAW OF ABROGATION AND SUBSTITUTION is the key to understanding the Quran.** Three surahs teach this law:

Sura 2:106

YUSUFALI: **None of Our revelations do We abrogate or cause to be forgotten, but We substitute something better or similar:** Knowest thou not that Allah Hath power over all things?

PICKTHAL: **Nothing of our revelation (even a single verse) do we abrogate or cause be forgotten, but we bring (in place) one better or the like thereof.** Knowest thou not that Allah is Able to do all things?

SHAKIR: **Whatever communications We abrogate or cause to be forgotten, We bring one better than it or like it.** Do you not know that Allah has power over all things?

Sura 13:39

YUSUFALI: Allah doth blot out or confirm what He pleaseth: with Him is the Mother of the Book.

PICKTHAL: Allah effaceth what He will, and establisheth (what He will), and with Him is the source of ordinance.

SHAKIR: Allah makes to pass away and establishes what He pleases, and with Him is the basis of the Book.

Sura 16:101

YUSUFALI: **When We substitute one revelation for another**,- and Allah knows best what He reveals (in stages),- they say, "Thou art but a forger": but most of them understand not.

PICKTHAL: And **when We put a revelation in place of (another) revelation**, - and Allah knoweth best what He revealeth - they say: Lo! thou art but inventing. Most of them know not.

SHAKIR: And **when We change (one) communication for (another) communication**, and Allah knows best what He reveals, they say: You are only a forger. Nay, most of them do not know.

Abrogate means, "Repealed, annulled, canceled, abolished by authority" (Oxford English Dictionary). **Muslim scholars interpret these verses to mean that the replaced verses stay in the Quran to deceive non-Muslims concerning their true intentions, but the replacement verses are practiced.**

Based on the above three surahs, Muslim scholars believe that surah 9:5—which they call, **"the verse of the sword"—replaces** most of the previous verses which taught peace, tolerance and non-retaliation. Surah 9:5 reads like this (shown in three translations):

YUSUFALI: But when the forbidden months are past, then **fight and slay the Pagans wherever ye find them, an seize them, beleaguer them, and lie in wait for them in every stratagem (of war)**; but if they repent, and establish regular prayers and practise regular charity, then open the way for them: for Allah is Oft-forgiving, Most Merciful.

PICKTHAL: Then, when the sacred months have passed, **slay the idolaters wherever ye find them, and take them (captive), and besiege them, and prepare for them each ambush**. But if they repent and establish worship and pay the poor-due, then leave their way free. Lo! Allah is Forgiving, Merciful.

SHAKIR: So when the sacred months have passed away, then **slay the idolaters wherever you find them, and take them captives and besiege them and lie in wait for them in every ambush**, then if they repent and keep up prayer and pay the poor-rate, leave their way free to them; surely Allah is Forgiving, Merciful.

Since the above surah (9:5) is one of the very last given (see Appendix A on page 173), it is the surah in effect today, replacing the earlier surahs teaching peace, tolerance, and non-retaliation.

2.4.2 Hadiths

The hadiths are stories supposedly from the time of Muhammad told about him by his associates, telling:

⇨ Some saying of Muhammad.

⇨ Something Muhammad did.

⇨ Something Muhammad approved or disapproved.

Most Muslim scholars consider the hadiths to be scripture almost as important, or as important, as the Quran.

2.5 The Ka'abah

The center of Islam is the black, cube-shaped Ka'abah toward which Muslims pray. In the beginning of Islam Muhammad was trying to attract Jews into Islam, and so he led Muslims to pray toward Jerusalem. But when the Jews rejected Muhammad and his teachings, he decided to have Muslims pray toward the Ka'abah in Mecca instead, which at the time still contained over 300 idols.

Figure 2.6: *The Ka'abah in Mecca.* [Photo ©Al-Fassam. *Licensed under the Creative Commons Attribution 2.0 Generic license.* `http://en.wikipedia.org/wiki/File:Kabaa.jpg`]

2.6 The five pillars of Islam

Muslims believe that they work their way to Heaven by performing five specific good works which they call the "five pillars of Islam."

2.6.1 Shahada

To become a Muslim all a person has to do is say the shahada. For most Muslims the shahada is: "There is no god but Allah, and Muhammad is his prophet." However, some Muslims believe that that shahada is polytheistic because it makes Muhammad equal to Allah. They say instead, "No god, only Allah." This will be discussed in greater detail in section 4.8.2 on page 62 of this book. The Arabic version of the polytheistic version of the shahada (shown below) is prominently displayed in the homes of the vast majority of Muslims in the world today.

Figure 2.7: *The polytheistic version of the shahada in Arabic.*

2.6.2 Salat

Salat is praying toward the Ka'abah five times each day. The bowing done with these prayers has to conform to specific rules.

2.6.3 Zakzt

Zakzt is giving alms to the poor. Requiring the giving of alms for a person to get to Heaven results in abuse. I have personally seen babies whose hand or foot had been cut off, lying on a mat under the hot sun on a sidewalk beside a tin cup to receive alms—their parents no where in sight. The mutilation appeared to be deliberate to cause pity. But even if it wasn't, to leave an infant baking for hours under the hot sun is extreme child abuse. And adult Muslim beggars are often very arrogant; they are after all—according to Islam—making it possible for the rich to work their way to Heaven!

2.6.4 Sawm

Sawm is fasting between dawn and sunset during the month of Ramadan. Then at night they have a big feast. **During the fasting month of Ramadan much more and more delicious food is consumed than during any other month of the year!** A great way to fast! Let's be blunt: that is phony fasting. That is feasting, not fasting.

Changing eating times is not true fasting. Muslims should consider that on the other side of the world from them Christians are fasting through the night at the same time that they are fasting through the day. Then in the morning Christians break fast (more commonly spelled "breakfast"). And Christians do this for twelve months each year, not just one. But only jokingly do they refer to that as "fasting." True fasting is refraining from eating throughout each 24 hour day (both day **and** night) for as long as the fast lasts, and should be done in private so as not to draw attention to one's self.

> Matthew 6:16 Moreover when ye fast, be not, as the hypocrites, of a sad countenance: for they disfigure their faces, that they may appear unto men to fast. Verily I say unto you, They have their reward. 17 But thou, when thou fastest, anoint thine head, and wash thy face; 18 That thou appear not unto men to fast, but unto thy Father which is in secret: and thy Father, which seeth in secret, shall reward thee openly.

2.6.5 Hajj

Muslims are obligated to make the hajj pilgrimage to Mecca at least once in their lifetime, where they walk counter-clockwise seven times around the Ka'abah, kiss or touch the Black Stone idol, then run seven times between the hills of As-Safa and Al-Marwah to symbolize Hagar's search for water and the miracle of the well, Zamzam. They spend the night at the village of Mina, then they meet at the plain of Arafat, about six miles from Mecca, and from noon to sunset pray quietly. Next, they climb a small mountain called the Mount of Mercy, and they ask God's forgiveness for their sins. They spend the night at Muzdalifah. Returning to Mina they "stone the devil" throwing pebbles at three pillars. On the tenth day, they sacrifice sheep or goats. Finally, they walk seven more times around the Ka'abah. Returning home, they celebrate for four days. Now the male pilgrim can boast that he is a hajji, and the female can brag that she is a hajjah. But the Bible says, "For by **grace** are

ye saved through **faith**; and that not of yourselves: it is the **gift** of God: **not of works, lest any man should boast**" (Ephesians 2:8-9). And what if a Muslim dies before getting to go to Mecca?

2.7 Jihad

Jihad is holy war for defending and spreading Islam. Jihad is one of the most dominate themes in the Quran; so jihad should concern Muslims and non-Muslims alike. There are at least 164 verses in the Quran which teach jihad against non-Muslims. As of August 9, 2011, **thereligionofpeace.com** website had documented **17,564** jihad terrorist attacks since 9/11/2001! And this figure only includes terrorist attacks reported in international news. Don't be deceived, Islam is a religion of war, not of peace.

Figure 2.8: *A screenshot of the very informative www.thereligionofpeace.com website.*

2.8 Mosques

Muslims worship in mosques which contain almost no furniture. Muslims sit on the floor on mats. In countries where Islam dominates, mosques often have powerful loudspeakers that blare the call to prayer for miles. The call to *fajr*, the first obligatory prayer, must be given long enough before the beginning of dawn to prompt people to get to the mosque by the beginning of dawn for the prayer. So, goodbye sleep if you live close to a mosque.

Figure 2.10: *There is virtually no furniture inside most mosques; Muslims sit on the floor.*

A Christian should never enter a mosque, because to do so he would have to honor the false god of Islam by removing his shoes.

Figure 2.11: *Modern mosques generally use loud-speakers to call people to the mosque to pray, and to intimidate the non-Muslims in the area.*

Figure 2.9: *A medium size mosque.*

Fertility rate, total (births per woman)
Total fertility rate represents the number of children that would be born to a woman if she were to live to the end of her childbearing years and bear children in accordance with current age-specific fertility rates. More info »

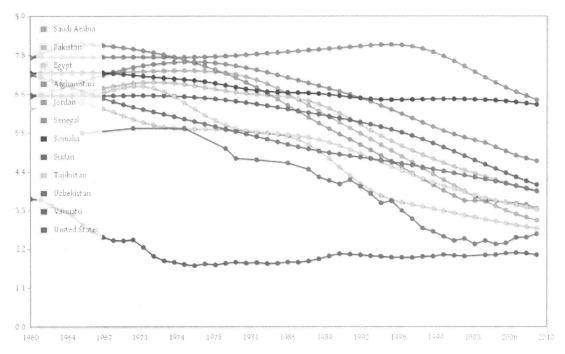

Data source: World Bank, World Development Indicators - Last updated March 2, 2011

Figure 2.12: *Although the atheist/humanist practice of birth control has influenced people of all religions, it has influenced Muslims far less than Christians. Note that the fertility rate in the USA (bottom line) is far less than in the Muslim countries listed above it. The fertility rate in most European countries is even less than that in the USA. This is rapidly tipping the balance of power in favor of the Muslims. Christians should love God enough to obey His command to "Be fruitful and multiply..." as given in Genesis 2:28. Otherwise, they very well may end up enslaved to Muslims. Having enough faith in God to not practice birth control caused the children of Israel to "wax exceeding mighty" in the days of Moses, resulting in their freedom from bondage. Read Exodus chapters 1-14. [Chart used with permission of IndexMundi:* http://www.indexmundi.com/ facts/indicators/SP.DYN.TFRT.IN/compare#country=af:eg:jo:pk:sa:sn:so:sd:tj:us:uz:vu]

Chapter 3

Is Muhammad the Comforter?

One of the most outrageous claims of Muslim teachers is the claim that Jesus was talking about Muhammad and not the Holy Spirit when he spoke about the Comforter. This claim is made to try to prove that the Bible teaches the coming of Muhammad. This chapter is a refutation of the lies concerning this subject told by Islamic teacher Akbarally Meherally in a document he posted on the World Wide Web many years ago. His document has since been copied to many other Islamic websites, which can be found by doing a web search. Meherally's teachings are very typical Islamic dogma. By dogma we mean strongly held opinions taught as authoritative by a religion or sect though there is no proof to back up those opinions.

Muslim teachers—and their trusting students—try to use the Bible of Christianity against Christians by taking verses out of context, by appealing to the Greek or Hebrew to try to make it look like the Bible is mistranslated, by using Bible translations made from corrupted manuscripts, or by claiming that the Quran contains quotes from the original Bible, and that the Bible of Christianity is a counterfeit of the original Bible. Of course, when Muslims are asked to produce a copy of that "original" Bible that agrees with the Quran they cannot do so, because such a Bible does not exist.

Let's examine the words of Muslim teacher Akbarally Meherally as he attempts to deceive the ignorant; then we will expose the deceptions. *Caution*: the words from Islamic teacher Akbarally Meherally's web pages are in boxes with black frames and gray backgrounds, like the one following this paragraph. **Please do not confuse his words with mine!** Let's begin now to examine Islamic deceptions.

Beware! Islamic deception follows:

University of Essex Islamic Society
Prophet Muhammad Prophesised in the Bible
by Akbarally Meherally

Note: The following is written in a language that is intended as an 'Invitation' (Daw'ah) to Christians, who have confused the concept of "Spirit of Truth" (a Paraclete) with "Holy Spirit".

Christians who have studied their Bibles are not confused in this matter. It is Meherally that is confused or rather who wants to confuse novice Christians, as will be proven step by step as the errors of his teachings are exposed in this book. Meherally's discourse is no doubt also intended to keep Muslims in confusion concerning Christianity. If Meherally's discourse is an invitation to Christians, it is only so in the sense of being an invitation to those who are weak and gullible to come and be deceived. The deception in Meherally's writing is so noticeable that no true Christian who knows his Bible well would ever be deceived by the obvious lies. It is those who have never read the Bible, and are therefore ignorant of its teachings that might be deceived. However, with a little help from this book even the most ignorant person can see the truth (and will thus no longer be ignorant), provided he sincerely wants to know the truth.

3.1   What is the core issue?

Before we refute Meherally's baseless claims, it is important to understand why he makes those claims. Why do Islamic teachers so desperately want to find predictions of Muhammad in the Bible? It is because of surah number 7:157 in the Quran (shown below in three translations):

> YUSUFALI: "Those who follow the messenger, the unlettered Prophet, **whom they find mentioned in their own (scriptures),- in the law and the Gospel;- ...."**

> PICKTHAL: Those who follow the messenger, the Prophet who can neither read nor write, **whom they will find described in the Torah and the Gospel (which are) with them. ...**

> SHAKIR: Those who follow the Messenger-Prophet, the Ummi, **whom they find written down with them in the Taurat and the Injeel**
> ...

In this verse Muhammad is said to be described in both the Torah[1] and the Gospel. Muhammad claimed to be the final prophet,

superior to and replacing Jesus. He further claimed that his authority to replace Jesus is based on the scriptures of both the Jews (the Torah) and the Christians (Gospel). So if no references to Muhammad can be found in the Torah or Gospel, then Muhammad is a fraud, and over a billion Muslims are following the lies of a false prophet—fooled by an impostor who supposedly couldn't even read or write!

3.2   Did Jesus Prophesy about Muhammad?

Yes, Jesus did prophesy that false prophets like Muhammad would come, but, no, Jesus did not say that Muhammad would replace Jesus.

Beware! Islamic deception follows:

Moses and Isaiah PROPHESIED the coming of JESUS.
Did Jesus and Isaiah PROPHESY the coming of MUHAMMAD?
To understand the prophecies made by Jesus on the subject, one has to begin with the First Epistle of John, Chapter 2, Verse 1. Here, Jesus Christ is called a "Paraclete" (Parakletos, Advocate, Comforter, Helper) by apostle John. The same term "Paraclete" is used by the apostle in his Gospel, in connection with a portentous prophecy made by Jesus Christ, before the end of his ministry upon this earth, for the coming of "another Paraclete". Prophet Moses also made a similar prophecy, before the end of his ministry, for the coming of his successor. Jesus Christ declared;
"And I will pray the Father, and He will give you another Paraclete, that he may abide

---

[1]The Torah is the Mosaic or Jewish law; hence, a name for the five books of the law (which are also the first five books in the Bible), also called the Pentateuch.

with you into the age (to come)."
John 14:16 Note: We often read the verse ending as; "with you for ever". However; "into the age" is the literal translation of the Greek phrase; 'eis ton aiona', used by John.

Before we critique what Meherally says about the Paraclete, please notice that the very verse Meherally quotes as a proof text refers to God as "**the Father.**" Jesus did not pray to the eunuch god, Allah, who cannot have children, but rather to the true God who is **the Father**. If Meherally wants to use this verse as a proof text, then he must concede that this important fact which disproves Islam.

3.3 Does Muhammad comfort you?

The reason that Meherally introduces the Greek word Parakletos ($\pi\alpha\rho\acute{\alpha}\kappa\lambda\eta\tau o\varsigma$) instead of simply using the English translation of that word, "Comforter," is because he wants to draw your attention away from the obvious fact that Muhammad was not a comforter. Muhammad brought distress and trouble to the world, not comfort. He was a terrorist who murdered many thousands of Christians. Muhammad taught, believed, and practiced terror, not comfort.

3.3.1 Jihad against all non-Muslims

Jihad is one of the most dominate themes in the Quran, so jihad should concern Muslims and non-Muslims alike. Yoel Natan has compiled the following list of 164 verses in the Quran which teach jihad (holy war) against non-Muslims: 002:178-179, 190-191, 193-194, 216-218, 244; 003:121-126,

Figure 3.1: *Does Muhammad comfort you? The World Trade Center moments before being struck by a second airplane which had been hijacked by Islamic terrorists, killing 2,753 people in premeditated, cold-blooded murder in the name of Islam's false god, Allah.*

140-143, 146, 152-158, 165-167,169, 172-173, 195; 004:071-072, 074-077, 084, 089-091, 094-095,100-104; 005:033, 035, 082; 008:001, 005, 007, 009-010, 012, 015-017, 039-048,057-060, 065-075; 009:005, 012-014, 016, 019-020, 024-026, 029,036, 038-039, 041, 044, 052, 073, 081, 083,086, 088, 092, 111, 120, 122-123; 016:110; 022:039, 058, 078; 024:053, 055; 025:052; 029:006, 069; 033:015, 018, 020, 023, 025-027, 050; 042:039; 047:004, 020, 035; 048:015-024; 049:015; 059:002, 005-008,

014; 060:009; 061:004, 011, 013; 063:004; 064:014; 066:009; 073:020; 076:008.[2]

Most Westerners consider the word **"terrorist"** a very dirty label. But Muslims who know the Quran well are proud to be called a **terrorist** because of verses like the following:

> YUSUFALI 8:60: **Against them** make ready your strength to the utmost of your power, **including steeds of war**, to strike **terror** into (the hearts of) the enemies, of Allah and your enemies, and others besides, whom ye may not know, but whom Allah doth know. Whatever ye shall spend in the cause of Allah, shall be repaid unto you, and ye shall not be treated unjustly.

> YUSUFALI 9:29–31: **Fight those who believe not in Allah** nor the Last Day, nor hold that forbidden which hath been forbidden by Allah and His Messenger, nor acknowledge the religion of Truth, **(even if they are) of the People of the Book** [meaning Jews and Christians who follow the Bible], until they pay the Jizya with willing submission, and feel themselves subdued. The Jews call 'Uzair a son of Allah, and **the Christians call Christ the son of Allah**. That is a saying from their mouth; (in this) they but imitate what the unbelievers of old used to say. **Allah's curse be on them**: how they are deluded away from the Truth! And **the Jews say: Uzair is the son of Allah; and the Christians say: The Messiah is the son of Allah**; these are the words of their mouths; they imitate the saying of those who disbelieved before; **may Allah destroy them**; how they are turned away!

Do those words sound like words of comfort? No. They are words of terror. Muhammad was not the Comforter; he was a **discomforter**.[3] Muhammad was a terrorist[4] who robbed camel caravans,[5] and allowed his men to rape the women[6] and murder their husbands. That is the reality of Muhammad.[7] And since Muhammad was a discomforter—the exact opposite of a comforter—, the Bible verses concerning the Comforter do not apply to him. This fact exposes Muhammad and Islam to be fraudulent.

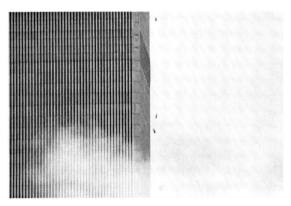

Figure 3.2: *Does remembering these Americans falling to their deaths from the burning World Trade Center comfort you? Never forget that followers of Muhammad caused this horror.*

---

[2]http://www.answering-islam.org/Quran/ Themes/jihad_passages.html

[3]Discomforter: "One who discomforts, discourages, or distresses" (Oxford English Dictionary).

[4]For detailed documentation proving that Muhammad was a murderer and terrorist read http://answering-islam.org/Silas/terrorism.htm See also http://www.faithfreedom.org/ Articles/sina/falwell.htm, noting especially the last paragraph.

[5]That this was robbery, and not retrieval of stolen property is documented here: http://www.thereligionofpeace.com/ Muhammad/myths-mu-raid-caravans.htm

[6]For a long article documenting that Muhammad allowed Muslim men to rape women taken captive in war, read http://www.answering-islam.org/ Quran/Tafsir/066.html

[7]For a extremely interesting article by Richard P. Bailey documenting and giving the history of the surahs teaching peace or jihad, see http://www. answering-islam.org/Bailey/jihad.html

3.4 Does the Bible prophesy the coming of Muhammad?

Meherally asked, "Did Jesus and Isaiah PROPHESY the coming of MUHAMMAD?" The answer is no, Muhammad is **never** named or referred to in the Bible, and, no, Islam is never named or referred to either. There is not even one verse in the entire Bible that validates the claim of Islam that Muhammad is the final and greatest prophet. According to the Bible, Jesus has—and always will have—the preeminence.

> Phillippians 2:5 Let this mind be in you, which was also in **Christ Jesus**: 6 Who, being in **the form of God**, thought it not robbery to be **equal with God**: 7 But made himself of no reputation, and took upon him the form of a servant, and was made in the likeness of men: 8 And being found in fashion as a man, he humbled himself, and became obedient unto death, **even the death of the cross**. 9 Wherefore God also hath **highly exalted him**, and given him a name which is **above every name**: 10 **That at the name of Jesus every knee should bow**, of things in heaven, and things in earth, and things under the earth; 11 And that **every** tongue should confess that **Jesus Christ is Lord**, to the glory of God the Father.

Muhammad is on his knees in Hell right now confessing that Jesus is Lord.

Although the Bible contradicts Muhammad's boastful claims, Jesus did prophesy about the **group** of prophets in which Muhammad is found:

> Mat. 7:15 Beware of **false prophets,** which come to you in sheep's clothing, but inwardly they are ravening wolves. 16 **Ye shall know them by their fruits.** Do men gather grapes of thorns, or figs of thistles? 17 Even so **every good tree bringeth forth good fruit; but a corrupt tree bringeth forth evil fruit.** 18 **A good tree cannot bring forth evil fruit, neither can a corrupt tree bring forth good fruit.** 19 Every tree that bringeth not forth good fruit is hewn down, **and cast into the fire.** 20 **Wherefore by their fruits ye shall know them.** 21 Not every one that saith unto me, Lord, Lord, shall enter into the kingdom of heaven; but he that doeth the will of my Father which is in heaven. 22 Many will say to me in that day, Lord, Lord, have we not prophesied in thy name? and in thy name have cast out devils? and in thy name done many wonderful works? 23 And then will I profess unto them, I **never** knew you: depart from me, ye that work **iniquity**.

3.5 What are Muhammad's fruits?

In the above verses the Bible says that you can know a false prophet by his evil fruits. So, what are Muhammad's evil fruits? Answer (to name just a few):

3.5.1 Extreme abuse of women.

Figure 3.3: *This 16 year old Bangladesh rape victim was given 101 lashes for getting pregnant. "Her rapist was pardoned by the elders." http://www.telegraph.co.uk/news/worldnews/ asia/bangladesh/7073191/Rape-victim-receives-101-lashes-for-becoming-pregnant.html*

Muhammad considered women inferior to men.

Volume 1, Book 6, Number 301:

Narrated Abu Said Al-Khudri: Once Allah's Apostle went out to the Musalla (to offer the prayer) o 'Id-al-Adha or Al-Fitr prayer. Then he passed by the women and said, "O women! Give alms, as **I have seen that the majority of the dwellers of Hell-fire were you (women)**." They asked, "Why is it so, O Allah's Apostle ?" He replied, "You curse frequently and are ungrateful to your husbands. **I have not seen anyone more deficient in intelligence and religion than you**. A cautious sensible man could be led astray by some of you." The women asked, "O Allah's Apostle! What is deficient in our intelligence and religion?" He said, "Is not the evidence of two women equal to the witness of one man?" They replied in the affirmative. He said, "This is the deficiency in her intelligence. Isn't it true that a woman can neither pray nor fast during her menses?" The women replied in the affirmative. He said, "This is the deficiency in her religion." (Hadith collection of Sahih Bukhari

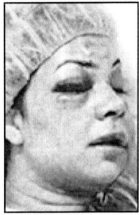

Figure 3.4: *Saudi TV presenter, Rania al-Baz, said her husband, Mohammed al-Fallatta, beat her so hard...that he broke her nose and fractured her face in 13 places. "It is considered a husband's rights that his wife should obey him," Abeer Mishkhas, of the Saudi English-language newspaper Arab News, told BBC News Online, "This can involve coercion or violence, and we know that the majority of cases of this kind go unreported and unnoticed."*

Because of his low regard for women, Muhammad allowed men to abuse them in many ways. For example:

3.5.1.1 Wife beating

SHAKIR 4:34: Men are the maintainers of women because Allah has made some of them to excel others and because they spend out of their property; the good women are therefore obedient, guarding the unseen as Allah has guarded; and (as to) those on whose part you fear desertion, admonish them, and leave them alone in the sleeping-places **and beat them**; then if they obey you, do not seek a way against them; surely Allah is High, Great.[8]

3.5.1.2 Prostitution in the guise of marriage

Narrated Abdullah: We used to participate in the holy wars carried on by the Prophet and we had no women (wives) with us. So we said (to the Prophet). "Shall we castrate ourselves?" But the Prophet forbade us to do that and thenceforth **he allowed us to marry a woman (temporarily)** by giving her even a garment, and then he recited: "O you who believe! Do not make unlawful the good things which Allah has made lawful for you." (Hadith collection of Sahih Bukhari Volume 6, Book 60, Number 139)[9]

---

[8]For an article documenting the teaching and practice of wife beating in Islam read http://answering-islam.org/Silas/wife-beating.htm A video all women should watch: http://www.youtube.com/watch?

v=tHwATEWqslw&NR=1 A video discussing the status of women in Islam: http://www.youtube.com/watch?v=6TftOBBdyGo

[9]http://www.usc.edu/schools/college/crcc/engagement/resources/texts/muslim/hadith/bukhari/060.sbt.html

In other words, Muhammad told his married men that its was OK for them to commit fornication and adultery with a prostitute, paying her with a piece of clothing. Furthermore, he said that Allah had made this lawful for a believer!

Christian girls beware! Some Muslim clerics are advising Muslim college students to marry a girl "temporarily" while studying in the USA or Europe.

3.5.1.3 Polygamy

Muslim men are allowed up to 4 wives at a time.

> PICKTHAL 4:3: And if ye fear that ye will not deal fairly by the orphans, **marry of the women, who seem good to you, two or three or four**; and if ye fear that ye cannot do justice (to so many) then one (only) or (the captives) that your right hands possess. Thus it is more likely that ye will not do injustice.

3.5.1.4 Rape of slaves

Muslim men are allowed to rape even their married female slaves.

> PICKTHAL : And all **married** women (are forbidden unto you) **save those (captives) whom your right hands possess**. It is a decree of Allah for you. Lawful unto you are all beyond those mentioned, so that ye seek them with your wealth in honest wedlock, not debauchery. And those of whom ye seek content (by marrying them), give unto them their portions as a duty. And there is no sin for you in what ye do by mutual agreement after the duty (hath been done). Lo! Allah is ever Knower, Wise.

In a video uploaded to YouTube on Jun 10, 2011, Egyptian Muslim imam, Shaykh Abu-Ishaq al-Huwayni, said: "When I want a sex slave, I just go to the market and choose the woman I like and purchase her."[10]

---

[10]http://www.youtube.com/watch?v=tssBq4jCWtw

3.5.2 Horrible self mutilation

Muhammad's teachings cause people to abuse and mutilate their own selves. The photograph below shows Muslim men in Basra, Iraq chopping open their own heads with large knives on Ashoura day. Muhammad and Allah inspire people to do this. Is this not demon possession and insanity? Does having people like this in the world comfort you? [11]

Figure 3.5: *Islam caused insanity—blood flows as Muslims in Basra, Iraq chop open their own heads with large knives on Ashoura day.*

3.5.3 Extreme racism

Many Muslims interpret the Quran to teach that Allah turned Jews into apes and pigs, and that Jews should now be wiped off the face of the earth.

---

[11]Warning: these videos are unbelievably horribly gory: http://www.youtube.com/watch?v=GkfV6eoGMzY http://www.youtube.com/watch?v=bvcwcw4Zyl8 Sunni Muslims say this is Shia, not Islam. But they do the same thing to themselves mentally. No, this is Islam.

3.5.3.1 Jews turned into apes

Below are the verses from the Quran which Muslim believe teach that Jews are apes. The contexts of these verses show that Jews were being discussed.

> YUSUFALI 7:166: When in their insolence they transgressed (all) prohibitions, We said to them: "**Be ye apes**, despised and rejected."

> YUSUFALI 2:65: And well ye knew those amongst you who transgressed in the matter of the Sabbath: We said to them: "**Be ye apes**, despised and rejected."

3.5.3.2 Jews turned into pigs

Here is a verse from the Quran that adds that these Jews also became swine.

> YUSUFALI 5:60: Say: "Shall I point out to you something much worse than this, (as judged) by the treatment it received from Allah? those who incurred the curse of Allah and His wrath, those of whom some **He transformed into apes and swine, those who worshipped evil**;- these are (many times) worse in rank, and far more astray from the even path!"

3.5.3.3 Jews turned into rats

Several hadiths also teach the transformation of Jews into animals, among them this one:

> Narrated Abu Huraira: The Prophet said, "A group of Israelites were lost. Nobody knows what they did. But I do not see them except that they were cursed and changed into rats, for if you put the milk of a she-camel in front of a rat, it will not drink it, but if the milk of a sheep is put in front of it, it will drink it." I told this to Ka'b who asked me, "Did you hear it from the Prophet?" I said, "Yes." Ka'b asked me the same question several times; I said to Ka'b. "Do I read the Torah? (i.e. I tell you this from the Prophet.)" (Sahih al-Bukhari, Volume 4, Book 54, Number 524)

These hateful, irrational verses prove that the Quran is not the words of the righteous God in Heaven. No sane intelligent person would ever believe that these verses are true. [12]

3.5.4 Hatred of Jews and Christians

The Quran demands that a Muslim never make friends with Jews or Christians, but rather should kill them wherever they are found, unless they submit to Islam.

> YUSUFALI 5:51 O ye who believe! **take not the Jews and the Christians for your friends and protectors**: They are but friends and protectors to each other. And he amongst you that turns to them (for friendship) is of them. Verily Allah guideth not a people unjust. [13]

3.5.5 Terrorism

Muhammad ruled by fear: threats, beheadings, and many other acts of violence—against civilians, including women and children. As has often been pointed out: not all Muslims are terrorists, but almost all terrorists are Muslims. That is just a fact.[14] Sure there are exceptions, but not many.

3.5.6 Murder of apostates

Muhammad commanded Muslims to murder any Muslims who leave Islam—no soul lib-

---

[12]This Islamic idea that Jews were turned into apes is documented here: http://www.answering-islam.org/Authors/Arlandson/jew_apes.htm And be sure to watch this video: http://www.youtube.com/watch?v=UXz_-MHHOHU

[13]To read this verse in other translations, go here: http://www.usc.edu/schools/college/crcc/engagement/resources/texts/muslim/quran/005.qmt.html Scroll down to 005.051.

[14]For many articles documenting this, see: http://www.answering-islam.org/Terrorism/index.html

erty whatsoever is allowed to a Muslim.[15]

Muhammad is a corrupt tree, whose teachings are presently causing the world more sorrow and misery than the teachings of any other religious leader. Because of Muhammad, terror, violence, and misery have misplaced peace in the world. Watch Muslims' faces—they are almost always angry and unhappy. They are never satisfied, and do not have peace in their hearts. The biggest lie of this century is that Islam is a religion of peace. Everyone knows that is a lie—even the Muslims and former president George W. Bush. Most of the wars presently being waged were started by followers of Muhammad. Jesus said this to those who think it is OK to murder and lie for the sake of their religion:

> John 8:44 **Ye are of your father the devil**, and the **lusts** of your father ye will do. He was a **murderer** from the beginning, and abode not in the truth, because **there is no truth in him**. When he speaketh a lie, he speaketh of his own: for he is a **liar**, and the father of it.

As you read through this book, count the lies and deceptions of Islamic teacher Meherally as I point them out. The above verse describes Muhammad—and the Muslim teachers following him—perfectly. No honest person can continue to be a Muslim after giving this book a fair reading.

---

[15]A long article documenting that death is the penalty for leaving Islam: http://www.answering-islam.org/Silas/apostasy.htm Video of Muslim imam admitting that death is the penalty for leaving Islam: http://www.youtube.com/watch?v=mgo4aGe1OGc&NR=1 Video of Rifqa Bary whose dad has threatened to kill her for leaving Islam: http://www.youtube.com/watch?v=p8C2ApyZD3o&feature=related

3.6 Are Muslim teachers Greek experts?

You cannot know if a person is a Greek expert unless you have a working knowledge of Greek yourself. Meherally implies that "with you for ever" is a wrong translation of John 14:16. Like most teachers of Islam, Meherally knows very little about Greek, but hopes that those whom he is trying to deceive will know nothing about Greek at all, and will think that Meherally knows a lot. The obvious fact is that Meherally doesn't even know English very well, much less Greek. As you will see in most of Meherally's writings, he constantly uses a language he hopes is foreign to you so that you must simply take him at his word. **Hot tip** (to borrow a phrase from Meherally): when discussing subjects that will determine your eternal destiny, never take someone at his word in blind faith—always check out everything he says. And remember that Christianity has many enemies besides Muslims. There are false prophets among Christians also—real Jesus haters; so don't be surprised if the false prophets of Islam quote the false prophets that have infiltrated Christianity.

> Jude 1:4 For there are **certain men crept in unawares**, who were before of old ordained to this condemnation, **ungodly men**, turning the grace of our God into lasciviousness, and denying the only Lord God, and our Lord Jesus Christ.

> 2 Peter 2:1 But there were **false prophets** also among the people, **even as there shall be false teachers among you**, who privily shall bring in **damnable heresies**, even denying the Lord that bought them, and bring upon themselves swift destruction. 2 And many shall follow their pernicious ways; by reason of whom the way of truth shall be evil spoken of. 3 And through covetousness shall they with **feigned words** make merchandise of you: whose judgment now of a long time lingereth not, and their damnation slumbereth not.

"Feigned" words are counterfeit, untrue words formed into clever lies purposely to deceive. God's word warns us that there shall be such deceivers claiming to be Christian preachers. So, **when Islamic teachers quote such heretics, it really carries no weight of authority at all**. The reader needs be aware that there is a fierce spiritual battle being waged between the true God and His followers versus Satan and his followers. It is a battle for the hearts, minds, and souls of men. Satan knows he is going to Hell, and he intends to take as many humans to Hell with him as possible. Don't let him take you!

3.7 Is it honest to quote out of context?

As is typical of Islamic teachers, Meherally almost always uses quotations out of context in an attempt to deceive people who are too trusting. The fact is, you can never trust a Muslim teacher. You must always suspect that he has taken quotes out of context—you must always check to see if what he told you is the truth or a lie. I'm not just saying this to put down Muslim teachers, but as a lesson learned from dealing with Muslims for many years. For example:

Beware! Islamic deception follows:

These two verses by John clearly demonstrate that Jesus Christ, while speaking of "another Paraclete", was speaking of the coming of "another male figure" like himself, some time in the future, after his departure. The passage quoted below also confirms that the original concept among the noted Christian scholars and populace, for the "Paraclete" was for the coming of a "male figure", but that concept was later confused with the "Holy Spirit". Here is an extract from the world renowned and

---

distinguished Anchor Bible Volume 29A: "The word parakletos is peculiar in the NT to the Johannine literature. In 1John ii1 Jesus is a parakletos (not a title), serving as a heavenly intercessor with the Father. ...Christian tradition has identified this figure (Paraclete) as the Holy Spirit, but scholars like Spitta, Delafosse, Windisch, Sasse, Butlmann and Betz have doubted whether this identification is true to the original picture and have suggested that the Paraclete was once an independent salvific figure, later confused with the Holy Spirit." (page 1135).

3.7.1 Quoting the Anchor Bible out of context

Meherally quotes from the Anchor Bible. The Anchor Yale Bible is a module of Logos Bible software. It is not actually a Bible, but is a set of 83 volumes comprising a commentary on the whole Bible. However, Spitta, Delafosse, Windisch, Sasse, Bultmann, and Betz were not authors of any of the volumes in the Anchor Yale Bible, as seems to be implied by Meherally. The author of the volume from which Meherally quoted is Raymond E. Brown, a Roman Catholic priest. Jochen Katz has this to say about this quotation (all emphasis is original with Katz):

> I agree, the Anchor Bible is "renowned and distinguished" as Mr. Meherally says. But this doesn't mean that any out of context quote is also distinguished and worthy of renown. In 1995, I wrote: "*Let me quote a bit more of this distinguished commentary and correct your (un)intentional mistakes. I leave it to you to decide if they were (un) or not.*" In 1995, I wanted to give Mr. Meherally the benefit of the doubt. The fact that he claims the same thing in 1997 after I have corrected him and shown him wrong cannot be seen other than deliberate deception of his readers. And this is how he corrupts the meaning:

First, he asserts that "*the passage quoted below from the world renowned and distinguished Anchor Bible **confirms** that the original concept among the noted Christian scholars and populace, for the Paraclete **was** for a male salvific figure, ...*"

This is obviously twisting the quotation. Mr. Meherally wants to give the impression that **the Anchor Bible states this as a fact** but the quotation actually only says that some "scholars like Spitta, ... and Betz have **doubted** and ... have **suggested** that ..." There is **no** mentioning in this quote of any certainty or conclusive evidence for this statement. Only that some scholars have presented this as a hypothesis.

Mr. Meherally wants to make his readers believe something to be the consensus of responsible scholarship which was only a suggestion for discussion. This is the first part of his deception. But the next part of this drama is a lot worse.

Not only does he present as certainty what was only a suggestion, the way he writes that "the passage ... from **the world renowned and distinguished Anchor Bible confirms** ..." he clearly wants to give the impression that this quotation is **in agreement** with the author of this commentary. But this is a plain lie, fabricated in the hope that the reader of article will not check the truthfulness of the quotation as we will show in the following.

Mr. Meherally failed to mention that this is **not** from the text of the commentary itself but from the appendix, where Dr. Raymond Brown (the author of this volume) is discussing some **other people's opinions and objections**. It is **not a valid interpretation** in the eyes of the author of the world renowned and distinguished Anchor Bible Commentary. But as for any scholarly commentary Dr. Brown also has to list opposing views and to carefully discuss them. This is the proper scholarly approach. Yet Mr. Meherally cited the **quote of the opposing view** - which the author is about to discuss in the pages that follow it - **as if it were the opinion of the author of the Anchor Bible**.

Please pay attention to the very next sentence in the same paragraph of the Anchor Bible after the place Mr. Meherally decided to cut short his quotation:

"... but scholars like Spitta, Delafosse, Windisch, Sasse, Bultmann and Betz have doubted whether this identification is true to the original picture and have suggested that the Paraclete was once an independent salvific figure, later confused with the Holy Spirit. **To test this claim, we shall begin by .... "**

and then follow several pages of analysis of the textual evidence. After completion of this analysis, on page 1139, Dr. Brown gives his own conclusion and writes:

"**It is our contention that John presents the Paraclete as the Holy Spirit** in a special role, namely, as the personal presence of Jesus in the Christian while Jesus is with the Father."

Is that quote not crystal clear? The renowned commentator has established after detailed analysis that **the Paraclete is the Holy Spirit**. This is **the exact opposite** of what Mr. Meherally claims the position of the Anchor Bible to be. Would anyone maintain that this was an honest quotation? Why does Mr. Meherally continue to to spread these lies in full knowledge (for two years) that he is lying? This is no longer an honest mistake.

And on page 1140 the commentary continues:

"..., we would stress that the identification of the Paraclete as the Holy Spirit in 14:26 is **not** an editorial mistake, for the similarities between the Paraclete and the Spirit are found in all the Paraclete passages.

The peculiarity of the Johannine portrait of the Paraclete/Spirit, and this is our second point, centers around the resemblance of the Spirit to Jesus. Virtually everything that has been said about the Paraclete has been said elsewhere in the Gospel about Jesus."

The emphasis in **boldface letters** in the above is mine, just so that the essential word is not overlooked. But otherwise it is the exact quotation from Dr. Brown's commentary in John from the world renowned and distinguished Anchor Bible.[16]

Clearly, Meherally has practiced deliberate deception, and this is typical of Muslim teachers. The truth just doesn't matter in Islam.

3.7.2 Quoting the Bible out of context

It is bad enough to quote a commentary or dictionary out of context. It is far worse to quote God's word out of context. Here is the context of the verses Meherally just quoted, so you can see for yourself how he misquoted them:

> John 14:16 And I will pray the Father, and he shall give you another **Comforter**, that he may abide with you for ever; 17 Even the **Spirit of truth**; whom **the world cannot receive, because it seeth him not**, neither knoweth him: but ye know him; **for he dwelleth with you, and shall be in you**. 18 I will not leave you comfortless: I will come to you. 19 Yet a little while, and the world seeth me no more; but ye see me: because I live, ye shall live also. 20 At that day ye shall know that I am in my Father, and ye in me, and I in you. 21 He that hath my commandments, and keepeth them, he it is that loveth me: and he that loveth me shall be loved of my Father, and I will love him, and will manifest myself to him. 22 Judas saith unto him, not Iscariot, Lord, how is it that thou wilt manifest thyself unto us, and not unto the world? 23 Jesus answered and said unto him, If a man love me, he will keep my words: and my Father will love him, and **we** will come **unto him, and make our abode with him**. 24 He that loveth me not keepeth not my sayings: and the word which ye hear is not mine, but the Father's which sent me. 25 These things have I spoken unto you, being yet present with you. 26 But **the Comforter, which is the Holy Ghost**, whom the Father will send in my name, he shall teach you all things, and bring all things

to your remembrance, whatsoever I have said unto you.

⇨ Note in verse 17 that the Comforter will dwell "with" the disciples of Christ and will be "in" the disciples of Christ. Muhammad does not dwell "with" the disciples of Christ and never has dwelt with them, and he was not "in" the disciples of Christ and never has been in them.

⇨ Note in verse 17 that the world could not receive the Comforter because "it seeth him not." Was Muhammad invisible so that the world could not see him? No. Muhammad was visible and thousands of people of the world saw him. Muhammad is not the Comforter.

⇨ Note also in verse 17 that the Comforter is the Spirit of truth—Muhammad was not a spirit, but an ordinary human being—and he didn't usually tell the truth, but rather lied a lot!

⇨ Note in verse 26 that **the Comforter is clearly said to be the Holy Ghost**, not Muhammad.

⇨ Note in these verses that God is said to be "the Father." The true God is not a eunuch like Allah who cannot father children.

The Islamic **interpretation** of the Bible is likewise very deceptive and dishonest, as is shown throughout this book.

| Beware! Islamic deception follows: |

The Bible tells us that Jesus Christ, besides being a "Messiah" was also a prophet like Moses, by his own admission. Please see John 5:46 and 9:17. Hence to say that the

---

[16]http://www.answering-islam.org/ Responses/Meherally/integrity.htm

coming of "another Paraclete" was similar to the coming of "another Prophet" like Jesus and Moses, would not be inaccurate. OTOH, the concept of "Holy Spirit" is unequivocally negated by the following verse: "But I tell you the truth, it is to your advantage that I go away; for if I do not go away, the Paraclete shall not come to you; but if I go, I will send him to you." John 16:7 This verse clearly tells us that the coming of the Paraclete was subject to the departure of Jesus. Whereas, the "Holy Spirit" was already present. It was in existence since the day of the Creation and was hovering upon the surface of the earth (Genesis 1:2). It was also present with the prophets of the Old Testament. The "Holy Spirit" happened to be present at River Jordan when Jesus Christ was being Baptised by John the Baptist, in the early part of his ministry. So, how could Jesus say; "but if I go, I will send Holy Spirit"?

That Jesus—not Muhammad—is the prophet like unto Moses mentioned in Deuteronomy 18:15, will be discussed later on in chapter 13 of this book. For now we will simply point out that, of course, the Holy Spirit was there, for the Holy Spirit is the omnipresent God. However, He was **not** there **as the Comforter** until Jesus **sent** Him, as the following verses from God's word very clearly show:

> John 7:37 In the last day, that great day of the feast, Jesus stood and cried, saying, If any man thirst, let him come unto me, and drink. 38 He that believeth on me, as the scripture hath said, out of his belly shall flow rivers of living water. 39 (But this spake he of **the Spirit**, which they that believe on him should receive: for **the Holy Ghost was not yet given**; because that Jesus was not yet glorified.)

These verses very clearly tell us that the Spirit which Jesus would send was the Holy Ghost—not Muhammad. Meherally will later tell

us that parentheses around words mean that those words were not in the original. He is not telling the truth in this matter, as he very well knows. Why not get an unaltered Textus Receptus Greek New Testament and see for yourself whether the words are there or not? You will find that the words are there.

Beware! Islamic deception follows:

"When the Paraclete comes, whom I will send to you from the Father, that is the Spirit of Truth, who proceeds from the Father, he will bear witness of me." John 15:26 This above verse clears the confusion. The Paraclete is called the "Spirit of Truth" and not the "Holy Spirit". These are two separate terms and two independent entities. The first takes the pronoun "he" being a male figure, whereas, the second one takes the pronoun "it".

"But the Paraclete, the Spirit, whom the Father will send in my name, he will teach you all things, and bring to your remembrance all that I said to you." John 14:26 Note:

1. In the older MSS, Codex Syriacus discovered in 1812 on Mount Sinai by Mrs.Agnes S. Lewis (and Mrs. Bensley), the text of 14:26 reads; "Paraclete, the Spirit"; and not "Paraclete, the Holy Spirit". "The Spirit" is a reference to "the Spirit of Truth" as in 15:26.

As was just shown, Meherally is lying here. The Paraclete (Comforter) was called the Holy Ghost in John 14:26:

> But the Comforter, **which is the Holy Ghost**, whom the Father will send in my name, he shall teach you all things, and bring all things to your remembrance, whatsoever I have said unto you.

In the old English of the King James Bible, "Ghost" and "Spirit" are translated from the exact same Greek word, and have the exact same meaning.

3.8 Does Codex Syriacus predict Muhammad?

The Codex Syriacus (not to be confused with the Codex Sinaiticus) is a **translation** of the Scriptures into the Syrian language. It is **not** a manuscript of the original Greek text. It is **not** equal or even more reliable than the text from which it was translated. Meherally is saying that because the word "Holy" is missing from John 14:26 in the Codex Syriacus translation, this proves that the verse predicts Muhammad. That is pure blind-faith conjecture[17] on his part. Frankly, his claim is totally baseless and silly. The only proof Meherally offers to defend his wild claims is his illogical dogmatic beliefs. He thinks that because he believes something that proves his beliefs to be true! It has to be true since he believes it!

3.9 Does the pronoun "it" validate Muhammad?

Concerning the pronoun "it" being associated with the Holy Spirit, again Meherally shows ignorance of the Greek language. Gender in Greek grammar "must not be confused with ideas of sex" (Alfred Marshall, *New Testament Greek Primer*, page 9).

---

[17]Conjecture means, "To form an opinion or supposition as to facts on grounds admittedly insufficient; to guess, surmise; to propose as a conjecture in textual or historical criticism, etc" (Oxford English Dictionary).

Beware! Islamic deception follows:

2. The word spirit, Greek. 'pneu'ma', is of neutral gender and takes pronoun "it". Whereas, in almost all the verses referring to Paraclete quoted above and below, the pronoun used is "he".

Again, Meherally is implying that in Greek grammar the pronouns indicate the sex of a person. That is not true in the Greek language and is not necessarily so in English. Note in verse 39 below, "it" refers to Christ:

> Luke 24:36 And as they thus spake, Jesus himself stood in the midst of them, and saith unto them, Peace be unto you. 37 But they were terrified and affrighted, and supposed that they had seen a **spirit**. 38 And he said unto them, Why are ye troubled? and why do thoughts arise in your hearts? 39 Behold my hands and my feet, that **it** is I myself: handle me, and see; for a spirit hath not flesh and bones, as ye see me have. 40 And when he had thus spoken, he shewed them his hands and his feet.

Another verse that shows that the Holy Ghost is the Comforter:

> Acts 9:31 Then had the churches rest throughout all Judaea and Galilee and Samaria, and were edified; and walking in the fear of the Lord, and in the **comfort of the Holy Ghost**, were multiplied.

This happened hundreds of years before the birth of Muhammad, and so could not possibly refer to Muhammad. Muhammad is not the Holy Ghost or Comforter. A discomforter cannot be the Comforter.

Even if Meherally were correct about the pronouns (he isn't), that still would not prove that "he" refers to Muhammad. "He" doesn't refer to Muhammad unless Muhammad was previously talked about in the text, and that obviously is not the case. Even if you look for 10,000 years you will not find the name Muhammad in the Bible.

3.10 Are spirits of truth (or of error) humans?

No, these terms are not used for human beings! These are **spirits** that **motivate** human beings, but they are spirits, not humans. The spirit of truth mentioned in these verses is the **Spirit of God** which indwells true men of God. The spirit of error is the spirit of Satan in false prophets such as Muhammad, who deny that God sent his only begotten Son into the world to be the propitiation for our sins. A propitiation is a sacrifice for sins that satisfies God's demand for justice, thereby appeasing God's wrath. Here is 1 John 4:6 in its context so that you can see for yourself (note in particular verses 9 and 10):

> 1 John 4:1 Beloved, believe not every spirit, but try the spirits whether they are of God: because many false prophets are gone out into the world. 2 Hereby know ye the Spirit of God: **every spirit that confesseth that Jesus Christ is come in the flesh is of God:** 3 **And every spirit that confesseth not that Jesus Christ is come in the flesh is not of God: and this is that spirit of antichrist,** whereof ye have heard that it should come; and even now already is it in the world. 4 Ye are of God, little children, and have overcome them: because greater is he that is in you, than he that is in the world. 5 They are of the world: therefore speak they of the world, and the world heareth them. 6 We are of God: he that knoweth God heareth us; he that is not of God heareth not us. Hereby know we **the spirit of truth,** and **the spirit of error.** 7 **Beloved, let us love one another: for love is of God; and every one that loveth is born**

of God, and knoweth God. 8 **He that loveth not knoweth not God; for God is love.** 9 In this was manifested the love of God toward us, because that **God sent his only begotten Son** into the world, that we might live through him. 10 Herein is love, not that we loved God, but that he loved us, and sent his **Son** to be the **propitiation** for our sins.

Note also in verse 8 above that a person who does not love other people does not know God, for God is love. The author of this book once quoted that verse to a particularly hateful hajj (a person that has made the pilgrimage to Mecca, and received training to be a Muslim teacher). He immediately stopped me and said, "That is what your book says; the Quran tells me to hate you, and so I do." This verse clearly declares that such a person has not been born of God, and does not know the true God.

If Meherally and other Islamic teachers want to use 1 John 4:1 as God's word, then they must also accept 1 John 4:2-10 as God's word, by admitting that Jesus is the Son of God and the propitiation for our sins. Otherwise they should stick to the Quran. A text taken out of context is pretext and deception.

3.11 Does history record Muhammad as an honest man?

Is this claim, made by all Islamic teachers, true?

Meherally offers no history records to prove this claim. But I can offer the following history record to prove that Muhammad was dishonest **after** he supposedly received the revelations. In the July 8, 1996 issue of *The New Republic* magazine, Yehoshua Porath, Professor of Middle Eastern History at the Hebrew University of Jerusalem, states:

> ...Arafat repeatedly equated the Oslo agreement with the Khudaybiya (sic) agreement, which the prophet Muhammad concluded during his wars with the Quraysh tribe. Muhammad broke the agreement eighteen months after its conclusion, when the balance of power changed in his favor, and it has become a guiding precedent in Islamic law for how to deal with non-Muslim powers. (July 8, 1996, p.9)

This historian is thus implying (correctly) that the Prophet Muhammad was a dishonest man. Muhammad gave his word at the Treaty of Hudaybiyya, and then by violating the treaty proved that he was a liar and not a man who could be trusted. Muslim leaders today use the Hudaybiyya agreement to justify signing agreements which they—like Muhammad—have no intention of keeping. They are just using the agreements to buy time to get into a position of strength so that they can defeat those with whom they make the agreements, reasoning that if it was right for Muhammad to lie to further Islam, then it is right for them to lie to further Islam also. Is it wise to believe a religion that practices lying to advance itself? Might not the teachers of that religion be telling lies to you also? Here is where the Quran says that Allah freed Muhammad from his obligations to keep the treaties he had made with non-Muslims:

009.001

YUSUFALI: **A (declaration) of immunity from Allah and His Messenger, to those of the Pagans with whom ye have contracted mutual alliances:-**

PICKTHAL: **Freedom from obligation (is proclaimed) from Allah and His messenger toward those of the idolaters with whom ye made a treaty.**

SHAKIR: **(This is a declaration of) immunity by Allah and His Messenger towards those of the idolaters with whom you made an agreement.**

009.002

YUSUFALI: Go ye, then, for four months, backwards and forwards, (as ye will), throughout the land, but know ye that ye cannot frustrate Allah (by your falsehood) but that Allah will cover with shame those who reject Him.

PICKTHAL: Travel freely in the land four months, and know that ye cannot escape Allah and that Allah will confound the disbelievers (in His Guidance).

SHAKIR: So go about in the land for four months and know that you cannot weaken Allah and that Allah will bring disgrace to the unbelievers.

009.003

YUSUFALI: **And an announcement from Allah and His Messenger, to the people (assembled) on the day of the Great Pilgrimage,- that Allah and His Messenger dissolve (treaty) obligations with the Pagans.** If then, ye repent, it were best for you; but if ye turn away, know ye that ye cannot frustrate Allah. And proclaim a grievous penalty to those who reject Faith.

PICKTHAL: And a proclamation from Allah and His messenger to all men on the day of the Greater Pilgrimage that **Allah is free from obligation to the idolaters, and (so is) His messenger.** So, if ye repent, it will be better for you; but if ye are averse, then know that ye cannot escape Allah. Give tidings (O Muhammad) of a painful doom to those who disbelieve,

SHAKIR: And an announcement from Allah and His Messenger to the people on the day of the greater pilgrimage that **Allah and His Messenger are free from liability to the idolaters;** therefore if you repent, it will be better for you, and if you turn back, then know that you will not weaken Allah; and announce painful punishment to those who disbelieve.

009.004

36

YUSUFALI: (But the treaties are) not dissolved with those Pagans with whom ye have entered into alliance and who have not subsequently failed you in aught, nor aided any one against you. So fulfil your engagements with them to the end of their term: for Allah loveth the righteous.

PICKTHAL: Excepting those of the idolaters with whom ye (Muslims) have a treaty, and who have since abated nothing of your right nor have supported anyone against you. (As for these), fulfil their treaty to them till their term. Lo! Allah loveth those who keep their duty (unto Him).

SHAKIR: Except those of the idolaters with whom you made an agreement, then they have not failed you in anything and have not backed up any one against you, so fulfill their agreement to the end of their term; surely Allah loves those who are careful (of their duty).

009.005

YUSUFALI: **But when the forbidden months are past, then fight and slay the Pagans wherever ye find them, an seize them, beleaguer them, and lie in wait for them in every stratagem (of war)**; but if they repent, and establish regular prayers and practise regular charity, then open the way for them: for Allah is Oft-forgiving, Most Merciful.

PICKTHAL: Then, when the sacred months have passed, **slay the idolaters wherever ye find them, and take them (captive), and besiege them, and prepare for them each ambush.** But if they repent and establish worship and pay the poor-due, then leave their way free. Lo! Allah is Forgiving, Merciful.

SHAKIR: So when the sacred months have passed away, then **slay the idolaters wherever you find them, and take them captives and besiege them and lie in wait for them in every ambush**, then if they repent and keep up prayer and pay the poor-rate, leave their way free to them; surely Allah is Forgiving, Merciful.

Here is Islamic interpretation of the above verses from the Quran:

(I have been commanded to fight the people until they testify that there is no deity worthy of worship except Allah and that Muhammad is the Messenger of Allah, establish the prayer and pay the Zakah.) **This honorable Ayah (9:5) was called the Ayah of the Sword**, about which Ad-Dahhak bin Muzahim said, **"It abrogated every agreement of peace between the Prophet and any idolator, every treaty, and every term."** Al-'Awfi said that Ibn 'Abbas commented: **"No idolator had any more treaty or promise of safety ever since Surah Bara'ah was revealed.** The four months, in addition to, all peace treaties conducted before Bara'ah was revealed and announced had ended by the tenth of the month of Rabi' Al-Akhir." (Tafsir ibn Kathir)[18]

So, not only was Muhammad a treaty breaker, and therefore not a man of his word, but Allah was the cause of his dishonesty![19]

Another amazing example of Muhammad's dishonesty—and Allah's encouraging dishonesty—is recorded in surah number 66 of the Quran, in which Allah prompts Muhammad to break a promise he made to his wives (verse 1), and declares it lawful for him and all Muslim men to break oaths in some cases (verse 2). Here are those two verses shown in three translations:

066.001

YUSUFALI: O Prophet! Why holdest thou to be forbidden that which Allah has made lawful to thee? Thou seekest to please thy consorts. But Allah is Oft-Forgiving, Most Merciful.

PICKTHAL: **O Prophet! Why bannest thou that which Allah hath made lawful for thee, seeking to please thy wives?** And Allah is Forgiving, Merciful.

SHAKIR: O Prophet! why do you forbid (yourself) that which Allah has made lawful for you;

---

[18]http://wikiislam.net/wiki/Abrogation_(Naskh)

[19]To learn more about Muslims breaking treaties, read: http://www.answering-islam.org/authors/shamoun/rebuttals/zawadi/hasan_islam1.html

you seek to please your wives; and Allah is Forgiving, Merciful.

066.002

YUSUFALI: **Allah has already ordained for you, (O men), the dissolution of your oaths** (in some cases): and Allah is your Protector, and He is Full of Knowledge and Wisdom.

PICKTHAL: **Allah hath made lawful for you (Muslims) absolution from your oaths** (of such a kind), and Allah is your Protector. He is the Knower, the Wise.

SHAKIR: **Allah indeed has sanctioned for you the expiation of your oaths** and Allah is your Protector, and He is the Knowing the Wise.

The Rauzatu'r Safâ, Volume II, p. 188, explains the history of surah 66:

Mary (the Copt) was a Christian slave given to Mohammed 7 A.H. (628 A.D.) by the Governor of Egypt, Elmokaukas. Her sister, Shereena was also given at the same time. Mohammed became intimate with Mary and she bore him Ibrahim, who died in 10 A.H. The intimacy took place in the home and bed of his wife Hafsah (daughter of Umar) who was absent at that moment and on the day which was either her or Ayshah's turn. When Hafsah found this out and questioned him he promised (on oath) not to touch Mary again if she would keep this a secret, and promised that Umar and Abu-Bakr should be his successors. Hafsah, however, told Ayshah about this event, and for a full month Mohammed had no dealings with any of his wives, living with Mary alone.

So, as a result of Muhammad sleeping with his slave, Mary, at the time he had promised to sleep with one of his wives, Muhammad brought great domestic discord upon himself. But...Allah to the rescue, telling Muhammad that it was OK for him to break promises and oaths! So we see that the truth doesn't matter to Allah, or Muhammad, or Islam. All that mattered to Muhammad was being able to

satisfy his carnal lusts, and get away with it.[20]

So, was Muhammad known for his truth and honesty? No, he was known for lying and committing fornication and adultery, then receiving a new surah from "righteous Allah" stating that since he was Allah's prophet these sins were not sins for him. And, of course, he received that surah just in time to save him from the consequences of those sins.

Surah 66 goes on to warn Muhammad's wives that if they don't repent (apparently for being offended by Muhammad's immorality and dishonesty), then they will have to face the wrath of Allah, who will cause Muhammad to divorce them to be replaced by better wives, and will then send them **and their families** to the fire of Hell! Allah commands Muhammad to be hard and firm with them if they refuse to believe this surah, in which case Hell will be their home. Quite a threat in the name of Allah! And no doubt believed, since they had seen Muhammad have many people beheaded. Here is surah 66:3–9 in three translations, so you can read the threats yourself.

066.003

YUSUFALI: When the Prophet disclosed a matter in confidence to one of his consorts, and she then divulged it (to another), and Allah made it known to him, he confirmed part thereof and repudiated a part. Then when he told her thereof, she said, "Who told thee this? "He said, "He told me Who knows and is well-acquainted (with all things)."

PICKTHAL: When the Prophet confided a fact unto one of his wives and when she afterward divulged it and Allah apprised him thereof, he made known (to her) part thereof and passed over part. And when he told it her she said: Who hath told thee? He said: The Knower, the Aware hath told me.

_____

[20]An enlightening article examining the history of surah 66 is found here: http://www.answering-islam.org/Quran/Tafsir/066.html

SHAKIR: And when the prophet secretly communicated a piece of information to one of his wives– but when she informed (others) of it, and Allah made him to know it, he made known part of it and avoided part; so when he informed her of it, she said: Who informed you of this? He said: The Knowing, the one Aware, informed me.

066.004

YUSUFALI: If ye two turn in repentance to Him, your hearts are indeed so inclined; But if ye back up each other against him, truly Allah is his Protector, and Gabriel, and (every) righteous one among those who believe,- and furthermore, the angels - will back (him) up.

PICKTHAL: If ye twain turn unto Allah repentant, (ye have cause to do so) for your hearts desired (the ban); and if ye aid one another against him (Muhammad) then lo! Allah, even He, is his Protecting Friend, and Gabriel and the righteous among the believers; and furthermore the angels are his helpers.

SHAKIR: If you both turn to Allah, then indeed your hearts are already inclined (to this); and if you back up each other against him, then surely Allah it is Who is his Guardian, and Jibreel and -the believers that do good, and the angels after that are the aiders.

066.005

YUSUFALI: It may be, if he divorced you (all), that Allah will give him in exchange consorts better than you,- who submit (their wills), who believe, who are devout, who turn to Allah in repentance, who worship (in humility), who travel (for Faith) and fast,- previously married or virgins.

PICKTHAL: **It may happen that his Lord, if he divorce you, will give him in your stead wives better than you**, submissive (to Allah), believing, pious, penitent, devout, inclined to fasting, widows and maids.

SHAKIR: Maybe, **his Lord, if he divorce you, will give him in your place wives better than you**, submissive, faithful, obedient, penitent, adorers, fasters, widows and virgins.

066.006

YUSUFALI: O ye who believe! **save yourselves and your families from a Fire whose fuel is Men and Stones**, over which are (appointed) angels stern (and) severe, who flinch not (from executing) the Commands they receive from Allah, but do (precisely) what they are commanded.

PICKTHAL: O ye who believe! Ward off from yourselves **and your families** a Fire whereof the fuel is men and stones, over which are set angels strong, severe, who resist not Allah in that which He commandeth them, but do that which they are commanded.

SHAKIR: O you who believe! save yourselves and your families from a fire whose fuel is men and stones; over it are angels stern and strong, they do not disobey Allah in what He commands them, and do as they are commanded.

066.007

YUSUFALI: (They will say), "**O ye Unbelievers! Make no excuses this Day! Ye are being but requited for all that ye did!**"

PICKTHAL: (Then it will be said): O ye who disbelieve! Make no excuses for yourselves this day. Ye are only being paid for what ye used to do.

SHAKIR: O you who disbelieve! do not urge excuses today; you shall be rewarded only according to what you did.

066.008

YUSUFALI: O ye who believe! Turn to Allah with sincere repentance: In the hope that your Lord will remove from you your ills and admit you to Gardens beneath which Rivers flow,- the Day that **Allah will not permit to be humiliated the Prophet** and those who believe with him. Their Light will run forward before them and by their right hands, while they say, "Our Lord! Perfect our Light for us, and grant us Forgiveness: for Thou hast power over all things."

PICKTHAL: **O ye who believe! Turn unto Allah in sincere repentance!** It may be that your Lord will remit from you your evil deeds and bring you into Gardens underneath which rivers flow, on the day when Allah will not abase the Prophet and those who believe with him. Their light will run before them and on their right hands; they will say: Our Lord! Perfect our light for us, and forgive us! Lo! Thou art Able to do all things.

SHAKIR: O you who believe! turn to Allah a sincere turning; maybe your Lord will remove from you your evil and cause you to enter gardens beneath which rivers flow, on the day on which Allah will not abase the Prophet and those who believe with him; their light shall run on before them and on their right hands; they shall say: Our Lord! make perfect for us our light, and grant us protection, surely Thou hast power over all things.

066.009

YUSUFALI: **O Prophet! Strive hard against the Unbelievers and the Hypocrites, and be firm against them. Their abode is Hell,- an evil refuge (indeed).**

PICKTHAL: O Prophet! Strive against the disbelievers and the hypocrites, and be stern with them. Hell will be their home, a hapless journey's end.

SHAKIR: O Prophet! strive hard against the unbelievers and the hypocrites, and be hard against them; and their abode is hell; and evil is the resort.

It seems that Allah had a habit of making sin and immorality into righteousness **just for Muhammad.** For example, Allah did not just permit, but "ordained" him to marry his adopted son's wife in surah 33:37–38.[21] And Allah allowed Muhammad—but no one else—to marry or have sex with just about any woman he wanted in surah 33:50. There were six groups of women permitted to him, so it takes five uses of "and" to list them all!

PICKTHAL: **O Prophet! Lo! We have made lawful unto thee** thy wives unto whom thou hast paid their dowries, **and** those whom thy right hand possesseth of those whom Allah

hath given thee as spoils of war, **and** the daughters of thine uncle on the father's side and the daughters of thine aunts on the father's side, **and** the daughters of thine uncle on the mother's side **and** the daughters of thine aunts on the mother's side who emigrated with thee, **and** a believing woman if she give herself unto the Prophet and the Prophet desire to ask her in marriage - **a privilege for thee only, not for the (rest of) believers** - We are Aware of that which We enjoined upon them concerning their wives and those whom their right hands possess - **that thou mayst be free from blame**, for Allah is ever Forgiving, Merciful.

So, Muhammad was allowed to have sex with his wives, his slaves, his cousins from both his mother's family and his father's family, and (a privilege just for Muhammad only) with any Muslim woman who gave herself to him in marriage (without the need for a legal guardian to give her away, and without Muhammad having to pay dowry)[22]—and apparently their were many such women.

Aisha, whom Muhammad had married when she was only six years old, clearly saw that this was wrong, and commented:

> **I used to look down upon those ladies who had given themselves to Allah's Apostle and I used to say, "Can a lady give herself (to a man)?"** But when Allah revealed: "You (O Muhammad) can postpone (the turn of) whom you will of them (your wives), and you may receive any of them whom you will; and **there is no blame on you** if you invite one whose turn you have set aside (temporarily)." (33.51) I said (to the Prophet), "**I feel that your Lord hastens in fulfilling your wishes and desires.**" (Sahih Al-Bukhari, Volume 6, Book 60, Number 311)[23]

---

[21]For a detailed exposition of this, see http://answering-islam.org/Shamoun/zaynab.htm

[22]For Muslim commentary of this, see http://altafsir.com/Tafsir.asp?tMadhNo=0&tTafsirNo=74&tSoraNo=33&tAyahNo=50&tDisplay=yes&UserProfile=0&LanguageId=2

[23]http://www.usc.edu/schools/college/

Aisha's conscience told her that Muhammad was actually committing adultery, but when surah 33 was issued she knew that she was powerless to stop it.

Surahs 33 and 66 prove that Allah is not righteous, and therefore is not the true God. They also completely undermine Muhammad's moral authority as an honest and righteous prophet.[24]

3.12 Is the Quran of God?

As anyone who has read both the Bible and the Quran knows, the two books contradict each other. They cannot both be of God. Yet Muslims claim to believe the Bible, and try to use it to convert Christians to Islam.

Beware! Islamic deception follows:

Jesus Christ did indicate what the Paraclete to come will do in his time. Did prophet Muhammad do those things? Let's examine;
1. "But when he, the Spirit of Truth, comes, he will guide you into all the truth; for he will not speak on his own initiative, but whatever he hears, he will speak..." Jn.16:13
Note: The Quran is a compilation of the "Divine Revelations" that were received by prophet Muhammad, over a period of 23 years, through the arch angel Gabriel. The prophet used to recite whatever he used to hear. Prophet's companions used to write down whatever was recited. The Quran does not contain the writings or teachings

---

of or by Muhammad, as often mentioned by some misinformed authors.

3.12.1 What the Bible says about the Quran

If Meherally and other Islamic teachers want to use the Bible to prove points, then they must accept all of what the Bible teaches in context. According to the Bible, the Quran could not possibly be of God. The Bible (God's word) very clearly teaches that the book of Revelation is the final book of God's word. Furthermore, the Bible pronounces curses upon anyone who adds anything to God's word.

> Rev. 22:18 For I testify unto every man that heareth the words of the prophecy of this book, **If any man shall add unto these things, God shall add unto him the plagues that are written in this book:** 19 And if any man shall **take away** from the words of the book of this prophecy, **God shall take away his part out of the book of life**, and out of the holy city, and from the things which are written in this book.

The Quran was Muhammad's attempt to **add** books to the Bible, and by denying many of the verses in the Bible, Muhammad also attempted to **take away** words from the Bible. Where then does this leave Muhammad? Answer: it leaves him cursed by Almighty God, and deleted from the book of life. In other words, Muhammad is eternally doomed to the Lake of Fire. The Bible does not authenticate Muhammad as a prophet. Rather it exposes him as an impostor, and condemns him to Hell.

3.12.2 Errors in Muhammad's recitations

Also, Muhammad did not guide people into truth, but rather into error.

---

crcc/engagement/resources/texts/muslim/
hadith/bukhari/060.sbt.html#006.060.311
[24]For a more detailed discussion of all the sexual relationships allowed to Muhammad, see http://answering-islam.org/authors/shamoun/marriage_without_guardian.html

3.12.2.1 Death in Heaven

For example, consider the following error found in the Quran (surah 56:21), shown below in four translations:

> **YUSUFALI**: And the flesh of fowls, any that they may desire.

> **PICKTHAL**: And flesh of fowls that they desire.

> **SHAKIR**: And the flesh of fowl such as they desire.

> **KHALIFA**: Meat of birds that they desire.

This verse is given in a passage discussing what Heaven will be like, and it says that those nearest to Allah will get to eat the flesh of fowls in Heaven. That implies that there will have to be death in Heaven for those fowls to become food. If there were death in Heaven then Heaven would cease to be Heaven!

The Bible portrays Heaven as a far better place than does the Quran:

> Revelation 21:1 And I saw a **new heaven** and a new earth: for the first heaven and the first earth were passed away; and there was no more sea. 2 And I John saw the holy city, new Jerusalem, coming down from God out of heaven, prepared as a bride adorned for her husband. 3 And I heard a great voice out of heaven saying, Behold, the tabernacle of God is with men, and he will dwell with them, and they shall be his people, and God himself shall be with them, and be their God. 4 And God shall wipe away all tears from their eyes; **and there shall be no more death**, neither sorrow, nor crying, neither shall there be any more pain: for the former things are passed away.

3.12.2.2 Sun sets in water

Now consider what the Quran says about the sun in surah 18:86:

> **YUSUFALI**: Until, when he reached the setting of the sun, he found it set in a spring of murky water: Near it he found a People: We said:

> "O Zul-qarnain! (thou hast authority,) either to punish them, or to treat them with kindness."

> **PICKTHAL**: Till, when he reached the setting-place of the sun, he found it setting in a muddy spring, and found a people thereabout. We said: O Dhu'l-Qarneyn! Either punish or show them kindness.

> **SHAKIR**: Until when he reached the place where the sun set, he found it going down into a black sea, and found by it a people. We said: O Zulqarnain! either give them a chastisement or do them a benefit.

> **KHALIFA**: When he reached the far west, he found the sun setting in a vast ocean, and found people there. We said, "O Zul-Qarnain, you can rule as you wish; either punish, or be kind to them."

Regardless of which translation one accepts, it is clear that the Quran is not scientifically accurate. The sun does not set in water. It is not possible to reach the setting of the sun. The sun does not set in a "place." The sun **appears** to set in a place on the horizon, but if you go that place you find that the sun is not there.

3.12.2.3 Babies come from blood clots

Another scientific discrepancy is found in surah 23:14

> **YUSUFALI**: Then We made the sperm into **a clot of congealed blood**; then of that clot We made a (foetus) lump; then we made out of that lump bones and clothed the bones with flesh; then we developed out of it another creature. So blessed be Allah, the best to create!

> **PICKTHAL**: Then fashioned We the drop **a clot**, then fashioned We the clot a little lump, then fashioned We the little lump bones, then clothed the bones with flesh, and then produced it as another creation. So blessed be Allah, the Best of creators!

> **SHAKIR**: Then We made the seed **a clot**, then We made the clot a lump of flesh, then We made (in) the lump of flesh bones, then We

clothed the bones with flesh, then We caused it to grow into another creation, so blessed be Allah, the best of the creators.

Note that the Quran says that "We made the sperm into a clot of congealed blood" before forming it into a foetus. We know today that that is not what happens. Congealed blood is dead blood. Sperm is not made into a blood clot, and then into a baby. The Quran is not even remotely scientifically accurate in this matter, so it could not be of God. If the Quran is actually from Allah, then Allah could not possibly be the true and living Creator God.

3.12.2.4 Relationship errors

The answering-islam.org website lists numerous errors found in the Quran. Nehls points out an interesting one:

> Christians read with surprise in Sura 19:28-29 that Mary, the mother of Jesus, was a sister of Aaron. Learned men of Islam, who are aware that between Miriam, the sister of Aaron, and Miriam or Mary, the mother of Jesus **there is a gap of 1500 years**, try to persuade us that Mary had a brother, who also happened to be an Aaron. We reject this possibility, because she is also described as the daughter of Imram (Sura 66:12), the Amram of Exodus 6:20. He was indeed the father of Aaron, Moses and Miriam. Besides that, Jelalood Deen has stated that Mary's mother was Hannah. The one who was mentioned in 1 Samuel, chapters 1-2, and who lived about a 1000 years before her "daughter".
>
> **All this is a hopeless mix-up of historical events** and no argument will convince one that in fact the Quran is right and the Christian have changed their Bibles, as in fact claimed by the Muslims.[25]

---

[25]http://www.answering-islam.org/Nehls/Ask/sources.html

3.12.2.5 Math errors

Would a God-inspired book contain math errors? Certainly not. Consider this critique of the Quran from the answering-islam.org website:

> Now we know that Muhammad could neither read nor write, but obviously he also could not do math either. Consider the Quran's rules concerning dividing the inheritance. When a man dies and leaves behind a mother, wife and one sister only, then according to surah 4:11 the mother gets 1/3 (because he has neither children nor a brother), the wife gets 1/4 according to surah 4:12 (because they have no children) and the sister gets 1/2 according to surah 4:176 (because he has no children). Not only do we have again distributed more than there exists [1/12 in overdraft], we also have the very strange result that the direct heirs [people of direct relationship = spouse, children, parents] get each less than the indirect heir which is his sister. It becomes even worse if he has more than one sister since they then get 2/3 instead of 1/2 and we get even more into overdraft.
>
> Anybody who has ever dealt with dividing out an inheritance will know how easily that can get nasty and how this can poison family relationships if people think they have been cheated. Promising certain people a definite share but not being able to pay them this share because more was promised than is available is the surest recipe for disaster.
>
> And there seems to be an awareness of this in the Qur'an since it does repeatedly in further verses stress the necessity of being just. And in the verses we have been looking at, we have the explicit statement at the end of 4:176 that "Allah makes clear to you, lest you go astray" as well as in 4:11–12 it says that "So Allah apportions" and "so Allah charges you" and (because?) He is the "All-wise". I am not sure there are many commands on the Qur'an which are explicitly given to make things clear and which are so completely unclear and contradictory and impossible to fulfill. Do we really want to charge God that he didn't know what

he was saying and that He is the author of confusion and contradiction? Or would it be more consistent with the confidence in God's wisdom to assume that this is NOT from God?[26]

Figure 3.7: *Muslims in England on Sept. 11, 2011, celebrating the Sept. 11, 2001 Muslim terrorist attack on the World Trade Center by disrupting a memorial service and setting fire to the USA flag.*

Figure 3.6: *According to the USAID website, "The mosque [pictured above] and its minaret are now restored. USAID funding helped reinforce the building's structure, ensuring that it will stand for future generations of Cypriots and pilgrims. The project also planted over 130 date and palm trees around the site to provide shade and restored the original footpath terraces that visitors have admired for centuries." This is a flagrant violation of the First Amendment. These are mosques being repaired or built with the taxes taken from people the majority of which very strongly disagree with the message and beliefs of Islam. That is against our law. Is it any wonder that Muslims consider Americans stupid fools, and are encouraged to keep fighting us? [Photo credit: UNOPS.* `http://www.usaid.gov/stories/ afghanistan/ba_af_survey_a_h.html]`

Figure 3.8: *At the same event as above, a Muslim preacher said: "Do not be fooled by the politicians. This is not about security;* **its about a war against all Islam—a war against belief.... It is a religious war** *against the Muslims.* **Open your own eyes, and look to the reality! We are fighting all this government, and the Americans are fighting against a belief. And** *you are doomed to failure." A must-watch video of this event is available here:* `http://www.youtube. com/watch?v=5_gPoE46eQo&feature=related`

---

[26]`http://answering-islam.org/Quran/ Contra/i001.html`

Figure 3.9: *Muhammad followers "comforting" people by threatening to behead them. So much for freedom of speech and religion.*

Figure 3.10: *This mosque and its grounds had deteriorated due to the humid climate of Cyprus, insect infestation, and water damage, and was restored with funds taken by taxation from USA citizens. The US government has given $770,000,000.00 dollars to restore mosques around the world. That is enough money to build 1,540 new buildings costing $500,000.00 each! In many third world countries that is enough money to build many thousands of medium-sided mosques. Using tax money this way is a flagrant violation of the First Amendment. [Photo credit: USAID/UNDP/Elias Karassellos.* `http://www.usaid.gov/stories/cyprus/ ba_cy_mosque_b_h.html]`

Chapter *4*

Did Muhammad glorify Jesus?

One of the most obvious lies Islamic teachers tell is that Muhammad—and now Islam—glorify Jesus. The deception usually begins as follows:

> **Beware! Islamic deception follows:**
>
> 2. "He shall glorify me." John 16:14
> Note: The Quran glorifies the birth of Jesus through Virgin Mary. The Quran also confirms, Jesus was a Messiah; a Messenger of God; the Spirit from God; the Word of God and the Righteous Prophet.

Note that when dealing with Christians, Meherally quotes only from the Bible—never from the Quran. Muslim teachers have learned from experience that the Quran has little influence on Christians—it just doesn't have the ring of truth.

4.1 Did Muhammad actually glorify Jesus?

NO. This is just another of Islam's lies. Consider the following facts:

➪ If Jesus had no earthly father as both the Bible and the Quran teach, then surely He had a Heavenly Father, which is what the Bible repeatedly teaches, but which Islam denies, saying He had no father at all! Muhammad denied that God was Jesus' Father. Muhammad did not glorify Jesus, but rather blasphemed Jesus.

➪ Jesus repeatedly claimed to be the Son of God. Muhammad taught that Jesus was not the Son of God. So, Muhammad did not glorify Jesus, but rather blasphemed Jesus.

➪ The Bible teaches that Jesus is "the" Messiah, not just "a" Messiah. Does it glorify Jesus to say that He is just "a" Messiah? No. Muhammad did not glorify Jesus, but rather blasphemed Jesus.

➪ If Jesus is "a Messenger of God; the Spirit from God; the Word of God and the Righteous Prophet," as Meherally implies Muhammad taught, did Jesus lie when He claimed to be the Son of God? Does implying that Jesus is a liar glorify Him? No. Muhammad did not glorify Jesus, but rather blasphemed Jesus.

➪ Muhammad—a sinful mortal man—claimed to be a greater prophet than the sinless Jesus—to actually supersede

47

Jesus. Does that glorify Jesus? No. Muhammad did not glorify Jesus, but rather blasphemed Jesus.

⇨ To confess that Jesus is God glorifies Jesus. Muhammad denied that Jesus is God. Does it glorify Jesus to say that He is a mere mortal man and not God? No. Muhammad did not glorify Jesus, but rather blasphemed Jesus.

Islam's claim to glorify Jesus is simply a lie. Islam does not glorify Jesus, but rather denies Jesus' glory and blasphemes Him.

Figure 4.1: *Graffiti left by Muslim jihadists in Maluku, Indonesia to "glorify" Jesus. It says, "Jesus is an animal—a dog." This shows the true feelings Islam causes Muslims to have toward Jesus.*

4.2   Did Muhammad glorify himself?

Note also that the Spirit of truth "shall **not** speak of himself" (John 16:13). A search for "Muhammad" in the Pickthall translation of the Quran finds 273 matches, while searching for "Jesus" finds only 25 matches. Muhammad recited something about himself 10.92 times for every one time he recited something about Jesus, thus proving without any shadow of doubt that he is **not** the Comforter.

While 25 times is 25 times more than the Bible mentions the name of Muhammad, 273 times is over 1,092 percent more times than the 25 times the Quran uses the name Jesus. Muhammad spoke of himself often, and so is clearly not the Comforter.

4.3   Did Muhammad speak the words of Christ?

> **Beware! Islamic deception follows:**
>
> 3. "He shall take mine and shall disclose it to you." Jn.16:14
> Note: Muhammad did declare himself a Messenger of God like Abraham, Moses and Jesus.

The correct reading of this verse is "...he shall receive of mine, and shall show it unto you." Muhammad did not do this. He did not show us what Jesus said. Instead he subtracted from and added to what Jesus said. Anyone can claim to be a prophet; that is no great thing. But a true prophet will not contradict the Bible, as Muhammad did repeatedly. The prophet Isaiah warned us about false prophets such as Muhammad:

> Isaiah 8:19 And when they shall say unto you, Seek unto them that have familiar spirits, and unto wizards that peep, and that mutter: should not a people seek unto their God? for the living to the dead? 20 **To the law and to the testimony: if they speak not according to this word, it is because there is no light in them.**

Muhammad did not speak according to the Bible because there is no light in him. Instead Muhammad muttered and peeped after being possessed of Satan in the cave of Hira, and that muttering and peeping became the Quran.

Muhammad even admitted that he thought he was being possessed of an evil spirit.[1]

The Quran does not teach a way of life. Rather Islam teaches a way of death, as do all false religions. The Bible says that Jesus is "the way, the truth, and the life." Islam refuses Jesus as the way of life, even as it falsely claims to believe the Bible. Islam glorifies suicide. Islam is a way of acting, but it is not a way of life. Muslims have often been in the news these last few years for bragging that they love death more than Christians love life.[2] It takes satanic possession to motive a person to send his own children on suicide bomber missions, or to go on one himself.

---

[1]The history of the spirit that possessed Muhammad to recite the Quran is documented here: http://answering-islam.org/Silas/spirit_of_islam.htm

[2]Examples: http://online.wsj.com/article/SB120450617910806563.html?mod=rss_opinion_main and http://www.freerepublic.com/focus/f-bloggers/2384170/posts

Many people quote Jesus every day. That does not make them prophets. And it certainly does not mean that they are the Comforter. But actually Muhammad did **not** quote Jesus. If anything, he very dishonestly misquoted Jesus. But in most cases he just made up new teachings to contradict the Bible. These contradictions, which are now repeated by his followers, are pointed out in this book over and over again.

Figure 4.2: *The graffiti witness of Muslim jihadists concerning Christ. It says: "Jesus is a wicked, cursed man."*

4.4 Did Muhammad bear witness of Christ?

If the Quran admits that Jesus is the Messiah of God, why then do Muslims not study and obey the teachings of Jesus as recorded in the Bible? There is a great inconsistency here that should cause sincere Muslims to lose faith in the Quran.

Note that Meherally bases his argument of Acts 2:22 and 3:13 from the New American Standard Bible (NASB), not from the King James Bible. The New Testament section of the NASB is translated from Novum Testamentum Graece which is a compiled text created by Eberhard Nestle and Kurt Aland based on the so-called "Critical Text" of Brooke Foss Westcott and Fenton John Anthony Hort. Westcott and Hort rejected the thousands of extant[3] Greek New Testament manuscripts which contain the Textus Receptus Greek text (so named because only that text was received by the early church as genuine), and instead created a new text merging all the corruptions found in two exceedingly corrupt manuscripts, Codex Sinaiticus (also known as Aleph) and Codex Vaticanus (also know as B), into one even more corrupt text which is now called the Critical Text or Westcott and Hort text. Aleph and B not only differed with the Textus Receptus but also with each other.

Wrote Dean Burgon, who lived contemporary with Westcott and Hort,

> Aleph, B, D are three of the most scandalously corrupt copies extant:—exhibit the most shamefully mutilated texts which are anywhere to be met with:—have become, by whatever process (for their history is wholly unknown), the depositories of the largest amount of fabricated readings ancient blunders, and intentional perversions of Truth,—which are discoverable in any known copies of the Word of God. (Dean John W. Burgon, *Revision Revised*, p. 16)[4]

The 27th edition of *Novum Testamentum Graece* and the 4th edition of the United Bible Societies Greek New Testament are the same text. Members of the Editorial Committee of the United Bible Societies' Greek New Testament were Kurt Aland, Barbara Aland, Matthew Black, Carlo Maria Martini, Bruce Metzger, Allen Wikgren, and Johannes Karavidopoulos. These people were all unbelievers, and their translations must be rejected by all true believers in the Lord Jesus Christ. For instance, Westcott denied the bodily resurrection of the Lord Jesus Christ; Bruce Metzger did not believe that all of the books in the Bible are inspired of God;[5] Kurt Aland so hated the Jesus described in the Gospel of John that he wrote, "(...if the Gospel of John was really written by the beloved disciple of Jesus), then the real question arises: was there really a Jesus?"[6] And Carlo Maria Martini was a very liberal Catholic cardinal.[7] Muslim teachers love the works of these arrogant people who worked so zealously to **change the content** of the Bible. Of course, Muslim teachers love the corrupt translations made by these people. Such corrupted translations help Muslims convert weak Christians to Islam. The Textus Receptus is the original and genuine New Testament text, and is the only text from which legitimate translations of the New Testament can be made. In the English language use only the King James Bible, and you will have in your hands a weapon that is "quick, and powerful, and sharper than any twoedged sword, piercing even to the dividing asunder of soul and spirit, and of the

---

[3]Extant means, "still existing" (Oxford English Dictionary).

[4]For more information about the corruption of Aleph and B, read http://www.deanburgonsociety.org/CriticalTexts/dbs2695.htm

[5]http://en.wikipedia.org/wiki/Bruce_Metzger

[6]http://www.trinitarianbiblesociety.org/site/articles/aland.pdf

[7]http://en.wikipedia.org/wiki/Carlo_Maria_Martini

joints and marrow, and is a discerner of the thoughts and intents of the heart" (Hebrews 4:12). Muslim's fear the King James Bible!

Not only is the NASB translated from a corrupt text, but its translators did not believe in the deity of Christ. Therefore they often translated words incorrectly on purpose in order to remove proof that Jesus was God and the Son of God.

The reason Meherally used the NASB is because the *true* reading of Acts 3:13 as found in the King James Bible is as follows:

> Acts 3:13 The God of Abraham, and of Isaac, and of Jacob, **the God of our fathers, hath glorified his Son Jesus**; whom ye delivered up, and denied him in the presence of Pilate, when he was determined to let him go. 14 But ye denied **the Holy One and the Just**, and desired a murderer to be granted unto you; 15 And killed the Prince of life, whom God hath raised from the dead; whereof we are witnesses.

Verse 13 says that Jesus is the "**Son**" of God, **not** "servant" of God! Verse 14 calls Jesus the "Holy One," a term used only for God. And verse 15 says that **Jesus died, was buried, and rose from the dead!** All of this Islam denies; and, therefore, Meherally does not want you to know it is in the Bible. Also, Acts 2:22 does not call Jesus a servant even in the NASB. See the deception of Islam!

The deception of the NASB translators must be exposed here also. The Greek word translated "Son" in Acts 2:22 and 3:13 in the King James Bible, and translated "Servant" in the NASB, is παῖδα. παῖδα is found five times in the New Testament. The NASB translators translated παῖδα "boy" in every case except where it referred to Jesus—in which case they translated παῖδα as "Servant." Even "boy" is wrong, as it removes the father-son relationship, but to translate παῖδα as "Servant" is nothing less than dishonest and deceitful.

4.5 What about Kedar?

Beware! Islamic deception follows:

Prophet Isaiah is considered to be one of the major prophets of the Old Testament. In the Book of Isaiah there are several prophecies about the coming of the Messiah. In chapter 42, Isaiah begins with a prophecy for the coming of prophet Jesus. After verse number nine, God declares through Isaiah, the "new things" that are to "spring forth" in the Land of Kedar.

In the Bible there is only one personality called Kedar. He was the grandson of prophet Abraham, through his son Ishmael (see Gen.25:13). Kedar's descendants had settled in Paran (Syno-Arabian dessert). In the Rabbinic literature Arabia is called the "Land of Kedar". Prophet Muhammad was a descendant of Kedar. God declares through Isaiah;

"Behold, the former things are come to pass, and the new things do I declare: before they spring forth I tell you of them. 'Sing unto the Lord a new song, and his praise from the end of the earth'. Let the wilderness and the cities thereof lift up their voices, the villages that Kedar doth inhabit: let the inhabitants of the rock sing, let them shout from the top of the mountains. Let them give glory unto the Lord, and declare His praise in the inlands." Chapter 42, Verses 9-12.

God did reveal in the Land of Kedar, through prophet Muhammad - a direct descendant of Kedar, a "New Song" - The Qur'an (Quran). This happens to be the only Scripture to be revealed in the language of the Kedarites. The verses of the Qur'an are recited like a poem. Nearly 1.2 billion Muslims, residing all over the world, recite this "new song" and Glorify Allah, in their daily prayers, five times in a day. The initial Revelation came to prophet Muhammad in a cave of Mount Hira near the city of Mecca. There are several mountains near Mecca. During the annual Islamic Pilgrimage called "Hajj", Muslims from all over the world, assemble in Mecca and shout Glory to the Lord from the top of Mount Arafat. The pilgrims continuously give Glory to Allah on their ways, to and from Mecca.

There is no indication whatsoever from the text that these verses mean what Meherally and other Islamic teachers say they mean. Meherally is simply imagining things to be as he wishes they were, but in fact are not. Neither the Quran, nor Islam, nor Muhammad are mentioned in these texts. To quote Meherally himself (see the paragraph numbered 2 in his Answer No.15 on page 130): "One can only SUBSTITUTE (of course with admissible logic), the original term *IF* the LITERAL translation of the used term fails to reconcile with the rest of the text." In the above text the literal translation of the used terms do not fail to reconcile with the rest of the text. Therefore substitution is not allowed, according to Meherally's own rule.

4.5.1 Who is the servant of Isaiah 42:1?

The context shows that this servant could not be Muhammad. When Muslim teachers quote a verse from the Bible, they almost always take it out of context. So, let's read the entire chapter to see if Muhammad's name is anywhere to be found:

> Isaiah 42:1 Behold **my servant**, whom I uphold; mine elect, in whom my soul delighteth; I have put my spirit upon him: he shall bring forth judgment to the Gentiles. 2 He shall not cry, nor lift up, nor cause his voice to be heard in the street. 3 A bruised reed shall he not break, and the smoking flax shall he not quench: he shall bring forth judgment unto truth. 4 He shall not fail nor be discouraged, till he have set judgment in the earth: and the isles shall wait for his law. 5 Thus saith God **the LORD**, he that created the heavens, and stretched them out; he that spread forth the earth, and that which cometh out of it; he that giveth breath unto the people upon it, and spirit to them that walk therein: 6 I **the LORD** have called thee in righteousness, and will hold thine hand, and will keep thee, and give thee for a covenant of the people, for a light of the Gentiles; 7 To open the blind eyes, to bring out the prisoners from the prison, and them that sit in darkness out of the prison house. 8 **I am the LORD: that is my name**: and my glory will I not give to another, neither my praise to graven images. 9 Behold, the former things are come to pass, and new things do I declare: before they spring forth I tell you of them. 10 **Sing unto the LORD a new song**, and his praise from the end of the earth, ye that go down to the sea, and all that is therein; the isles, and the inhabitants thereof. 11 Let the wilderness and the cities thereof lift up their voice, the villages that **Kedar** doth inhabit: let the inhabitants of the rock sing, let them shout from the top of the mountains. 12 **Let them give glory unto the LORD**, and declare his praise in the islands. 13 **The LORD** shall go forth as a mighty man, he shall stir up jealousy like a man of war: he shall cry, yea, roar; he shall prevail against his enemies. 14 I have long time holden my peace; I have been still, and refrained myself: now will I cry like a travailing woman; I will destroy and devour at once. 15 I will make waste mountains and hills, and dry up all their herbs; and I will make the rivers islands, and I will dry up the pools. 16 **And I will bring the blind by a way that they knew not; I will lead them in paths that they have not known: I will make darkness light before them, and crooked things straight. These things will I do unto them, and not forsake them.** 17 They shall be turned back, they shall be greatly ashamed, that trust in graven images, that say to the molten images, Ye are our gods. 18 Hear, ye deaf; and look, ye blind, that ye may see. 19 Who is blind, but my servant? or deaf, as my messenger that I sent? who is blind as he that is perfect, and blind as **the LORD'S servant**? 20 Seeing many things, but thou observest not; opening

the ears, but he heareth not. 21 **The LORD** is well pleased for his righteousness' sake; he will magnify the law, and make it honourable. 22 But this is a people robbed and spoiled; they are all of them snared in holes, and they are hid in prison houses: they are for a prey, and none delivereth; for a spoil, and none saith, Restore. 23 Who among you will give ear to this? who will hearken and hear for the time to come? 24 Who gave Jacob for a spoil, and Israel to the robbers? did not **the LORD**, he against whom we have sinned? for they would not walk in his ways, neither were they obedient unto his law. 25 Therefore he hath poured upon him the fury of his anger, and the strength of battle: and it hath set him on fire round about, yet he knew not; and it burned him, yet he laid it not to heart.

Did you see the name "Muhammad" in those verses? No. Meherally is using **substitution** in violation of his own rule (see his Answer No. 15 on page 130). It is clear from the context that it is not Muhammad who is being talked about here. In verse 19, we see that this servant is "**the LORD'S servant**" (JE-HOVAH's servant), not Allah's slave. The translators of the King James Bible often translated "JEHOVAH" (God's name) as "the LORD" (using all capital letters). Note verse eight: "**I am the LORD: that is my name.**" Allah is not JEHOVAH, and JEHOVAH is not Allah.

So, who is the servant mentioned in verse one of Isaiah chapter forty-two? We do not have to speculate about this like the Muslim scholars do. **The Bible clearly reveals that servant to be Jesus Christ**.

Matthew 12:14 Then the Pharisees went out, and held a council against him, how they might destroy him. 15 But when **Jesus** knew it, he withdrew himself from thence: and great multitudes followed him, and he healed them all; 16 And charged them that they should not make him known: 17 **That it might be fulfilled which was spoken by Esaias the prophet**, saying, 18 Behold **my servant**, whom I have chosen; my beloved, in whom my soul is well pleased: I will put my spirit upon him, and he shall shew judgment to the Gentiles. 19 He shall not strive, nor cry; neither shall any man hear his voice in the streets. 20 A bruised reed shall he not break, and smoking flax shall he not quench, till he send forth judgment unto victory. 21 And in his name shall the Gentiles trust.

4.5.2 What is the "new song" of Isaiah 42:10?

What about the "new song" mentioned in Isaiah 42:10? Is that the Quran, as Islamic teachers claim? Well, no, not according to the Bible. According to the Bible this new song is a song of praise to the Lord Jesus Christ for "redeeming us to God" with His blood.

Revelation 5:1 And I saw in the right hand of him that sat on the throne a book written within and on the backside, sealed with seven seals. 2 And I saw a strong angel proclaiming with a loud voice, Who is worthy to open the book, and to loose the seals thereof? 3 And no man in heaven, nor in earth, neither under the earth, was able to open the book, neither to look thereon. 4 And I wept much, because no man was found worthy to open and to read the book, neither to look thereon. 5 And one of the elders saith unto me, Weep not: behold, **the Lion of the tribe of Juda, the Root of David**, hath prevailed to open the book, and to loose the seven seals thereof. 6 And I beheld, and, lo, in the midst of the throne and of the four beasts, and in the midst of the elders, stood **a Lamb as it had been slain**, having seven horns and seven eyes, which are the seven Spirits of God sent forth into all the earth. 7 And he came and took the book out of the right hand of him that sat upon the throne. 8 And when he had taken the book, the four beasts and four and twenty elders fell down before **the Lamb**, having every one of them harps, and golden vials full of odours, which are the prayers of saints. 9 And they sung a **new song**, saying, **Thou art worthy to take the book, and to open the seals thereof: for thou wast slain, and**

hast redeemed us to God by thy blood out of every kindred, and tongue, and people, and nation; 10 And hast made us unto our God kings and priests: and we shall reign on the earth.

Dear reader, if you will place your faith in the Lord Jesus Christ, then you also will have a new song in your heart, knowing that your sins are forgiven, and that you are eternally saved by grace through faith in Christ's blood. Even in the land of Kedar there are a few people that have believed in the Lord Jesus Christ to the saving of their souls, and that therefore know this joy.

4.5.3 Do Kedarites preach truth and peace?

It is true that Kedar was one of the sons of Ishmael. But note what else the Bible says about Kedar:

> Psalm 120:1 In my distress I cried unto the LORD, and he heard me. 2 Deliver my soul, O LORD, from **lying lips, and from a deceitful tongue.** 3 What shall be given unto thee? or what shall be done unto thee, thou false tongue? 4 Sharp arrows of the mighty, with coals of juniper. 5 **Woe is me, that I sojourn in Mesech, that I dwell in the tents of Kedar! 6 My soul hath long dwelt with him that hateth peace. 7 I am for peace: but when I speak, they are for war.**

"Woe" means "distressed, afflicted, unfortunate, grieved." That is how the psalmist felt while dwelling in the tents of Kedar. Why? Because the Kedarites had lying lips and deceitful tongues, and because the Kedarites hated peace. And while the psalmist was for peace, the Kedarites were for war. And that is still the way it is with the Kedarites. In the year 2000, the Israelis were willing to give Muslim leader Yasser Arafat virtually everything he demanded in exchange for peace. Amazingly, Arafat rejected the deal, and instead started what he called the Al-Aqsa Intifada, that

killed almost 1000 Israelis, and maimed thousands of others...At the height of the intifada, there were nine suicide attacks in Israel—killing 85 Israelis in just one month (March 2002)...Yasser Arafat started the intifada in September 2000, just weeks after he had rejected at Camp David Israel's offer of withdrawal, settlement evacuation, sharing of Jerusalem and establishment of a Palestinian state. Arafat wanted all that, of course, but without having to make peace and recognize a Jewish state. Hence the terror campaign—to force Israel to give it all up unilaterally."[8]

Being a descendant of Kedar is therefore not a plus for Muhammad, but implies that he is one of the lying, deceitful, peace-hating Kedarites that bring woe and discomfort upon the world. And history proves that to be the case.

Beware! Islamic deception follows:

"The Lord shall go forth as a mighty man, he shall stir up jealousy like a man of war: he shall cry, yea, roar; he shall prevail against his enemies." Verse 13.

In the Old Testament the God often speaks "I" will do this, or "I" have done this; whereas, He has chosen human beings like us, to do these jobs. (see 2 Samuel 12:7-12). Muhammad did go forth as a mighty prophet of Allah, did stir up jealousy among the most influential and dominating tribe of the pagan Arabs in Arabia. Finally with a war cry and roar, Muhammad did prevail upon the enemies of Lord - the idolaters, fulfilling the above prophecy.

Consider carefully what Meherally said in the above paragraph. According to Meherally, the "Lord" that went forth as a "man of war" was not actually God, but

[8] http://seattletimes.nwsource.com/html/opinion/2001960796_krauthammer21.html

Muhammad! Muhammad was the "man of war." Meherally says, "Finally with a **war cry** and roar, **Muhammad** did prevail upon the enemies of Lord." It was Muhammad that issued the "war cry." And it is obvious that the "enemies of the Lord" in Meherally's belief were actually just anyone who didn't agree with Muhammad. Muhammad used war to spread Islam. He did not go forth peaceably trying to persuade people. Islam is not a religion of tolerance. Instead he forced people to either convert to Islam, pay a tax as a non-Muslim, or else be beheaded. That is what Muslims call tolerance. Muhammad was a man of war and violence, not a man of peace. And Islam is a religion spread by war, and is not a religion of peace.

Remember that the God mentioned in Isaiah chapter 42 is "JEHOVAH," not Allah. Muhammad did not go forth from JEHOVAH. Muhammad was an Ishmaelite, and in Psalms 83 the Ishmaelites are listed among the enemies of JEHOVAH God. Muhammad did not go forth "from" JEHOVAH, but rather went forth to **oppose** JEHOVAH.

Beware! Islamic deception follows:

"I have long time holden my peace; I have been still, and refrained myself, now will I cry like a travailing woman; I will destroy and devour at once." Verse 14.
The prophets that came before Muhammad had all tried with peaceful missions. But, the concept of sharing God's Glory continued to surface again and again, in one way or other. It was with the war cry, through the descendants of Kedar (Arabs), these sinful practices were destroyed and devoured, inside and outside of Arabia. The spread of Islam was swift, wide spread and at once.
"And I will bring the blind by a way they knew not; I will lead them in paths that they have not known; I will make darkness light before them, and crooked things straight.

These things I will do unto them, and not forsake them." Verse 16.
It is an undeniable fact that before the advent of Islam, the pagan Arabs were like the blinds. Their religious and social concepts were crooked. The revelation of this "new song" brought them out of that darkness. Earlier, God had not sent any prophet to these people.

It is true that before the advent of Islam the pagan Arabs were like blind men. It is also true that after the advent of Islam they were even more blind than before. Because after Muhammad their freedom of speech was taken from them, and with it their freedom to consider the truth and accept it. Muhammad's song is a song of enslavement. Islamic nations are now the most enslaved areas on earth. By their own admission, Muslims hate freedom of speech and freedom in general.

In contrast, Jesus Christ and his Bible bring true freedom to every nation that embraces them.

John 8:31 Then said Jesus to those Jews which believed on him, **If ye continue in my word**, then are ye my disciples indeed; 32 **And ye shall know the truth, and the truth shall make you free.**

Note that Meherally said, "The prophets that came before Muhammad had all tried with **peaceful** missions. But ..." not Muhammad. Muhammad came "with a **war** cry" and a sword, to use violence against anyone who did not want to submit to his religion. This proves that the Islam brought by Muhammad was not a religion of peace.

Figure 4.3: *Muslims protesting cartoonist's drawings of Muhammad. Islam does not free, it enslaves.*

4.6 Was Ishmael the son of a bondwoman?

Beware! Islamic deception follows:

By sending Muhammad, God fulfilled His above promise and also the following promise to Abraham:
"And also of the son of the bondwoman I will make a nation, because he is thy seed." Genesis 21:13.

This is an interesting admission of an important truth by Meherally—Ishmael is the son of the bondwoman. This proves that

Muhammad is not a prophet of the true God, and that the Quran is not of God. As Meherally says later on in this document, "The call of sincerity demands that if believing in the Truth is the honest intent then one could only pass an ethical judgment after reflecting upon all the relevant texts." So let us reflect upon all the texts to see what the Bible really teaches about Ishmael so that all honest seekers of truth can pass ethical judgment concerning Ishmael or his seed receiving the covenant of God. Let's consider some important Bible facts about Ishmael.

4.6.1 Ishmael—a result of unbelief

Ishmael was a product of Sarah's unbelief; had Sarah believed God, Ishmael would never have been born. God promised to give Abraham a son, and Sarah was Abraham's only wife, so the son would be born through her womb.

> Genesis 15:1 After these things the word of **the LORD** came unto **Abram** in a vision, saying, Fear not, Abram: I am thy shield, and thy exceeding great reward. 2 **And Abram said**, Lord GOD, **what wilt thou give me, seeing I go childless**, and the steward of my house is this Eliezer of Damascus? 3 **And Abram said**, Behold, to me thou hast given no seed: and, lo, one born in my house is mine heir. 4 And, behold, **the word of the LORD** came unto him, saying, **This shall not be thine heir; but he that shall come forth out of thine own bowels shall be thine heir.** 5 And he brought him forth abroad, and said, Look now toward heaven, and tell the stars, if thou be able to number them: and he said unto him, So shall thy seed be. 6 And he believed in the LORD; and he counted it to him for righteousness.

But Sarah was old and barren, and so when she did not quickly get pregnant she lost faith in God's promise, and even laughed at the promise.

Genesis 18:1 And **the LORD** appeared unto him in the plains of Mamre: and he sat in the tent door in the heat of the day; 2 And he lift up his eyes and looked, and, lo, three men stood by him: and when he saw them, he ran to meet them from the tent door, and bowed himself toward the ground, 3 And said, My Lord, if now I have found favour in thy sight, pass not away, I pray thee, from thy servant: 4 Let a little water, I pray you, be fetched, and wash your feet, and rest yourselves under the tree: 5 And I will fetch a morsel of bread, and comfort ye your hearts; after that ye shall pass on: for therefore are ye come to your servant. And they said, So do, as thou hast said. 6 And **Abraham** hastened into the tent unto **Sarah**, and said, Make ready quickly three measures of fine meal, knead it, and make cakes upon the hearth. 7 And Abraham ran unto the herd, and fetcht a calf tender and good, and gave it unto a young man; and he hasted to dress it. 8 And he took butter, and milk, and the calf which he had dressed, and set it before them; and he stood by them under the tree, and they did eat. 9 And they said unto him, **Where is Sarah thy wife?** And he said, Behold, in the tent. 10 And he said, I will certainly return unto thee according to the time of life; and, lo, **Sarah thy wife shall have a son.** And Sarah heard it in the tent door, which was behind him. 11 Now Abraham and Sarah were old and well stricken in age; and it ceased to be with Sarah after the manner of women. 12 **Therefore Sarah laughed within herself, saying, After I am waxed old shall I have pleasure, my lord being old also?** 13 **And the LORD said unto Abraham, Wherefore did Sarah laugh, saying, Shall I of a surety bear a child, which am old?** 14 **Is any thing too hard for the LORD? At the time appointed I will return unto thee, according to the time of life, and Sarah shall have a son.** 15 Then Sarah denied, saying, I laughed not; for she was afraid. **And he said, Nay; but thou didst laugh.**

As a result of Sarah's unbelief, she told Abraham to sleep with her bondmaid, Hagar, and Ishmael was born.

4.6.2 Ishmael—a work of the flesh

Ishmael was a product of trying to do God's work in the strength of the flesh using human reasoning instead of having faith in God and letting God do God's own work God's way.

Genesis 16:1 Now **Sarai Abram's wife bare him no children:** and she had an handmaid, an Egyptian, whose name was **Hagar.** 2 And **Sarai said** unto Abram, Behold now, **the LORD hath restrained me from bearing: I pray thee, go in unto my maid; it may be that I may obtain children by her.** And Abram hearkened to the voice of Sarai. 3 **And Sarai Abram's wife took Hagar her maid the Egyptian, after Abram had dwelt ten years in the land of Canaan, and gave her to her husband Abram to be his wife.** 4 **And he went in unto Hagar, and she conceived: and when she saw that she had conceived, her mistress was despised in her eyes.**

This was a horrible sin of immorality on Sarai's[9] part for which her descendants have suffered down to this day.

4.6.3 Ishmael—conceived in uncircumcision

Ishmael was conceived before Abraham was circumcised, and was therefore a product of uncleanness.

Genesis 17:23 And Abraham took Ishmael his son, and all that were born in his house, and all that were bought with his money, every male among the men of Abraham's house; and circumcised the flesh of their foreskin in the selfsame day, as God had said unto him. 24 And Abraham was ninety years old and nine, when he was circumcised in the flesh of his foreskin. 25 And Ishmael his son was thirteen years old, when he was circumcised in the flesh of his

_____
[9]Sarah's name before it was changed to Sarah in Genesis 17:15.

57

foreskin. 26 **In the selfsame day was Abraham circumcised, and Ishmael his son.** 27 And all the men of his house, born in the house, and bought with money of the stranger, were circumcised with him.

In verse 26 above, we read that Abraham and Ishmael were circumcised on the same day. Verse 25 tells us that Ishmael was 13 years old at the time. Therefore it is clear that Ishmael was conceived 13 years before Abraham was circumcised, while Abraham was **uncircumcised** and therefore unclean.

4.6.4 Ishmael—a persecutor

Ishmael was born after the "flesh," and therefore "persecuted" him that was born after the "Spirit." The Oxford English Dictionary defines a persecutor as "One who persecutes; 'one who harasses others with continued malignity' (J.); esp. one who harasses others on account of opinions or belief."

> Galatians 4:28 Now we, brethren, as Isaac was, are the children of promise. 29 But as then **he that was born after the flesh persecuted him that was born after the Spirit**, even so it is now. 30 Nevertheless what saith the scripture? Cast out the bondwoman and her son: for the son of the bondwoman shall not be heir with the son of the freewoman. 31 So then, brethren, we are not children of the bondwoman, but of the free.

Ishmael and his descendants have persecuted spiritual people from his day to this day.

4.6.5 Ishmael—a mocker

Ishmael was a mocker of (and therefore an enemy of) God's chosen one, Isaac.

> Genesis 21:9 **And Sarah saw the son of Hagar the Egyptian, which she had born unto Abraham, mocking.** 10 Wherefore she said unto Abraham, Cast out this bondwoman and her son: for the son of this bondwoman shall not be heir with my son, even with Isaac. 11

And the thing was very grievous in Abraham's sight because of his son. 12 And God said unto Abraham, Let it not be grievous in thy sight because of the lad, and because of thy bondwoman; in all that Sarah hath said unto thee, hearken unto her voice; for in Isaac shall thy seed be called. 13 And also of the son of the bondwoman will I make a nation, because he is thy seed.

4.6.6 Ishmael—given no inheritance

Ishmael was the son of the bondwoman, not the son of the freewoman, and therefore was sent away without inheritance.

> Genesis 25:1 Then again Abraham took a wife, and her name was Keturah. 2 And she bare him Zimran, and Jokshan, and Medan, and Midian, and Ishbak, and Shuah. 3 And Jokshan begat Sheba, and Dedan. And the sons of Dedan were Asshurim, and Letushim, and Leummim. 4 And the sons of Midian; Ephah, and Epher, and Hanoch, and Abida, and Eldaah. All these were the children of Keturah. 5 **And Abraham gave all that he had unto Isaac.** 6 But unto the sons of the concubines, which Abraham had, Abraham gave gifts, **and sent them away from Isaac his son**, while he yet lived, eastward, unto the east country.

> Galatians 4:30 Nevertheless what saith the scripture? **Cast out the bondwoman and her son:** for **the son of the bondwoman shall not be heir with the son of the freewoman.**

4.6.7 Ishmael—rejected as an illegitimate son

God considered Isaac to be Abraham's "only begotten son," therefore rejecting Ishmael as illegitimate, and not fit to be the heir.

> Hebrews 11:17 By faith Abraham, when he was tried, offered up **Isaac**: and he that had received the promises offered up his **only begotten son**, 18 Of whom it was said, That **in**

Isaac shall thy seed be called: 19 Accounting that God was able to raise him up, even from the dead; from whence also he received him in a figure.

4.6.8 Ishmael—excluded from the covenant

God established His covenant with Isaac, not with Ishmael.

Genesis 17:1 And when **Abram** was ninety years old and nine, **the LORD** appeared to Abram, and said unto him, **I am the Almighty God**; walk before me, and be thou perfect. 2 And I will make my covenant between me and thee, and will multiply thee exceedingly. 3 And Abram fell on his face: and God talked with him, saying, 4 As for me, behold, my covenant is with thee, and thou shalt be a father of many nations. 5 Neither shall thy name any more be called Abram, but thy name shall be Abraham; for a father of many nations have I made thee. 6 And I will make thee exceeding fruitful, and I will make nations of thee, and kings shall come out of thee. 7 **And I will establish my covenant between me and thee and thy seed after thee in their generations for an everlasting covenant, to be a God unto thee, and to thy seed after thee.** 8 And I will give unto thee, and to thy seed after thee, the land wherein thou art a stranger, all the land of Canaan, for an everlasting possession; and I will be their God. 9 And God said unto Abraham, Thou shalt keep my covenant therefore, thou, and thy seed after thee in their generations. 10 **This is my covenant, which ye shall keep, between me and you and thy seed after thee; Every man child among you shall be circumcised.** 11 And ye shall circumcise the flesh of your foreskin; and it shall be a token of the covenant betwixt me and you. 12 And he that is eight days old shall be circumcised among you, every man child in your generations, he that is born in the house, or bought with money of any stranger, which is not of thy seed. 13 He that is born in thy house, and he that is bought with thy money, must needs be circumcised: and my covenant shall be in your flesh for an everlasting covenant. 14 And the uncircumcised man child whose flesh of his foreskin is not circumcised, that soul shall be cut off from his people; he hath broken my covenant. 15 And God said unto Abraham, As for Sarai thy wife, thou shalt not call her name Sarai, but Sarah shall her name be. 16 And I will bless her, and give thee a son also of her: yea, I will bless her, and she shall be a mother of nations; kings of people shall be of her. 17 Then Abraham fell upon his face, and laughed, and said in his heart, Shall a child be born unto him that is an hundred years old? and shall Sarah, that is ninety years old, bear? 18 And Abraham said unto God, O that **Ishmael** might live before thee! 19 **And God said, Sarah thy wife shall bear thee a son indeed; and thou shalt call his name Isaac: and I will establish my covenant with him for an everlasting covenant, and with his seed after him.** 20 And as for Ishmael, I have heard thee: Behold, I have blessed him, and will make him fruitful, and will multiply him exceedingly; twelve princes shall he beget, and I will make him a great nation. 21 **But my covenant will I establish with Isaac**, which Sarah shall bear unto thee at this set time in the next year.

Since this covenant is contained in the word of God, this proves that the Quran did not originate with God, and that Muhammad is not God's prophet.

4.6.9 Ishmael—living in bondage

Allegorically, Hagar (also called Agar), Ishmael's mother, is Mt. Sinai in Arabia. Mt. Sinai is where the 10 commandments were given. Thus Hagar, the bondwoman, represents the bondage people are in when trying to keep the law in order to save their own souls. Hagar also represents the present Jerusalem—the center of the present Jewish religion—which also has rejected Jesus as God's only begotten Son, and therefore remains in spiritual bondage, trying vainly to save themselves by good works.

Galatians 4:25 For this **Agar** is mount Sinai in Arabia, and answereth to Jerusalem which now is, **and is in bondage with her children.**

Sarah, Isaac's mother—the free woman who gave birth to a free son—, represents the "Jerusalem which is above which is free," thus representing the freedom people experience when they trust not in their own good works to save them from Hell, but rather trust only in the finished work of the Lord Christ on the cross of Calvary.

Galatians 4:21 Tell me, **ye that desire to be under the law**, do ye not hear the law? 22 For it is written, that Abraham had two sons, the one by a bondmaid, the other by a freewoman. 23 But he who was of the bondwoman was born after the flesh; but he of the freewoman was by promise. 24 Which things are an allegory: for these are the **two covenants**; the one from the mount Sinai, **which gendereth to bondage**, which is **Agar**. 25 For this Agar is mount Sinai in Arabia, and answereth to Jerusalem which now is, and is in bondage with her children. 26 But Jerusalem which is above is free, which is the mother of us all. 27 For it is written, Rejoice, thou barren that bearest not; break forth and cry, thou that travailest not: for the desolate hath many more children than she which hath an husband. 28 Now we, brethren, as Isaac was, are the children of promise. 29 But as then he that was born after the flesh persecuted him that was born after the Spirit, even so it is now. 30 Nevertheless what saith the scripture? Cast out the bondwoman and her son: for the son of the bondwoman shall not be heir with the son of the freewoman. 31 **So then, brethren, we are not children of the bondwoman, but of the free.**

4.6.10   Ishmael—a wild man

Ishmael was a "wild man," his hand against every man, and every man's hand against him.

Genesis 16:3 And Sarai Abram's wife took **Hagar** her maid the Egyptian, after Abram had dwelt ten years in the land of Canaan, and gave her to her husband Abram to be his wife. 4 And he went in unto Hagar, and she conceived: and when she saw that she had conceived, her mistress was despised in her eyes. 5 And Sarai said unto Abram, My wrong be upon thee: I have given my maid into thy bosom; and when she saw that she had conceived, I was despised in her eyes: the LORD judge between me and thee. 6 But Abram said unto Sarai, Behold, thy maid is in thy hand; do to her as it pleaseth thee. And when Sarai dealt hardly with her, she fled from her face. 7 And the angel of the LORD found her by a fountain of water in the wilderness, by the fountain in the way to Shur. 8 And he said, Hagar, Sarai's maid, whence camest thou? and whither wilt thou go? And she said, I flee from the face of my mistress Sarai. 9 And the angel of the LORD said unto her, Return to thy mistress, and submit thyself under her hands. 10 And the angel of the LORD said unto her, I will multiply thy seed exceedingly, that it shall not be numbered for multitude. 11 **And the angel of the LORD said unto her, Behold, thou art with child, and shalt bear a son, and shalt call his name Ishmael**; because the LORD hath heard thy affliction. 12 **And he will be a wild man; his hand will be against every man, and every man's hand against him**; and he shall dwell in the presence of all his brethren.

And so it is down to this day. The descendants of Ishmael are, for the most part, wild, angry, violent people who cannot control their tempers, and who holler and scream and destroy things in fits of rage—except for those of them who have accepted the Lord Jesus Christ as personal Lord and Savior, and have therefore been changed into new creatures in Christ.

2 Corinthians 5:14 For **the love of Christ** constraineth us; because we thus judge, that if one died for all, then were all dead: 15 **And that he died for all, that they which live should not henceforth live unto themselves, but unto him which died for them, and rose again.** 16 Wherefore henceforth know we no man after the flesh: yea, though we have known Christ

after the flesh, yet now henceforth know we him no more. 17 **Therefore if any man be in Christ, he is a new creature: old things are passed away; behold, all things are become new.** 18 And all things are of God, who hath reconciled us to himself by Jesus Christ, and hath given to us the ministry of reconciliation; 19 To wit, that **God was in Christ, reconciling the world unto himself**, not imputing their trespasses unto them; and hath committed unto us the word of reconciliation. 20 **Now then we are ambassadors for Christ, as though God did beseech you by us: we pray you in Christ's stead, be ye reconciled to God.** 21 For he hath made him to be sin for us, who knew no sin; that we might be made the righteousness of God in him.

4.7 Did God make a covenant with Ishmael?

> **Beware! Islamic deception follows:**
>
> "And also of the son of the bondwoman I will make a nation, because he is thy seed." Genesis 21:13.
> Please note the word "also" in above promise. The nations of Judaism and Christianity came out from the descendants of Abraham and Sarah. The nation of Islam came out from the descendants of Abraham and Hagar. Judaism, Christianity and Islam are three children of Abraham by God's Covenants with Abraham.
> This also fulfills the following prophecy by Jesus:
> "Howbeit when he, the Spirit of Truth, is come, he will guide you into all truth; for he shall not speak of himself; but what soever he shall hear, that shall he speak: and he will show you thing to come." John 16:13

God did make a great (in the sense of large) nation out of Ishmael. But God did not make His covenant with Ishmael. God established His covenant with Isaac, not with Ishmael. This is made very clear in Genesis chapter 17:

> 18 And Abraham said unto God, O that Ishmael might live before thee! 17:19 And God said, **Sarah thy wife shall bear thee a son indeed; and thou shalt call his name Isaac: and I will establish my covenant with him for an everlasting covenant, and with his seed after him.** 17:20 And as for Ishmael, I have heard thee: Behold, I have blessed him, and will make him fruitful, and will multiply him exceedingly; twelve princes shall he beget, and I will make him a great nation. 21 **But my covenant will I establish with Isaac,** which Sarah shall bear unto thee at this set time in the next year.

Since the covenant is contained in the Word of God, and the covenant was given to Isaac not Ishmael, this proves that the Quran—which came from Ishmael's descendants—did not originate with God.

Let us point out again that John 16:13 says that the Spirit of truth "shall not speak of himself." Muhammad, however, spoke of himself 273 times in the Quran. Therefore Muhammad does not qualify to be the Comforter.

4.8 Did Muhammad destroy idolatry in Mecca?

The Oxford English Dictionary defines an idol as: "1. An image or similitude of a deity or divinity, used as an object of worship: applied to those worshiped by pagans, whence, in scriptural language, = false god, a fictitious divinity which 'is nothing in the world' (1 Cor. viii. 4). 2. Any thing or person that is the object of excessive or supreme devotion, or that usurps the place of God in human affection."

> **Beware! Islamic deception follows:**
>
> For further details about "the Paraclete" and "the Spirit of Truth" please see Section 1 of this article.
>
> "They shall be turned back, they shall be greatly ashamed, that trust in graven images; they say to the molten images, 'Ye are our gods.'" Isaiah 42 Verse 17.
>
> History records that Prophet Muhammad did put the pagan idolaters to great shame when he demolished before them, their 365 idols that were installed in Ka'bah (Mecca), the most respected place of pilgrimage in the whole of Arabia. Today, Ka'bah is the Grand Mosque of Islam. Muslims from all over the world face towards Ka'bah while reciting their daily ritual prayers.

4.8.1 The Black Stone

Muhammad destroyed all the idols in the Ka'bah but one—the Black Stone, which Muslims bow down to kiss in great admiration and reverence. Muhammad himself kissed this idol. If that is not idolatry nothing is.

> Leviticus 26:1 Ye shall make you no idols nor graven image, neither rear you up a standing image, **neither shall ye set up any image of stone in your land**, to bow down unto it: for I am the LORD your God.

Can you imagine all the disease that has been spread by people kissing that stone idol. The preceding person who kissed the idol may have had a terrible disease such as TB or AIDS and a bleeding sore on his lips.

> In 1674, according to Johann Ludwig Burckhardt, someone smeared the Black Stone with excrement so that "every one who kissed it retired with a sullied beard".[10]

---

[10]For a history of the Black Stone, see: http://en.wikipedia.org/wiki/Black_Stone

Has that excrement all been kissed off yet?

Of course, Muslims don't want to admit that the black stone is an idol. Most idol-worshipers won't admit that their idol is an idol—they say it is just to remind them of their god. But if one bows down and kisses it in reverence, it is his idol. Islam blinds people's minds so that they can't see that it is an idol right in front of their face as they kiss it.

Umar ibn al-Khattab (580-644) was the second Caliph. Narrated 'Abis bin Rabia in the ahadith collection of Sahih Bukhari (2:26:667):

> Umar came near the Black Stone and kissed it and said "No doubt, I know that you are a stone and can neither benefit anyone nor harm anyone. Had I not seen Allah's Apostle kissing you I would not have kissed you." [11]

Obviously, Umar knew in his heart that kissing that stone was idolatry, and would not have done it had he not seen Muhammad do it, and therefore felt forced to do it. Muslims should admit the obvious truth, and repent before it is too late!

4.8.2 Shahada

There is also one other god in Islam besides Allah and the Black Stone. Muslims also worship Muhammad! Muslims deny this, of course, but their actions speak louder than their words. And the Quran contradicts itself by encouraging this deification of Muhammad. For example, consider surah 3:31 from the Quran (shown below in three translations):

> YUSUFALI: **Say: "If ye do love Allah, Follow me**: Allah will love you and forgive you your sins: For Allah is Oft-Forgiving, Most Merciful."
>
> PICKTHAL: **Say, (O Muhammad, to mankind): If ye love Allah, follow me; Allah

---

[11]http://www.cmje.org/religious-texts/hadith/bukhari/026-sbt.php

Figure 4.4: *A Muslim kisses the Black Stone idol.*

will love you and forgive you your sins. Allah is Forgiving, Merciful.

SHAKIR: **Say: If you love Allah, then follow me**, Allah will love you and forgive you your faults, and Allah is Forgiving, MercifuL.

Note that this surah doesn't say, If you love Allah, then follow Allah. No, it says, then follow Muhammad. The direct implication of the rest of the verse is that forgiveness of a person's sin is totally dependent on following Muhammad.

And in surah 4:136 people are commanded to believe in Allah **and** his messenger, thus putting Muhammad on the same level as Allah.

YUSUFALI: O ye who believe! **Believe in Allah and His Messenger**, and the scripture which He hath sent to His Messenger and the scripture which He sent to those before (him). Any who denieth Allah, His angels, His Books, His Messengers, and the Day of Judgment, hath gone far, far astray.

PICKTHAL: O ye who believe! **Believe in Allah and His messenger** and the Scripture which He hath revealed unto His messenger, and the Scripture which He revealed aforetime. Whoso disbelieveth in Allah and His angels and His scriptures and His messengers and the Last Day, he verily hath wandered far astray.

SHAKIR: O you who believe! **believe in Allah and His Messenger** and the Book which He has revealed to His Messenger and the Book which He revealed before; and whoever disbelieves in Allah and His angels and His messengers and the last day, he indeed strays off into a remote error.

SHAHADA[12] (meaning testimony)—the first pillar of Islam—is another example of Muhammad being an idol of Islam. This is especially the case of Sunni Muslims. Below is how the Madinah Masjid of Carrolton, Texas explains the shahada and the glorification of Muhammad. (For the sake of space, much of the original Arabic is deleted, and only the translation given, but it is still a **very** long statement of praise to Muhammad).

The Islamic Creed, the first pillar of Islam, LA-ILAHA-ILLA-ALLAH, MUHAMMADUR-RASUL-ULLAH. (i.e. There is no god but Allah, **Muhammad is the Messenger of Allah**)....

The first pillar starts with the most essential faith in unseen, (i.e. to believe in unseen). We have not seen Allah , yet we are to believe "LA-ILAHA ILLA-ALLAH" (There is no god but ALLAH). "There is no god but Allah, **Muhammad is the Messenger of Allah**". "Allah" of the first pillar is :the Lord of the worlds" (Rabbul Alameen, Quran, 1:1) **and Muhammad is "the Blessings for the worlds"** (Rahmatul-lil-Alameen: Quran, 21:107).

---

[12]The first pillar of Islam is also called "Kalima."

63

The first pillar if Islam is the fundamental and basic need of human, Prophet Muhammad said: "I have been ordered to fight against people until they testify that there is no god but Allah **and the Muhammad is the Messenger of Allah.**" (Sahi-Bukhari, Muslim). **It clearly indicates that we must have faith in** <u>both</u> **the parts of the first pillar of Islam.**...

You will find people of knowledge of a **lower order** saying, "The Holy Prophet (Salla'llahu' alaihi wa sallam) is just a mortal like us."

Yet you will find great intellectual giants of this 20 C like the great Sir Muhammad Iqbal (r.a.) who as a poet of Islam is incomparable with anyone else before him except, Maulana Jalaludin Rumi (Rahmatullah-alai), saying

"That possessor of knowledge of the parts of guidance, that terminator of the office of divine Messenger ship, that leader of all creation, who illuminates the sand below the feet of the caravan of his followers into the illuminated sand of Sinai. From the point of view of love and approach to the problem in depth; **it is he who is the first and it is he who is the last, and it is he who is the Qur'aan and it is he who is the standard of right and wrong in this entire universe.**" ...

According to the Qur'aan, the Holy Prophet has a double status. The one aspect of his personality is universal and the other is mundane (earthly)

The Holy Qur'aan says in S 21 V 107 - Al-Ambiya **"O! Prophet (Sallallahu alai hi wa sallam) I have not sent you but as a mercy to all the worlds." All the worlds, beyond this earth and humanity. This is called the cosmic or universal level. He is the mercy for the entire creation of Allah i.e. The universe.** His mundane status is , as the Qur'aan say in S 18 V 110 - Kahaf "O! Prophet proclaim to the people that I am nothing more than a human being' Mislukum'."

Many people have stumbled on this verse because this word Mislukum can be translated in two ways . One translation leads to Kufr whilst the other translation is the translation of Imaan. It has been translated by some as being " like you" This is the translation on the basis of Kufr. This statement is the greatest falsehood against the Qur'aan and Hadith and is blasphemous against the personality of the Holy prophet. Blasphemy leads a person to Kufr. **No human being is like the Holy Prophet**, What do they mean when they translate it in this ugly fashion? Like whom? A robber, murderer, drunkard, thief, devil incarnate, like whom? **Who has that standard of piety and status that he can be likened to the Holy Prophet?** The connotation of the verse is to emphasize the humanity of the Holy Prophet so that Muslims do not fall prey, like others have, in view of his great qualities and miraculous powers that Allah has given him. They may not fall into the misconception that he is God or son of God like others have fallen before them. It is his divinity that is being denied here, not that he is like us. He is a human being - We are human beings.

Students of science and physics know that charcoal is pure carbon and diamond is also pure carbon. It is only the frequency of molecules of the electronic particles of the diamond that makes one a diamond and the other charcoal. Black - illuminous . Medicinal value. Monetary value. World of difference. **The Holy Prophet is human being and we are human beings, but he is diamond and we are charcoal.**...

The source of grace as established by Allah is only the Holy Prophet. There is no other source. ...Not only is the Prophet honorable but the soil upon which he walks becomes honorable.

The Qur'aan says this in s 90 v 1-4 "I swear by this city of Makkah, not because this city contains the Kaaba, but because your blessed feet touch the soil of this city" **Not only is the Holy Prophet venerable but even the particles of dust that touch the soles of his blessed shoes become venerable.**...

Moulana Zakarriya quotes in his book

"the virtues of Hajj" in the chapter "behaviour in Madinah and its virtues" that **the portion of the earth in the immediate vicinity of the holy body of Rasulullah is even higher**

in rank than the Kaaba and the Throne of Allah. He quotes on the authority of Qaadi Ayaadh, Imam Maalik and ibn Asaakir. Â UNIVERSAL/ COSMIC STATUS.

The Quraan says in s 21 v 107 - al ambiya "**O Prophet**(Salla'llahu'alaihi wa sallam)) **I Have not sent thee but as a mercy unto the entire universe**"

and in another verse s 5 v 15 maida

"Verily their has come unto you a **light** and a clear book...."

The wow here is the wow of conjunction, the noor is something different and the kitaab is something different. **Their is a difference of opinion amongst the commentators , some say ' light ' here refers to the Holy Prophet others say that it does not, but only to the guidance he has brought.** Here again the same problem comes in, ' fikre har kast be kadre himmate woh ' , but the Prophet was commissioned by God to explain every intricate verse of the Qur'aan, and it says

'O Prophet I have commissioned thee to to expound, explain and make clear that which has been revealed in the book' li tu bayyina lin naasi na nuzzila ilayhim Here comes in hadith as the authority .

Let us ask the Holy Prophet what is the reference to the word noor here. In the Hadith quoted on the authority of Muhaddith ' abd ar Razzaq the eminent fore runner of Imam Bukhari and (and even quoted by non-Ahle-Sunnah scholar like Moulana Ashraf Ali Thanvi one of the very eminent ulema of Deoband in his kitaab Nashrut teeb fi zikre Habeeb). Hazrat Jaber bin Abd ullah bi Ansari reports that **the Holy Prophet informed him that:**

"The first thing which Allah created was my light, and every other creation was created from my light."

This Hadith compels us to side with those commentators who say that noor here refers to the Holy Prophet . It has been the consensus of Muslim belief which was challenged only in this period of Muslim decay and degeneration, under the impact of modern materialism, that **the**

Holy Prophet is the centre of creation, that Allah created the light of the Holy Prophet and from that light He created the whole universe. Allah is indivisible, so the meaning in the Hadith is sababbiya, not from the light, but because of the light. The Qur'aan also bears testimony to this that the Holy Prophet was the first of creation, when it explicitly affirms this fact, when it says: s6 v 163 al Anaam

"I am the first among Muslims."

Muslim here refers to the first thing or being to submit to the will of Allah and not the misuse it has been put to in these days of bickering. Muslim means he or she that submits his/her will entirely to the will of God. In another verse Allah says, s 3 v 83 al Imraan

"everything in the heaven and earth is Muslim"

Then what would "I am the first among the Muslims mean" ? That **the first being to be created by Allah was the Holy Prophet.**

. . . the essential **Holy** Prophet **transcends the limitations of space and time** and thus, he is a **living** Prophet t**hat is approachable every where**. . . . . . .

Meraj—see entire universe—including Allah—-from highest point. s53 v7-9 "Whilst he was at the highest level, then he approached and came closer, and was at a distance of but two bow lengths or nearer."

All differences were abolished here, except one, he is the created whilst Allah is the creator. The Quraan says in s4 v150 "**do not make differences between Allah and His Rasul.**"

If we are to make no differences between Allah and Muhammad, then we are to treat Muhammad as we would treat Allah! Muslims believe that Allah is God, so that is pretty high treatment.

Note the attributes of God that this mosque claims for Muhammad in the above discourse:

⇨ **HOLINESS.** Muhammad is called the "Holy Prophet," his dead body the "holy body." But this is no ordinary holiness being claimed here, for the claim they made is that "**No human being is like the Holy Prophet**, What do they mean when they translate it in this ugly fashion? Like whom? A robber, murderer, drunkard, thief, devil incarnate, like whom? **Who has that standard of piety and status that he can be likened** to the **Holy** Prophet?" Compare that to what the Bible says about God: "There is none holy as the LORD: for there is none beside thee: neither is there any rock like our God" (1 Samuel 2:2).

↪ OMNIPRESENCE. It is claimed that "the essential **Holy** Prophet **transcends the limitations of space**."

↪ ETERNAL. It is claimed that "the essential **Holy** Prophet **transcends the limitations of…time**."

↪ THE LIGHT. According to 1 John 1:5 "God is light." So, if Muhammad is the light, then he is God.

↪ THE ORIGIN OF THE WHOLE UNIVERSE. If it be true that "Allah created the light of the Holy Prophet and from that light He created the whole universe," then Allah created God (Muhammad) who is the origin of the universe.

↪ THE ONLY SOURCE OF GRACE AND MERCY. In John 1:17 the Bible tells us that "…the law was given by Moses, but grace and truth came by Jesus Christ." Jesus is God. So when Islam puts Muhammad in the place of Jesus, they are claiming Muhammad to be God.

↪ THE FIRST AND THE LAST. In Revelation 1:17, Jesus declares "I am the first and the last." Jesus is God. So when Muslims say that "Muhammad is the first and the last," they are claiming that he is God.

↪ THE STANDARD OF RIGHT AND WRONG FOR THE WHOLE UNIVERSE. Only God is the standard of right and wrong. So if Muhammad is that standard then he is God.[13]

↪ THE BLESSINGS FOR THE WORLDS. This statement too places Muhammad on the level of Jesus Christ, and thus implies that he is God.

↪ VENERABLE. According to the *Oxford English Dictionary*, venerable means, "Worthy of being venerated, revered, or highly respected and esteemed, on account of character or position." These Muslims are actually claiming that "the **portion of the earth** in the immediate vicinity of the **holy** body of Rasulullah **is even higher in rank than…the Throne of Allah**." So Muhammad is so glorious that **where he walked** is higher in rank than even **the throne of Allah**! That makes Muhammad even more glorious than Allah! Since Muslims believe Allah to be God, they are placing Muhammad even **above** God!

---

[13]Consider what a joke this claim is. Is Muhammad—the robber of camel caravans, the man who raped a woman after murdering her father, brother, and husband, the pedophile who married a six year old girl, the polygamist who said a man could have no more than four wives, but took three times that many for himself, the deceiver who made treaties with the intention of breaking them, the liar who made promises to his wives, but didn't keep them, the man who practiced slavery and sex slavery, the sinner who admitted he was going to Hell—the standard of right and wrong? We are to imitate such a vile man? Isaiah 5:20 comes to mind: "Woe unto them that call evil good, and good evil; that put darkness for light, and light for darkness; that put bitter for sweet, and sweet for bitter!" This is why Islam is so evil and wicked. Muslims believe that if Muhammad did a certain sin, then it isn't sin, and they can do it also.

Holy Spit! So highly exalted did Muslims consider Muhammad, they would even rub his **spit** on their faces! And he allowed such worship. The following is from the hadith Sahih Bukhari Volume 3 Book 50 Number 874:

> Before embracing Islam Al-Mughira was in the company of some people. He killed them and took their property and came (to Medina) to embrace Islam. The Prophet said (to him, "As regards your Islam, I accept it, but as for the property I do not take anything of it. (As it was taken through treason). Urwa then started looking at the Companions of the Prophet. By Allah, **whenever Allah's Apostle spat, the spittle would fall in the hand of one of them (i.e. the Prophet's companions) who would rub it on his face and skin; if he ordered them they would carry his orders immediately; if he performed ablution, they would struggle to take the remaining water; and when they spoke to him, they would lower their voices and would not look at his face constantly out of respect.**"[14]

Even some Muslims can see that including "Muhammad is the messenger of Allah" in the shahada is blasphemy and idolatry. Here is what the Islamic website Submission.Org says:

> Verse 3:18 states the First Pillar of Islam (Submission): "God bears witness that there is no other god besides Him, and so do the angels and those who possess knowledge."
>
> This most crucial pillar has been distorted. **Millions of Muslims have adopted Satan's polytheistic version, and insist upon mentioning the name of Muhammad besides the name of God.** However, the Quran's great criterion in 39:45 stamps such Muslims as disbelievers:
>
> "When God ALONE is mentioned, the hearts of those who do disbelieve in the Hereafter shrink with aversion, but when others are mentioned with Him, they become satisfied."
>
> I have conducted extensive research into this criterion, and I have reached a startling conclusion: the **idol worshipers** who do not uphold the First Pillar of Islam as dictated in 3:18 are forbidden by God from uttering the correct Shahadah. They simply cannot say: "Ash-hadu Allaa Elaaha Ellaa Allah" by itself, without mentioning the name of Muhammad. Try it with **any idol worshiper who claims to be a Muslim.** Challenge them to say: "Ash-hadu Allaa Elaaha Ellaa Allah." They can never say it. Since this is the religion of Abraham (2:130, 135; 3:95; 4:125; 6:161; 12:37-38; 16:123; 22:78; Appendix 9), the ONLY creed must be "LAA ELAAHA ELLAA ALLAH (there is no god except the One God)". **Muhammad did not exist on earth before Abraham.**

A Gross Blasphemy

> **There is no greater blasphemy than distorting the Quran to idolize the prophet Muhammad** against his will. Verse 19 of Sura "Muhammad" (47:19) states: "You shall know that there is no god except the one God."[15]

So, we see the unholy trinity of Islam: Allah, Muhammad, and the Black Stone. Muslims claim with their mouths to be monotheists, but with their actions they show clearly that they are polytheists—idolaters. Where does Muhammad glorify Jesus in all this? He doesn't. Muhammad blasphemes Jesus.

---

[14]http://www.usc.edu/schools/college/ crcc/engagement/resources/texts/muslim/ hadith/bukhari/050.sbt.html#003.050.891

[15]http://www.submission.org/suras/ app13.html

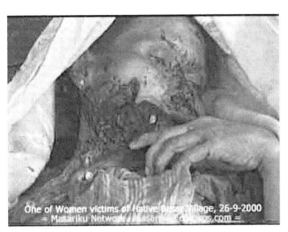

Figure 4.7: *Does burning churches glorify Jesus?*

Figure 4.5: *Does chopping innocent Christian women in the mouth with a sword glorify Jesus? No, none of the atrocities committed by the followers of Muhammad glorify Jesus. But they do show what a evil and wicked influence Muhammad has on his followers, who have no love or compassion for other people. Are Muhammad's followers ever happy? Only when they succeed in doing harm to other people. Otherwise, they are always unhappy and angry. How they need the joy of Christ!*

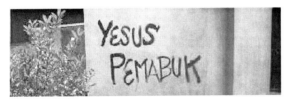

Figure 4.6: *"Yesus pemabuk" is Indonesian for "Jesus is a drunk." Muslims wrote this on a wall in a Christian village they attacked in Maluku, Indonesia. Does calling Jesus a drunk glorify Jesus?*

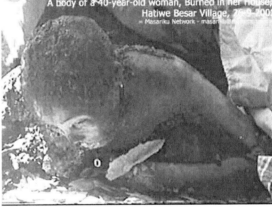

Figure 4.8: *Does burning Christians alive in their homes glorify Jesus?*

Chapter 5

Deceptive Muslim Answers To Christian's Questions 1–4

Chapters 5 through 10 of this book critique another article from Meherally in which he answers Christian's questions. After each of Meherally's answers a section will follow in which I expose the deception of his answers. It is especially needful for the reader to pay special attention to who is speaking. Notice that words from Meherally's article are in boxes with grey backgrounds. Please don't confuse his words with mine! Note also that the questions asked by Christians have been put in **boldface** to visually separate them from Meherally's answers.

5.1   Are Jesus and God the Father One?

Beware! Islamic deception follows:

ANSWERS TO FAQ BY CHRISTIANS FROM THE BIBLE
Note: The following is written in the language that is intended as an invitation (Daw'ah) to Christians, from their biblical perspective.

A Christian asks a legitimate question:

Question No.1 [from a Christian to Islamic teacher Meherally.]

Jesus said: "I and the Father are one" (Jn.10:30), therefore, is not Jesus the same, or, "co-equal" in status with his Father?

Beware! Islamic deception follows:

Answer No.1
In Greek, 'heis' means 'one' numerically (masc.) 'hen' means 'one' in unity or essence (neut.) Here the word used by John is 'hen' and not 'heis'. The marginal notes in New American Standard Bible (NASB) reads; one - (Lit.neuter) a unity, or, one essence. If one wishes to argue that the word 'hen' supports their claim for Jesus being "co-equal" in status with his Father, please invite his/her attention to the following verse: Jesus said: "And the glory which Thou hast given me, I have given to them (disciples); that they may be one, just as we are one." (John 17:22). If he/she was to consider/regard/believe the Father and Je-

sus Christ to be "one" meaning "co-equal" in status on the basis of John 10:30, then that person should also be prepared to consider/regard/believe "them" - the disciples of Jesus, to be "co-equal" in status with the Father and Jesus ("just as we are one") in John 17:22. I have yet to find a person that would be prepared to make the disciples (students) "co-equal" in status with the Father or Jesus. The unity and accord was of the authorized divine message that originated from the Father, received by Jesus and finally passed on to the disciples. Jesus admitted having accomplished the work which the Father had given him to do. (Jn.17:4)

Hot Tip: (precise and pertinent)
Jesus said: "I go to the Father; for the Father is greater than I." (Jn.14:28). This verse unequivocally refutes the claim by any one for Jesus being "co-equal" in status with his Father.

This is another example of Islam not glorifying Jesus.

The *Gingrich Greek New Testament Lexicon* lists as one definition of "hen" (ἕν): "For emphasis **one and the same**." Jesus is one and the same with the Father—they are one God. The word has several meanings depending on the context in which it is used. Meherally constantly steps into error because he ignores context. Meherally either knows little about Greek, or else is purposely deceiving. He wants to discuss the meaning of Greek words for two reasons: (1) because most English speaking people don't know Greek, so won't know if he is lying, and (2) to distract the reader from the context that disproves Islam. That Meherally is not being honest about the meaning of John 10:30 is immediately clear when we look at the **context** in which that was used. **Always look at the context.**

John 10:24 Then came the Jews round about him, and said unto him, How long dost thou make us to doubt? If thou be the Christ, tell us

plainly. 25 **Jesus** answered them, I told you, and ye believed not: the works that I do in **my Father's** name, they bear witness of me. 26 But **ye believe not, because ye are not of my sheep**, as I said unto you. 27 **My sheep hear my voice, and I know them, and they follow me: 28 And I give unto them eternal life; and they shall never perish, neither shall any man pluck them out of my hand. 29 My Father**, which gave them me, is greater than all; and no man is able to pluck them out of **my Father's** hand. 30 **I and my Father are one.** 31 Then the Jews took up stones again to stone him. 32 Jesus answered them, Many good works have I shewed you from **my Father**; for which of those works do ye stone me? 33 The Jews answered him, saying, **For a good work we stone thee not; but for blasphemy; and because that thou, being a man, makest thyself God.** 34 **Jesus** answered them, Is it not written in your law, I said, Ye are gods? 35 If he called them gods, unto whom the word of God came, and the scripture cannot be broken; 36 Say ye of him, whom **the Father** hath sanctified, and sent into the world, Thou blasphemest; because I said, **I am the Son of God**? 37 If I do not the works of **my Father**, believe me not. 38 But if I do, though ye believe not me, believe the works: that ye may know, and believe, **that the Father is in me, and I in him.** 39 Therefore they sought again to take him: but he escaped out of their hand, 40 And went away again beyond Jordan into the place where John at first baptized; and there he abode. 41 And many resorted unto him, and said, John did no miracle: but **all things that John spake of this man were true.** 42 And many believed on him there.

The following teachings from the above verses all disprove Islam:

⇨ The true God is the Father, not the eunuch. Verses 25, 29, 30, 32, 36, 37, and 38.

⇨ Jesus is the Son of God. Verse 36.

⇨ Jesus gives believers eternal life—not temporary life. Verse 28.

⇨ Believers in Jesus will never perish—it is impossible for a believer in Jesus to go to Hell. Verse 28.

⇨ No one can pluck the believer out of Jesus' hand—the believer is eternally secure. Verse 28.

⇨ Jesus and the Father are one. Verse 30.

⇨ By saying the above things Jesus was claiming to be God—that is why the Jews took up stones to stone him. Please read verses 31-33 again carefully.

Note also that Meherally misrepresents the Bible teachings concerning the Trinity. The Bible teaches that the Father, Son and Holy Spirit are all equally God for they are all **one and the same** God. True Christians do not believe in three equal Gods, but rather in **only one** true and living God. However, the Father, Son, and Holy Spirit as Persons are separate, different, and not equal in authority. Always the Son is in submission to the Father.

There is no such thing as a one person God. To deny the Son is to deny the Father also.

> 1 John 2:22 Who is a **liar** but he that denieth that Jesus is the Christ? **He is antichrist, that denieth the Father and the Son. 23 Whosoever denieth the Son, the same hath not the Father**: but he that acknowledgeth the Son hath the Father also.

Consider carefully what this verse means. **Muhammad denied the Son, so he was an antichrist, and does not have God.**

5.2 Is Jesus the ONLY way of salvation?

Question No.2 [from a Christian to Islamic teacher Meherally.]
Jesus said: "I am the way, ...no one comes to the Father, but through me."

(Jn.14:6), therefore, is not the Salvation through Jesus, ALONE?

Beware! Islamic deception follows:

Answer No.2
Before Jesus spoke these words, he said; "In my Father's house are many mansions (dwelling places); if it were not so, I would have told you; for I go to prepare a mansion (a dwelling place) for you." (John 14:2).
The above explicit statement confirms that Jesus was going to prepare "a" mansion and not "all" the mansions in "my Father's house". Obviously, the prophets that came before him and the one to come after, were to prepare the other mansions for their respective followers. The prophet that came after Jesus had evidently shown the current "way" to a modern mansion in the kingdom of heaven. Besides; the verse clearly states; Jesus was the "WAY" to a mansion. It is a folly to believe that Jesus (or any prophet) was the "DESTINATION".

John 14:6 very clearly states that Jesus is the way to "**the Father**," **not** the way to a mansion. The **Father** is the destination. Meherally is simply trying to distract from a question he is unable to answer. The vital question: is Jesus the only way to get to God the Father in Heaven? And the answer is, Yes, Jesus is the **only** way. Remember, always look at the context of a verse.

> John 14:1 Let not your heart be troubled: **ye believe in God, believe also in me.** 2 In **my Father's** house are many mansions: if it were not so, I would have told you. I go to prepare a place for you. 3 And if I go and prepare a place for you, I will come again, and receive you unto myself; that where I am, there ye may be also. 4 And whither I go ye know, and the way ye know. 5 Thomas saith unto him, Lord, we know not whither thou goest; and how can we know the way? 6 **Jesus saith unto him, I am the way, the truth, and the life: no man cometh unto the Father, but by me.** 7 If ye had known me, ye should have known **my**

Father also: and from henceforth ye know him, and have seen him. 8 Philip saith unto him, Lord, shew us the Father, and it sufficeth us. 9 **Jesus** saith unto him, Have I been so long time with you, and yet hast thou not known me, Philip? **he that hath seen me hath seen the Father**; and how sayest thou then, Shew us the Father?

Here is another verse where the Bible teaches that Jesus is the only way:

Acts 4:10 Be it known unto you all, and to all the people of Israel, that by the name of **Jesus Christ** of Nazareth, whom ye **crucified, whom God raised from the dead**, even by him doth this man stand here before you whole. 11 This is the stone which was set at nought of you builders, which is become the head of the corner. 12 **Neither is there salvation in any other: for there is none other name under heaven given among men, whereby we must be saved.**

Muslim teachers lie when they claim that the Bible teaches Islamic doctrines. Note carefully what the above verses from the book of Acts teach:

⇨ **Jesus Christ was crucified.** The idea of many Islamic teachers that it was Judas Iscariot or some other person instead of Jesus whom the people of Israel crucified, and not Jesus Christ is just a lie.

⇨ **God raised Jesus from the dead.** The Islamic teaching that Jesus was taken to Heaven without first dying, being buried, and rising from the dead is just a lie.

⇨ **There is no salvation in any person other than Jesus.** The Islamic teaching that there is salvation through the teachings of Muhammad is just a lie.

⇨ **It is only in the name of Jesus that we can be saved.** There is no saving power in the name Muhammad or in the name Allah.

So clearly, the Bible teaches that Jesus is the only Savior and the only way to get to God the Father in Heaven. Therefore, according to the Bible, Islam is not **the** way to Heaven. Islam is not even **a** way to Heaven. Islam is a way to Hell.[1]

Beware! Islamic deception follows:

Jesus said; "I am the door" to find the pasture. (Jn.10:9). A sheep that walks through the "door" will find the pasture. A sheep that circles around the "door" will never find the pasture.

True. If you trust in Jesus as the door to Heaven you will get there. If you try to get to Heaven by circling around Him or by any other "way" you will end up in Hell instead.

Beware! Islamic deception follows:

One who crosses over the "way" will reach the mansion. Anyone that stops on the "way" and believes the "way" to be the end of his/her journey, will be out in the open without any shelter and a roof.

The way to get from America to Europe is to get in a trustworthy ship or airplane, and sit down (stop working) until you get to Europe. If you do not have enough faith to do so, and instead try to swim there, or flap your arms to fly there in your own strength you will not get to Europe. Jesus is the only trustworthy

---

[1]There are many contradictions in the Quran concerning the death or not of Jesus. There are also many conflicting theories about Jesus' death given by Muslim teachers. These contradictions prove that the Quran is not inspired of God. For an article that documents these contradictions in the Quran and other Muslim writings, see http://answering-islam.org/Shamoun/crucifixion.htm

"ship" to the Father in Heaven. If you will get into Him, and stop working to save yourself, Jesus will absolutely for certain get you to God the Father in Heaven.

At this point, the context of John 10:9 needs to be pointed out. Since Meherally appeals to the Bible as the word of God to prove his points, he must be made to take it in context. He must accept the context also as the word of God. We will not allow him to pick out of context only what pleases him, while he rejects the context which clearly proves him wrong. Here is the context:

> John 10:7 Then said **Jesus** unto them again, Verily, verily, I say unto you, **I am the door of the sheep.** 8 All that ever came before me are thieves and robbers: but the sheep did not hear them. 9 **I am the door: by me if any man enter in, he shall be saved**, and shall go in and out, and find pasture. 10 **The thief cometh not, but for to steal, and to kill, and to destroy: I am come that they might have life, and that they might have it more abundantly. 11 I am the good shepherd: the good shepherd giveth his life for the sheep.** 12 But he that is an hireling, and not the shepherd, whose own the sheep are not, seeth the wolf coming, and leaveth the sheep, and fleeth: and the wolf catcheth them, and scattereth the sheep. 13 The hireling fleeth, because he is an hireling, and careth not for the sheep. 14 I am the good shepherd, and know my sheep, and am known of mine. 15 As the Father knoweth me, even so know I the Father: and **I lay down my life for the sheep.** 16 And other sheep I have, which are not of this fold: them also I must bring, and they shall hear my voice; and there shall be one fold, and one shepherd. 17 **Therefore doth my Father love me, because I lay down my life, that I might take it again. 18 No man taketh it from me, but I lay it down of myself. I have power to lay it down, and I have power to take it again.** This commandment have I received of **my Father**. 19 There was a division therefore again among the Jews for these sayings. 20 And many of them said, He hath a devil, and is mad; why hear ye him? 21 Others said, These

are not the words of him that hath a devil. Can a devil open the eyes of the blind?

Note the following things in these verses that Islam denies:

⇨ Whosoever enters in through Jesus will be saved. (verse 9)

⇨ Jesus came that we might have life, and that more abundantly. (verse 10)

⇨ Jesus came to give his life for the sheep, that is, for those who believe in him. (verses 11, 15, 17, and 18)

⇨ Jesus came to rise from the dead after dying for our sins. (verses 17 and 18)

⇨ Jesus did all these things at the commandment of his Father (verse 18). So, Jesus does have a Father, and his Father is God.

So again we see that the Bible does not prove Islamic doctrines as Muslim teachers claim, but rather disproves Islamic doctrines.

> **Beware! Islamic deception follows:**
>
> Hot Tip: (precise and pertinent)
> Jesus said; "Not every one that says to me; 'Lord, Lord,' will enter the kingdom of heaven; but he who does the will of my Father, who is in heaven." (Mt.7:21).

True. Jesus' Father is the Heavenly Father—Meherally inadvertently admits it now! And what is the will of Jesus' Father? The book of John tells us:

> John 6:35 And **Jesus** said unto them, **I am the bread of life: he that cometh to me shall never hunger; and he that believeth on me shall never thirst.** 36 But I said unto you, That ye also have seen me, and believe not. 37 All that the Father giveth me shall come to me; and **him that cometh to me I will in**

73

no wise cast out. 38 For I came down from heaven, not to do mine own will, but the will of him that sent me. 39 **And this is the Father's will which hath sent me, that of all which he hath given me I should lose nothing, but should raise it up again at the last day.** 40 **And this is the will of him that sent me, that every one which seeth the Son, and believeth on him, may have everlasting life: and I will raise him up at the last day.** 41 The Jews then murmured at him, because he said, I am the bread which came down from heaven. 42 And they said, Is not this Jesus, the son of Joseph, whose father and mother we know? how is it then that he saith, I came down from heaven? 43 Jesus therefore answered and said unto them, Murmur not among yourselves. 44 No man can come to me, except the Father which hath sent me draw him: and I will raise him up at the last day. 45 It is written in the prophets, And they shall be all taught of God. Every man therefore that hath heard, and hath learned of the Father, cometh unto me. 46 Not that any man hath seen the Father, save he which is of God, he hath seen the Father. 47 Verily, verily, I say unto you, **He that believeth on me hath everlasting life.** 48 I am that bread of life. 49 Your fathers did eat manna in the wilderness, and are dead. 50 This is the bread which cometh down from heaven, that a man may eat thereof, and not die. 51 **I am the living bread which came down from heaven: if any man eat of this bread, he shall live for ever: and the bread that I will give is my flesh, which I will give for the life of the world.** 52 The Jews therefore strove among themselves, saying, How can this man give us his flesh to eat? 53 Then Jesus said unto them, Verily, verily, I say unto you, Except ye eat the flesh of the Son of man, and drink his blood, ye have no life in you. 54 **Whoso eateth my flesh, and drinketh my blood, hath eternal life; and I will raise him up at the last day.**

Two things are said to be God's will in these verses.

1. It is God's will that we believe on God's Son, Jesus Christ, so that we might have

everlasting life. Verse 40.

2. It is God's will that Jesus not lose anyone the Father has given to him, but will raise that person up at the last day. Verses 39 and 54.

Closely related to the above two truths, the person that comes to Jesus will never hunger, and the person that believes on Jesus will never thirst (verse 35). Jesus totally satisfies our hunger and thirst for forgiveness and salvation and a relationship with God. The person that believes in Jesus has everlasting life (verse 47). And everlasting does not mean temporary; it means forever. In other words, once a person believes in Jesus, that person is saved for ever. It is impossible for that person to go to Hell. The Father gives to Jesus all who believe the gospel, and of those whom the Father gives to Jesus, Jesus will lose nothing, but will resurrect them at the last day.

Jesus was not just a messenger from God, but is God Himself "come down from Heaven" (verse 41), to become the perfect, sinless human sacrifice to save us from our sins.

And there is even more good news: Jesus promises that if you come to Him in faith He will receive you; and, having received you, will in no wise cast you out (verse 37). Jesus invites you to come to Him today to be saved by Him today.

5.3 Is seeing Jesus seeing God the Father?

Question No.3 [from a Christian to Islamic teacher Meherally.]

Jesus said: "He who has seen me has seen the Father" (Jn.14:9), does this not prove that Jesus Christ and his Father were one and the same?

Beware! Islamic deception follows:

Answer No.3

One day to prove a point and settle an argument, Jesus picked up a child and said to his disciples; "Whoever receives this child in my name receives me; and whoever receives me receives Him who sent me;" (Luke 9:48).

Jesus said; "He who believes in me does not believe in me, but in Him who sent me." (John 12:44) "He who hates me hates my Father also. ...but now they have both seen and hated me and my Father as well." (John 15:23-24) "And this is eternal life, that they may know Thee the only true God, and Jesus Christ whom Thou hast sent." (John 17:3).

The call of sincerity demands that if believing in the Truth is the honest intention then one could only pass an ethical judgement after reflecting upon all the relevant texts. John 17:3 (quoted above), if read with the following verse clears the air.

It is true that "The call of sincerity demands that if believing in the Truth is the honest intention then one could only pass an ethical judgment after reflecting upon all the relevant texts." We have shown (and will continue to show) that Meherally does not abide by his own principle.

There is another basic principle of interpretation that Meherally needs to learn: A text taken out of context is pretext.[2] By putting the above verses into a different context, Meherally makes them seem to mean something quite different from their true meaning. "He who has seen me has seen the Father" (John 14:9) taken in its true context **does** mean that Jesus and the Father are one and the same God. Said Jesus clearly, "I and my

---

[2]Pretext means, "That which is put forward to cover the real purpose or object; the ostensible reason or motive of action; an excuse, pretence, specious plea." (Oxford English Dictionary).

Father are one" (John 10:30). Since this was discussed earlier, we will not repeat it here. However, here is another verse to consider:

> 1 Timothy 3:16 And without controversy great is the mystery of godliness: **God** was manifest in the **flesh**, justified in the Spirit, seen of angels, preached unto the Gentiles, believed on in the world, received up into glory.

"God was manifest in the flesh" is a clear reference to Jesus Christ. Jesus is God manifest in human flesh.

Beware! Islamic deception follows:

Hot Tip: (precise and pertinent)

Jesus said; "Truly, truly, I say to you, a slave is not greater than his master; neither one who is sent greater than the one who sent him." (John 13:16). During his ministry, Jesus repeatedly said he was sent by his Father.

Note that the context in which Meherally makes the above statement proves that Meherally realizes that the Father which sent Jesus is God. If God is the Father (and of course He is), than God must have a Son.

Also, Meherally again misrepresents the doctrine of the Trinity. The Bible does not teach that there are three Gods, but rather that the one and only God is three persons. The concept of a God without these three persons is not a concept of the true God. The Father is this one God. The Son is this one God. And the Holy Spirit is this one God. As God, these three cannot be separated, for they are one and the same God.

He that hath seen Jesus hath seen the Father, for they are one and the same God. However, while these three persons are one and the same God, they are not one and the same person. They are distinctly different persons, with Jesus, the Son, sent by, and in perfect submission, to the Father. And this is not grievous for Jesus, for He is in perfect harmony with the Father. They are of the same mind and thoughts. They are one and the same God.

5.4   Is John 3:16 true?

Question No.4 [from a Christian to Islamic teacher Meherally.]

The Bible; "For God so loved the world, that He gave His only begotten son, that whoever believes in him should not perish, but have eternal life." (John 3:16); should you not believe in Jesus to have eternal life?

Beware! Islamic deception follows:

Answer No.4
Of course, we believe in Jesus for what he was and we do not believe in what he was not. We Muslims believe Jesus was a Messiah; "Spirit from God"; "Word of God"; the righteous Prophet as well as Messenger of God and the son of Virgin Mary. But, we do not believe Jesus was "the begotten son of God." The truth of the matter is apostle John never ever wrote; Jesus was "the begotten" son of God. Please obtain a copy of the 'Gideon Bible' from a Hotel or Motel near you. It is distributed free since 1899, all over the world, by The Gideon Society. In the beginning of this famous Bible, John 3:16 is translated in 26 popular world languages. You may be amazed to discover that in the English translation, the editors have used the traditionally accepted term "His only begotten son." Whereas, in several other languages the editors have used the term "His unique son" or "His one of a kind son." In 1992, when I discovered this textual variations, I wrote letters to various universities in North America requesting them to confirm the original Greek term used by John. Below is a copy of the response received from The George Washington University:- John 3:16 and John 1:18 each have the word 'monogenes' in Greek. This word ordinarily means "of a single kind". As a result, "unique" is a good translation. The reason you sometimes find a translation that renders the word as "only begotten" has to do with an ancient heresy within the church. In response to the Arian claim that Jesus was made but not begotten, Jerome (4th century) translated the Greek term 'monogenes' into Latin as 'unigenitus' ("only begotten"). Paul B. Duff, 22 April, 1992. Professor Duff's response was based upon 'Anchor Bible', volume 29, page 13-14. The Greek term for "begotten" is 'gennao' as found in Mt.1:2, which John did not use.

Let all Christians note how the modern perversions of the Bible undermine the Deity and Sonship of Christ Jesus, providing ammunition to the enemies of Christianity. The only way Muslims such as Meherally can prove their points is by using one of the modern translations from the corrupt composite texts based on exceedingly corrupt Codex Aleph and Codex B. Translations made from these corrupt texts amount to nothing less than treason and sedition to the Christian faith. When dealing with the Textus Receptus Greek New Testament or any accurate translation from the Textus Receptus (such as the King James Version of 1611) Muslims are powerless to prove their points.

From Meherally's comments it should be clear to all true Christians that the words "only begotten" cannot be left out of John 3:16 without stripping it of its basic message. For if Jesus is not the only begotten Son of God, then He cannot save us from our sins. Meherally is, of course, wrong; μονογενῆ (monogena) as found in John 3:16, and ἐγέν-νησε (egennase) as found in Mat. 1:2 are both from the very same root word, γεννάω (gennao), and, when used in reference to a child, both of these words always refers to a literal birth. Jesus is not God's Son in a figurative or allegorical sense, but has always been God's Son by His position in the Godhead, and is now God's only begotten Son by virtue of a literal physical birth from the virgin Mary.

Always use the King James Bible[3] when dealing with English-speaking Muslims, and you will be able to cut their phony arguments to shreds.

The conjecture that reaction to an ancient Arian heresy caused Jerome to translate μονογενῆ (monogena) as "unigenitus" is often parroted, but did Jerome say that was the cause? No. That is just a myth being spread by modern Arian heretics who love the corrupt codices Aleph and B because they give credibility to their heresy. They can give no real proof for that Christ-belittling idea. It is far more realistic to believe that Jerome translated μονογενῆ (monogena) as "unigenitus" (the Latin word for "only begotten") because he considered "only begotten" to be the correct translation. Michael D. Marlowe has written a long article about this from which comes the following quote:

> The Greek word μονογενής is an adjective compounded of μονος "only" and γενος "species, race, family, offspring, kind." In usage, with few exceptions it refers to an only son or daughter. **When used in reference to a son, it cannot mean "one of a kind," because the parent is also of the same kind. The meaning is, the son is the only offspring of the parent, not the only existing person of his kind.** And so in the Greek translation of the book of Tobit, when Raguel praises God for having mercy on δυο μονογενεις (8:17), he does not mean that his daughter Sara and Tobias were two "unique" persons; he means

that they were both only-begotten children of their fathers. In Luke's Gospel, the word is used in reference to an only child in 7:12, 8:42, and 9:38. In the Epistle to the Hebrews, it is said that when Abraham was ready to sacrifice Isaac he was offering up τον μονογενή, "his only-begotten" (11:17), because although Abraham had another son, God had said that only in Isaac shall Abraham's seed (σπερμα) be named. (Πίστει προσενήνοχεν Ἀβραὰμ τὸν Ἰσαὰκ πειραζόμενος, καὶ τὸν μονογενῆ προσέφερεν ὁ τὰς ἐπαγγελίας ἀναδεξάμενος, πρὸς ὃν ἐλαλήθη ὅτι Ἐν Ἰσαὰκ κληθήσεταί σοι σπέρμα). (1) When the word μονογενής is used in reference to a son or daughter, it always means "only-begotten." ...

If the word "begotten" as applied to Christ has had such importance in the history of Christian doctrine, **why have some modern versions of the Bible omitted the "begotten" in their renderings of the verses quoted above?**

It is because many modern scholars have rejected the interpretation of Scripture embodied in the Nicene Creed. These scholars maintain that the Nicene Creed's interpretation of Scripture is wrong, and they argue that the traditional rendering "only begotten" represents a dogmatically-motivated misinterpretation of the Greek word μονογενής. As one Baptist scholar puts it,

"The phrase 'only begotten' derives directly from Jerome (340?-420 A.D.) who replaced unicus (only), the reading of the Old Latin, with unigenitus (only begotten) as he translated the Latin Vulgate. Jerome's concern was to refute the Arian doctrine that claimed the Son was not begotten but made. This led Jerome to impose the terminology of the Nicene creed (325 A.D.) onto the New Testament" [Christopher Church, "Only Begotten," in the Holman Bible Dictionary (Broadman & Holman, 1991].

This author [Christopher Church] **gives the translators who have preferred "only begotten" too little credit, as if this phrase in the early English versions were merely an unthinking imitation of the Vulgate's unigenitus, and retained in some modern versions only by the force of a verbal tra-**

---

[3]Be aware that the editors of of the so-called New King James Version introduced corruptions to its text—it is not a genuine King James Bible. Buy and use the Authorized King James Version of 1611 with updated spelling.

dition. **But the translators of the King James Version were not just imitating the Vulgate when they translated** μονογενής **as "only begotten." They translated it thus because they understood it thus, in agreement with the interpretation of the word given in the Nicene Creed. And the author's [Christopher Church's]contention that Jerome imposed the terminology of the Nicene creed onto the Scriptures when he used unigenitus is unjustifiable. It is no imposition on the word to translate it thus. (13) Athanasius and the other Greek Fathers of the early fourth century did not need any Latin version to interpret this word for them, and in their disputes with the Arians they frequently explained it in the sense, "only-begotten," with exegetical emphasis on the "begotten."** If this were not enough, modern scholarly support for this understanding of the word is certainly not lacking either. "Only-begotten" is given as a sense for μονογενής in Lust's Greek-English Lexicon of the Septuagint (2nd ed., Stuttgart: Deutsche Bibelgesellschaft, 2003). In the 2nd ed. of the BAGD lexicon (1979) it is said that "the meanings only, unique may be quite adequate for all its occurrences" in the Johannine literature (p. 527), but the lexicon also presents the traditional view, in which the word is understood to mean "only-begotten." See also the article on monogenes by Büchsel in Kittel's Theological Dictionary of the New Testament, vol. 4, pp. 737-41. Büchsel concludes that in John's Gospel the word denotes "more than the uniqueness or incomparability of Jesus," because it also "denotes the origin of Jesus ... as the only-begotten." For a full discussion of this matter see John V. Dahms, "The Johannine Use of Monogenes Reconsidered," New Testament Studies 29 (1983), pp. 222-232. **Dahms concludes, "the external evidence, especially from Philo, Justin, and Tertullian, and the internal evidence from the context of its occurrences, makes clear that 'only begotten' is the most accurate translation after all."** ...

The truth is, those who do not acknowledge this meaning of the word μονογε-

νής **in the Johannine writings are themselves dogmatically motivated.** Their preferred translation—"only"—is an undertranslation which hides from view a Scriptural datum that supports the Christology of the ancient Creed but which happens to be unpopular with modern theologians.[4]

So to conclude this section, of course John 3:16 is true. "... yea, let God be true, but every man a liar" (Romans 3:4).

Jesus being the only-begotten Son of God will be discussed in more detail in chapter 6 under subheading 7.1.1.

5.5 Did God physically have sex with Mary?

> **Beware! Islamic deception follows:**
>
> Hot Tip: (precise and pertinent)
> Jesus said to Mary; "...go to my brethren, and say to them, I ascend to my Father and your Father..." (John 20:17). This verse demonstrates that the usage of term 'Father' was purely metaphorical. As for Jesus being a "unique son", he, unlike us, was created without a physical Father.

It is true that Jesus did not have a physical Father in the sense that He had no human father. God, the Father of Jesus, is a spiritual being, not a physical being. However, it is equally true that God the Father is the biological Father of Jesus. The usage of the term "Father" was not metaphorical as Meherally claims. Mat. 1:18 very plainly states this: "Now the birth of Jesus Christ was on this wise: When as his mother Mary was espoused to Joseph, **before** they came together, she was found with child **of the Holy Ghost.**" In Mat. 1:20 the angel of the Lord

---

[4]http://www.bible-researcher.com/only-begotten.html

again emphasized the fact: "for that which is conceived in her **is of the Holy Ghost**." Jesus **is** the only begotten Son of God.

Islam claims that it is not fitting for God to have a Son, for (claims Islam) "begetting a son is a physical act depending on the needs of men's animal nature".[5] Islam is misrepresenting the conception of Christ with such words. God the Father is a Spirit, and has no physical body with which to lie with a woman. There was no physical sex act between God and the virgin Mary, such as between a human husband and his wife. Rather, the Holy Ghost impregnated the virgin Mary by the process of a miracle. And she was just as much a virgin **after** conceiving Jesus of the Holy Ghost as she was **before**.

> Matthew 1:18 **Now the birth of Jesus Christ was on this wise**: When as his mother Mary was espoused to Joseph, **before they came together**, she was found **with child of the Holy Ghost**. 19 Then Joseph her husband, being a just man, and not willing to make her a publick example, was minded to put her away privily. 20 But while he thought on these things, behold, the angel of the Lord appeared unto him in a dream, saying, Joseph, thou son of David, fear not to take unto thee Mary thy wife: for **that which is conceived in her is of the Holy Ghost**. 21 And she shall bring forth a **son**, and thou shalt call his name **JESUS**: for **he shall save his people from their sins**. 22 Now all this was done, that it might be fulfilled which was spoken of the Lord by the prophet, saying, 23 Behold, a **virgin** shall be with child, and shall bring forth a **son**, and **they shall call his name Emmanuel, which being interpreted is, God with us**. 24 Then Joseph being raised from sleep did as the angel of the Lord had bidden him, and took unto him his wife: 25 **And knew her not** till she had brought forth her **firstborn** son: and he called his name **JESUS**.

If a woman has sexual intercourse she is no longer a virgin. The only way a virgin could be with child is for her to have conceived that child without physically having sex. Mary did not physically have sex with God, but rather her conception was a miracle of the Holy Ghost.

It is important to understand also that God the Son did not come into being at the birth of Jesus in Bethlehem, but at that time merely took upon Himself a human body, so that **as a human** He could die to take the punishment for our sins so that we could be saved. Jesus existed **before** He was born of the virgin Mary. In eternity past He already was.

> Micah 5:2 But thou, Bethlehem Ephratah, though thou be little among the thousands of Judah, yet out of thee shall he come forth unto me that is to be ruler in Israel; **whose goings forth have been from of old, from everlasting.**

> John 8:58 Jesus said unto them, Verily, verily, I say unto you, **Before** Abraham was, **I am.**

> John 17:1 These words spake **Jesus**, and lifted up his eyes to heaven, and said, **Father**, the hour is come; glorify **thy Son**, that **thy Son** also may glorify thee: 2 As thou hast given him power over all flesh, **that he should give eternal life to as many as thou hast given him**. 3 **And this is life eternal, that they might know thee the only true God, and Jesus Christ, whom thou hast sent.** 4 I have glorified thee on the earth: I have finished the work which thou gavest me to do. 5 And now, O **Father**, glorify thou me with thine own self with the glory **which I had with thee before the world was**....24 Father, I will that they also, whom thou hast given me, be with me where I am; that they may behold my glory, which thou hast given me: **for thou lovedst me before the foundation of the world.**

---

[5]Footnote 2487 in the Abdullah Yusuf Ali translation of the Quran.

79

Figure 5.1: *Muslims "glorified" Jesus by "comforting" this young Christian girl in the Maluku islands of Indonesia. Her parents probably never dreamed that followers of the "religion of peace" would do this to "their" daughter—but they did. You probably have never dreamed that the same might happen to your daughter—but it very well might if you don't take steps to stop the rapid spread of Islam in the USA. It is very foolish to think it can't happen here, because it can.*

Chapter 6

Deceptive Muslim Answers To Christians' Questions 5–8

6.1 Are you "born again"?

> **Question No.5 [from a Christian to Islamic teacher Meherally.]**
>
> **Jesus said: "Truly, truly. I say to you, unless one is born again, he cannot see the kingdom of God." (John 3:3); I am a "born again" Christian, are you a "born again" Muslim?**
>
> **Beware! Islamic deception follows:**
>
> Answer No.5
> The truth of the matter is apostle John did not use the phrase "born again". The Greek text reveals, the phrase used by John is "born from above". The Greek word used by John is 'anothen' ('ano' + 'then'). 'ano' means 'above' and the suffix 'then' denotes 'from'. Hence, what Jesus said was "unless one is born from above, he cannot see the kingdom of God." And, that sounds logical. Since none of the living creature is "born from above", no one can see the kingdom heaven during his life time.

Meherally immediately uses Greek to distract us. Notice that he doesn't answer the question. That is obviously because Meherally knows that he is not "born again." And that means that he is spiritually blind: "he **cannot see** the kingdom of God." "And if the blind lead the blind, both shall fall into the ditch" (Matthew 15:14). It also means "he **cannot enter into** the kingdom of God" (John 3:5). Except he repent, and believe in Jesus, he is doomed.

By his comments, Meherally again displays his ignorance of the Greek language. The Greek word ἄνωθεν (anothen) does sometimes mean "from above." However, in other cases it means "again." It all depends on the usage of the word in its context. The men who produced the King James Version of 1611 translation were experts in the Greek language, knowing the meanings of each Greek word as it was found in its context. Meherally is not an expert in the Greek language, and therefore is in no position to correct the work of the translators of the King James Bible.

To give an example in English, the word "saw" can mean "to see" (past tense) or "to cut with a special toothed tool." What saw means depends on the way it is used. Meherally is like a man who insists that saw always means "to see" no matter in what context it is used.

In Galatians 4:9 the word ἄνωθεν (anothen) is used in such a way that it could not possibly mean "from above": "...ye desire again (anothen) to be in bondage." To say, "ye desire **from above** to be in bondage" would obviously be incorrect. ἄνωθεν means "again" in this case. It is used this same way in John 3:3. Again we see that the King James Version of the Bible is correct, and Meherally is wrong. Meherally is no Greek expert.

6.1.1 Is being born again the same as being baptized?

> **Beware! Islamic deception follows:**
>
> The concept of being "born again" to see the kingdom of heaven is an innovation to instill the concept of Baptism.

Wrong again! Being born again is **not** the same as baptism. Baptism pictures a death, burial, and resurrection, not a birth.

> Romans 6:3 Know ye not, that so many of us as were **baptized** into Jesus Christ were **baptized** into his **death**? 4 Therefore we are **buried** with him by **baptism** into **death**: that like as Christ was **raised up** from the **dead** by the glory of the Father, even so we also should walk in newness of life.

A birth is not a burial.

> **Beware! Islamic deception follows:**
>
> The same word 'anothen' appears in the same Gospel and in the same chapter in verse 31. Here the editors have translated the word as "from above" and not "again". This further supports the logic of Jesus having said; "born from above".

In verse 31 "anothen" is used in a different way and therefore has a different meaning, as has already been explained on the current page.

6.1.2 Is salvation by works?

How to be saved from sins is the most important teaching of any religion. How can a person be sure that he will avoid Hell and go to Heaven when he dies? What does Islam teach about this most important doctrine? Let's see:

> **Beware! Islamic deception follows:**
>
> To enter the Kingdom of Heaven one has to keep the Commandments.

The above statement of Mr. Meherally is a very major false doctrine. In fact this is Islam's most fatal flaw. Mr. Meherally, do you keep the Commandments? No, like all men you break the Commandments—you sin.

> Ecclesiastes 7:20 There is **not** a man upon the earth that doeth good and sinneth not.
>
> Romans 3:10 As it is written, There is **none** righteous, **no, not one**: 11 There is **none** that understandeth, there is **none** that seeketh after God. 12 They are **all** gone out of the way, they are together become unprofitable; there is **none** that doeth good, **no, not one**.
>
> Romans 3:23 For **all** have **sinned** and come short of the glory of God.

Since you do not keep the commandments, are we to conclude that you are going to Hell? Of course you are going to Hell if "To enter the Kingdom of Heaven one has to keep the Commandments" as Islam teaches. The truth is that keeping the Commandments has never enabled anyone to enter the Kingdom of Heaven, except Jesus; for no one but Jesus has ever perfectly kept the Commandments.

James 2:11 For whosoever shall keep the **whole** law, and yet offend in **one point**, he is **guilty** of **all**.

Galatians 2:16 Knowing that a man is **not** justified by the works of the law, but by the faith of Jesus Christ, even we have believed in Jesus Christ, that we might be justified by the faith of Christ, and **not** by the works of the law: **for by the works of the law shall no flesh be justified**.

The Islamic idea that to get to Heaven one must "keep the commandments" is the root cause of Muslims becoming suicide bombers. Muslims are taught that no matter how sinful they have been, all their sins will be forgiven if they die waging jihad against the kafir (non-muslims). Narrated Abu Huraira:

> The Prophet said, **"The person who participates in (Holy battles) in Allah's cause** and nothing compels him to do so except belief in Allah and His Apostles, **will be recompensed by Allah either with a reward, or booty (if he survives) or will be admitted to Paradise (if he is killed in the battle as a martyr).** Had I not found it difficult for my followers, then I would not remain behind any sariya going for Jihad and I would have loved to be martyred in Allah's cause and then made alive, and then martyred and then made alive, and then again martyred in His cause."[1]

Even the top Muslim leaders are involved in immorality. When US Navy Seals raided Osama bin Laden's house in Pakistan, they found an extensive collection of pornography.[2] Obviously, Osama was not a holy man, but a very sinful man. Another example recently in the news is Islamic scholar

[1]From the hadith collection of Sahih Bukhari as translated by M. Muhsin Khan. http://www.usc.edu/schools/college/crcc/engagement/resources/texts/muslim/hadith/bukhari/002.sbt.html#001.002.035

[2]http://www.reuters.com/article/2011/05/13/us-binladen-porn-idUSTRE74C4RK20110513

Al-Awlaki, "who was convicted a couple of times for trolling for street hookers while living in California."[3]

Is circumcision necessary for salvation?

> **Beware! Islamic deception follows:**
>
> God's distinguished Command known as the 'Covenant of Circumcision' (physically, "in the flesh of your foreskin") was an everlasting Covenant (Compact,Treaty) between God and man. See Genesis 17:10-14.

Wrong! Circumcision was not the everlasting Covenant, but was "a **token** of the covenant."

Genesis 17:11 And ye shall circumcise the flesh of your foreskin; and it shall be a **token** of the covenant betwixt me and you.

A token is a sign or symbol of something. A token represents something besides itself, but is not in reality what it represents. This is always understood by wise people.

The Everlasting Covenant itself was explained as follows:

Genesis 17:7 And I will establish **my covenant** between me and thee and thy seed after thee in their generations for an everlasting covenant, to be a God unto thee, and to thy seed after thee. 8 **And I will give unto thee, and to thy seed after thee, the land wherein thou art a stranger, all the land of Canaan, for an everlasting possession; and I will be their God.**

The everlasting Covenant was that God gave the land of Canaan to Abraham's seed, and would be their God. This covenant was with Isaac, not with Ishmael.

[3]http://www.thesmokinggun.com/buster/prostitution/al-awlaki-prostitution-arrets-970612

Genesis 17:18 And Abraham said unto God, O that Ishmael might live before thee! 19 And God said, **Sarah thy wife shall bare thee a son indeed: and thou shalt call his name Isaac: and I will establish my covenant with him for an everlasting covenant**, and with his seed after him. 20 And as for Ishmael, I have heard thee: Behold, I make him fruitful, and will multiply him exceedingly; twelve princes shall he begat, and I will make him a great nation. 21 **But my covenant will I establish with Isaac**, which Sarah shall bear unto thee at this set time in the next year.

Therefore the land of Canaan belongs to the Jews not to the Arabs.

```
Beware! Islamic deception follows:
```

Can an everlasting Treaty be abrogated or revoked unilaterally? Did Jesus abrogate it? No. Jesus was circumcised in the flesh (Luke 2:21). We, Muslim males, are circumcised. Are the male Christians circumcised in the "flesh of their foreskins"? If not, please read the following verse:- Hot Tip: ^^^^^^^^ Jesus said; "Whoever then annuls (discards) one of the least of these commandments, and so teaches others, shall be called least in the kingdom of heaven; but whoever keeps and teaches them, he shall be called great in the kingdom of heaven." (Matt. 5:19).

God commanded that circumcision be performed on the **eighth day** after birth.

Leviticus 12:2 Speak unto the children of Israel, saying, If a woman have conceived seed, and born a man child: then she shall be unclean seven days; according to the days of the separation for her infirmity shall she be unclean. 3 And **in the eighth day** the flesh of his foreskin shall be circumcised.

Are Muslim males circumcised the eighth day after birth, or does Islam annul (discard) this commandment? No, they are **not** circumcised on the eight day! Instead, they wait until the child is much older to circumcise him or her—often 13 years old like Ishmael was when he was circumcised. So, Muslims sin by discarding this commandment! Jesus, however, was circumcised the eighth day in perfect obedience to the law of God.

Luke 2:21 And when **eight days** were accomplished for the circumcising of the child, his name was called JESUS, which was so named of the angel before he was conceived in the womb.

Circumcision has always been only a symbol, and never has had power to save the soul.

Galatians 5:1-11 Stand fast therefore in the **liberty** wherewith **Christ** hath made us **free**, and be not entangled again with **the yoke of bondage**. 2 Behold, I Paul say unto you, that **if ye be circumcised, Christ shall profit you nothing**. 3 For I testify again to every man that is circumcised, that he is a debtor to do the whole law. 4 Christ is become of no effect unto you, whosoever of you are justified by the law; ye are fallen from grace. 5 For we through the Spirit wait for the hope of righteousness by faith. 6 **For in Jesus Christ neither circumcision availeth any thing, nor uncircumcision; but faith which worketh by love**. 7 Ye did run well; who did hinder you that ye should not obey the truth? 8 This persuasion cometh not of him that calleth you. 9 A little leaven leaveneth the whole lump. 10 I have confidence in you through the Lord, that ye will be none otherwise minded: but he that troubleth you shall bear his judgment, whosoever he be. 11 And I, brethren, if I yet preach circumcision, why do I yet suffer persecution? then is the offence of the cross ceased.

The context shows that the words "if ye be circumcised, Christ shall profit you nothing" are referring to how to be saved from Hell. In other words, "if ye be circumcised [thinking that will save you], Christ shall profit you nothing." So, if you believe that circumcision will save your soul, then you do not believe in Christ to save your soul, and so you are lost and on your way to Hell.

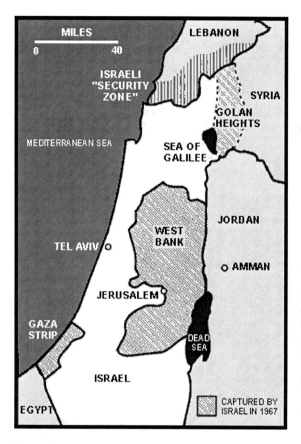

Figure 6.1: *Present day Israel possesses only a part of the land God gave them. The Gaza Strip, the West Bank, part of Jordan, part of present day Lebanon, and part of present day Syria also belong to Israel.*

Figure 6.2: *This map shows how God divided the land of Israel among the 12 tribes in Joshua chapters 18-19. Note that God gave Israel both the east and west banks of the Jordan river.*

Galatians 6:15 For in Christ Jesus neither circumcision availeth any thing, nor uncircumcision, but a new creature.

Being circumcised will not get a person to Heaven. If you want to get to Heaven, you must be born again, so that you become a new creature in Christ.

Now to answer Meherally's question: "Can an everlasting Treaty be abrogated or revoked unilaterally?" No, it cannot. Therefore, the Land of Canaan will always belong to the Jews. That is God's everlasting covenant that shall never be broken.

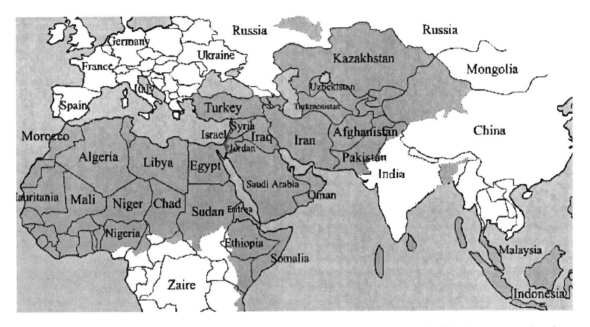

Figure 6.3: *The land of Israel (shaded black) surrounded by Muslim lands (shaded dark grey). Look at how much land the Muslims have, while Israel is so small that it almost takes a magnifying glass to see it on this map. The word "Israel" takes up three or four times more space on the map than the whole country itself takes. Yet Islam makes Muslims so hateful and greedy that they want Israel's land too. And they are ready to murder every Israeli there in order to steal it from them.*

Chapter 7

Deceptive Muslim Answers To Christians' Questions 9–13

7.1 Does Mat. 28:19 prove the Trinity?

Question No.6 [from a Christian to Islamic teacher Meherally.]

Jesus said; "Go therefore and make disciples of all the nations, baptizing them in the name of the Father and the Son and the Holy Spirit," (Matthew 28:19); does this not prove that the 'Doctrine of Trinity' and its present day formula was communicated and promulgated by Jesus Christ himself?

Beware! Islamic deception follows:

Answer No.6
With all due respect, we tend to disagree in view of the following compelling evidences:- 1. 'Peake's Commentary on the Bible' published since 1919, is universally welcomed and considered to be the standard reference book for the students of the Bible. Commenting on the above verse it records; "This mission is described in the language of the church and most commentators doubt that the trinitarian formula was original at this point in Mt.'s Gospel, since

the NT elsewhere does not know of such a formula and describes baptism as being performed in the name of the Lord Jesus (e.g. Ac. 2:38, 8:16, etc.)."

Meherally did not tell the truth in saying that "Peake's Commentary on the Bible published since 1919, is universally welcomed and considered to be the standard reference book for the students of the Bible." That statement simply is not true. In fact, *Peake's Commentary*—especially the revised edition—is welcomed only by advocates of the corrupt Codex Aleph and Codex B manuscripts. Other Bible scholars do not value it even as a secondary reference. It is not authoritative, and certainly cannot override the Bible. The authors of *Peake's Commentary* can doubt all they want; all infidels doubt. But they did not live back in the days when Matthew 28:19 was written, and so they do not know. The important thing to see here is that Islamic teachers know that the Bible doesn't actually teach Islamic doctrines, so they must somehow convince you that it is mistranslated, or words were added or subtracted by some scribe, or try to discredit the Bible by quoting other unbelievers like themselves, such as the authors of *Peake's Com-*

mentary. As you have already seen, the truth is that the Bible very effectively disproves Islamic teachings.

> **Beware! Islamic deception follows:**
>
> 2. Tom Harpur, author of several bestsellers and a former professor of New Testament, writes in his book 'For Christ's Sake'; "All but the most conservative of scholars agree that at least the latter part of this command was inserted later. The formula occurs nowhere else in the New Testament, and we know from the only evidence available (the rest of the New Testament) that the earliest Church did not baptise people using these words - baptism was "into" or "in" the name of Jesus alone."

Tom Harpur "is a proponent of the Christ myth theory, the idea that Jesus did not exist historically, but is a mythical figure."[1] Meherally quotes Harper as an authoritative source. So does Meherally also believe that Jesus never exited? If so, Meherally does not believe the Quran, for even the Quran admits Jesus existed. Like most Muslim teachers, Meherally's fatal flaw is that he ignores context, and just picks what he thinks will help him win arguments. He is not concerned about the truth.

Harpur says, "All but the most conservative of scholars agree..." The fact is, no truly conservative scholar would agree with Harper. In Christian circles the title "conservative" is used of scholars who are true Christians who believe the record that God gave of His Son. Liberals such as Harpur are unbelieving infidels, who decide that the Bible is in error even before they study it. They hate the Bible because it tells them that many of the things they love to do are sin. Usually (like Meherally has done above) they do not really study the Bible directly, but only study what other infidels have said about the Bible. Liberal scholarship is therefore neither true nor honest scholarship, but is simply infidels quoting other infidels. Liberals are lost men. Harpur and Meherally can offer no proof that the Trinitarian formula was inserted later except the foolish conjecture of other unbelieving lost men like themselves.

Harpur also believes that the Bible is just "a collection of holy myths."[2] If this is what Meherally also believes, then why is he quoting from the Bible trying to prove Islam? And if the Bible is not just a collection of myths, then why doesn't Meherally believe what it says? The truth is that the Isa Almasih of the Quran is the myth (among many other myths in the Quran).

> **Beware! Islamic deception follows:**
>
> 3. The above command (authentic or otherwise) does not indicate that the three names mentioned in the formula are or were, "coequal" in their status, as well as, were "coeternal" in the time frame, to conform with the acknowledged 'Doctrine of Trinity'.

Oh, but it does indicate that the three names mentioned in the formula are "coequal" in their status, as well as, "co-eternal" in their time frame, for it says "baptizing them in the name [singular, **not** "name**s**" plural] of the Father, and of the Son, and of the Holy Ghost."

---

[1] http://www.thedailybell.com/1859/ Anthony-Wile-with-Tom-Harpur-on-Bible-Mythology-and-Why-He-says-Jesus-Christ-Never-Lived-Historically.html

[2] Ibid.

7.1.1 Was Jesus God's Son before being born of Mary?

Muslim teachers think God is limited like a human being. In truth, however, God's word reveals to us that God is unlimited and His thoughts are higher than our thoughts, and His ways higher than our ways.

> Isaiah 55:8 For my thoughts are not your thoughts, neither are your ways my ways, saith **the LORD**. 9 For as the heavens are higher than the earth, **so are my ways higher than your ways, and my thoughts than your thoughts.**

The Bible plainly states that "God is not a man."

> Numbers 23:19 **God is not a man**, that he should lie; neither the son of man, that he should repent: hath he said, and shall he not do it? or hath he spoken, and shall he not make it good?

Muslim teachers have "changed the glory of the uncorruptible God into an image made like to corruptible man."

> Romans 1:18 For the wrath of **God** is revealed from heaven against all ungodliness and unrighteousness of men, who hold the truth in unrighteousness; 19 Because that which may be known of God is manifest in them; for God hath shewed it unto them. 20 For the invisible things of him from the creation of the world are clearly seen, being understood by the things that are made, **even his eternal power and Godhead**; so that they are without excuse: 21 **Because that, when they knew God, they glorified him not as God**, neither were thankful; but became vain in their imaginations, and their foolish heart was darkened. 22 Professing themselves to be wise, they became fools, 23 **And changed the glory of the uncorruptible God into an image made like to corruptible man**, and to birds, and fourfooted beasts, and creeping things.

In particular, Muslim teachers deny God's eternal power and Godhead. That is the reason they can't understand how God can do the seemingly impossible things He claims to have done. This is particularly true concerning the birth of God's Son. Consider the following Muslim questions:

Beware! Islamic deception follows:

4. If the Father and His Son were both in "existence" from the Day One, and no one was, a micro second before or after, and, no one was "greater or lesser" in status, than why is one called the Father and the other His begotten Son? 5. Did the act of "Begetting" take place? If YES, where was the "Begotten Son" before the act? If NO, why call him the "Begotten Son"?

There are two important Bible teachings which Muslim teachers—because of their low concept of God—can't understand how they can possibly be: (1) that Jesus is the eternal God who has no beginning because He has always existed, and (2) that Jesus is also the "only begotten Son of God." This just seems totally impossible to them. But they need to be reminded of what Jesus said in Matthew 19:26, "With men this is impossible; but **with God all things are possible.**" What impotent Allah cannot do, the true God can easily do.

The three persons of the Godhead, the Father, the Son, and the Holy Spirit, had no beginning, but have always existed, for they are eternal. In Hebrews 9:14 the Holy Ghost is called the "eternal Spirit." In eternity past the Son of God was the One God with the Father, but was in submission to the Father as a person. The Son of God is mentioned in the book of Daniel:

> Daniel 3:24 Then Nebuchadnezzar the king was astonied, and rose up in haste, and spake, and said unto his counsellors, Did not we cast **three** men bound into the midst of the fire? They answered and said unto the king, True, O king. 25 He answered and said, Lo, I see **four** men loose, walking in the midst of the fire, and

they have no hurt; and the form of the fourth is like **the Son of God**.

This was in the Old Testament **long before** the Son of God was born of the virgin Mary.

Consider also the following passage of Scripture from the New Testament which declares that Jesus is "a priest for ever after the order of Melchisedec."

Hebrews 7:1 For this **Melchisedec**, king of Salem, priest of the most high God, who met Abraham returning from the slaughter of the kings, and blessed him; 2 To whom also Abraham gave a tenth part of all; first being by interpretation King of righteousness, and after that also King of Salem, which is, King of peace; 3 **Without father, without mother, without descent, having neither beginning of days, nor end of life; but made like unto the Son of God**; abideth a priest continually. 4 Now consider how great this man was, unto whom even the patriarch Abraham gave the tenth of the spoils. 5 And verily they that are of the sons of Levi, who receive the office of the priesthood, have a commandment to take tithes of the people according to the law, that is, of their brethren, though they come out of the loins of Abraham: 6 But he whose descent is not counted from them received tithes of Abraham, and blessed him that had the promises. 7 And without all contradiction the less is blessed of the better. 8 And here men that die receive tithes; but there he receiveth them, of whom it is witnessed that he liveth. 9 And as I may so say, Levi also, who receiveth tithes, payed tithes in Abraham. 10 For he was yet in the loins of his father, when Melchisedec met him. 11 If therefore perfection were by the Levitical priesthood, (for under it the people received the law,) what further need was there that another priest should rise after the order of Melchisedec, and not be called after the order of Aaron? 12 For the priesthood being changed, there is made of necessity a change also of the law. 13 For he of whom these things are spoken pertaineth to another tribe, of which no man gave attendance at the altar. 14 For it is evident that **our Lord** sprang out of Juda; of which tribe Moses spake nothing concerning

priesthood. 15 And it is yet far more evident: for that after the similitude of Melchisedec there ariseth another priest, 16 Who is made, not after the law of a carnal commandment, but after the power of **an endless life**. 17 For he testifieth, **Thou art a priest for ever after the order of Melchisedec.** 18 For there is verily a disannulling of the commandment going before for the weakness and unprofitableness thereof. 19 **For the law made nothing perfect, but the bringing in of a better hope did**; by the which we draw nigh unto God. 20 And inasmuch as not without an oath he was made priest: 21 (For those priests were made without an oath; but this with an oath by him that said unto him, The Lord sware and will not repent, Thou art a priest for ever after the order of Melchisedec:) 22 By so much was **Jesus** made a surety of a better testament. 23 And they truly were many priests, because they were not suffered to continue by reason of death: 24 **But this man, because he continueth ever, hath an unchangeable priesthood. 25 Wherefore he is able also to save them to the uttermost that come unto God by him, seeing he ever liveth to make intercession for them. 26 For such an high priest became us, who is holy, harmless, undefiled, separate from sinners, and made higher than the heavens;** 27 Who needeth not daily, as those high priests, to offer up sacrifice, first for his own sins, and then for the people's: for this he did once, when he offered up himself. 28 For the law maketh men high priests which have infirmity; but the word of the oath, which was since the law, maketh **the Son**, who is consecrated for evermore.

Verse two above directly implies that the Son of God is "without father, without mother, without descent, having neither beginning of days, nor end of life." That is because Jesus' Sonship in eternity past was by **position**, not by birth. In eternity past Jesus had no father in the birth sense, for he has always existed—he had no beginning. At that time Jesus was God's Son by **position**.

That Jesus was God's Son before being begotten is confirmed in Hebrews chapter one:

> Hebrews 1:1 **God**, who at sundry times and in divers manners spake in time past unto the fathers by the prophets, 2 Hath in these last days spoken unto us by **his Son**, whom he hath appointed heir of all things, **by whom also he made the worlds**; 3 Who being the brightness of his glory, and the express image of his person, and upholding all things by the word of his power, when he had **by himself purged our sins**, sat down on the right hand of the Majesty on high; 4 Being made so much better than the angels, as he hath by inheritance obtained a more excellent name than they. 5 For unto which of the angels said he at any time, Thou art **my Son**, this day have I begotten thee? And again, **I will be to him a Father, and he shall be to me a Son**? 6 And again, when he bringeth in the **firstbegotten** into the world, he saith, And let all the angels of God worship him. 7 And of the angels he saith, Who maketh his angels spirits, and his ministers a flame of fire. 8 But unto **the Son** he saith, Thy throne, **O God**, is for ever and ever: a sceptre of righteousness is the sceptre of thy kingdom. 9 Thou hast loved righteousness, and hated iniquity; therefore God, even thy God, hath anointed thee with the oil of gladness above thy fellows. 10 And, Thou, **Lord, in the beginning hast laid the foundation of the earth; and the heavens are the works of thine hands:** 11 They shall perish; but thou remainest; and they all shall wax old as doth a garment; 12 And as a vesture shalt thou fold them up, and they shall be changed: but thou art the same, and thy years shall not fail. 13 But to which of the angels said he at any time, Sit on my right hand, until I make thine enemies thy footstool? 14 Are they not all ministering spirits, sent forth to minister for them who shall be heirs of salvation?

Verse two above tells us that the worlds were made by God's Son. And in verse 8 God tells us that his Son is God. And in verse 10 God tells us that his Son is **the Lord** who created the earth and the heavens. Obviously, creation took place **before** Jesus was begotten of God from the the virgin Mary. But verse

5 tells us that there came a **day** when Jesus was "**begotten**." From that day, Jesus was no longer the Son of God only by position, but also by physical birth. He was from that point forward the "**only begotten** Son of God."

The word "begotten" is especially important because it implies an actual birth. The book of Isaiah predicted the actual physical birth of God's Son:

> Isaiah 7:14 Therefore the Lord himself shall give you a sign; Behold, **a virgin** shall **conceive**, and **bear** a son, and shall call his name **Immanuel**.

> Isaiah 9:6 For unto us a child is **born**, unto us a **son** is given: and the government shall be upon his shoulder: and his name shall be called Wonderful, Counsellor, **The mighty God**, **The everlasting Father**,[3] The Prince of Peace.

These prophecies were fulfilled when the virgin Mary gave birth to Jesus:

> Matthew 1:19 Then Joseph her husband, being a just man, and not willing to make her a publick example, was minded to put her away privily. 20 But while he thought on these things, behold, the angel of the Lord appeared unto him in a dream, saying, Joseph, thou son of David, fear not to take unto thee Mary thy wife: **for that which is conceived in her is of the Holy Ghost.** 21 And she shall bring forth a **son**, and thou shalt call his name JESUS: for he shall save his people from their sins. 22 **Now all this was done, that it might be fulfilled which was spoken of the Lord by the prophet, saying,** 23 Behold, a virgin shall be with child, and shall bring forth a son, and they shall call his name Emmanuel, which being interpreted is, God with us. 24 Then Joseph being raised from sleep did as the angel of the Lord had bidden him, and took unto him his wife: 25 And **knew her not** till she had brought forth her **firstborn son**: and he called his name JESUS.

---

[3]The Son is called the "everlasting Father" because all the fullness of the Triune Godhead dwells in Jesus' body (Colossians 2:9).

Psalms chapter two is always quoted in the New Testament as referring to the Lord Jesus Christ.

> Psalms 2:7 I will declare the decree: **the LORD** hath said unto me, Thou art **my Son**; **this day** have I **begotten** thee. 8 Ask of me, and I shall give thee the heathen for thine inheritance, and the uttermost parts of the earth for thy possession. 9 Thou shalt break them with a rod of iron; thou shalt dash them in pieces like a potter's vessel. 10 Be wise now therefore, O ye kings: be instructed, ye judges of the earth. 11 Serve the LORD with fear, and rejoice with trembling.12 Kiss **the Son**, lest he be angry, and ye perish from the way, when his wrath is kindled but a little. Blessed are all they that put their trust in him.

Jesus was the Son of JEHOVAH God **from eternity past**, but He did not become the "only begotten Son" until He was born of the virgin Mary some 2,000 years ago **on a certain "day,"** thus taking upon Himself a human body so that as a human He could die for the sins of all humans on earth so that we might be saved from our sins. The New Testament commentary concerning the above verses makes this very clear:

> Acts 13:26 Men and brethren, children of the stock of Abraham, and **whosoever among you feareth God**, to you is the word of this salvation sent. 27 For they that dwell at Jerusalem, and their rulers, because they knew him not, nor yet the voices of the prophets which are read every sabbath day, they have fulfilled them in condemning him. 28 And though **they found no cause of death in him**, yet desired they Pilate that he should be slain. 29 **And when they had fulfilled all that was written of him, they took him down from the tree, and laid him in a sepulchre. 30 But God raised him from the dead:** 31 And he was seen many days of them which came up with him from Galilee to Jerusalem, who are his witnesses unto the people. 32 And we declare unto you glad tidings, how that the promise which was made unto the fathers, 33 **God** hath fulfilled the same unto us their children, in that **he hath raised up Jesus again**; as it is also written in the second psalm, Thou art **my Son, this day** have I **begotten** thee. 34 And as concerning that he raised him up from the dead, now no more to return to corruption, he said on this wise, I will give you the sure mercies of David. 35 Wherefore he saith also in another psalm, Thou shalt not suffer thine Holy One to see corruption. 36 For David, after he had served his own generation by the will of God, fell on sleep, and was laid unto his fathers, and saw corruption: 37 **But he, whom God raised again, saw no corruption.** 38 Be it known unto you therefore, men and brethren, that **through this man** is preached unto you **the forgiveness of sins**: 39 And **by him all that believe** are **justified** from **all things**, from which ye could not be justified by the law of Moses. 40 Beware therefore, lest that come upon you, which is spoken of in the prophets; 41 Behold, ye despisers, and wonder, and perish: for I work a work in your days, a work which ye shall in no wise believe, though a man declare it unto you.

Note in verse 28 above that they found no cause of death in Jesus. Because He was the only begotten, virgin born Son of the Holy God, He did not inherit a depraved nature inclined to sin from his Father and was sinless, and was thus able to die for **our** sins. In verses 28 and 29 we read that Jesus died in the manner predicted in the Old Testament, and was buried. And in verses 30, 33, and 37 we read that God raised him from the dead. Why did all these things happen? Verses 38 through 39 tell us that these things happened so that we might have forgiveness of sins, and be justified from all things through Christ. And verse 39 warns us that we cannot be justified by trying to keep the law of Moses, but only by believing in Jesus Christ. You and I sin, and so cannot save ourselves by our (not so good) works. But Jesus' life and works were perfect, so He is the perfect and only Savior.

> Hebrews 5:1 For **every high priest taken from among men** is ordained for men in things pertaining to God, that he may offer both gifts and sacrifices for sins: 2 Who can have compassion on the ignorant, and on them that are

out of the way; for that he himself also is compassed with infirmity. 3 And by reason hereof he ought, as for the people, so also for himself, to offer for sins. 4 And no man taketh this honour unto himself, but he that is called of God, as was Aaron. 5 So also **Christ** glorified not himself to be made an high priest; but he that said unto him, **Thou art my Son, to day have I begotten thee.** 6 As he saith also in another place, **Thou art a priest for ever after the order of Melchisedec.** 7 Who in the days of his flesh, when he had offered up prayers and supplications with strong crying and tears unto him that was able to save him from death, and was heard in that he feared; 8 Though he were a **Son**, yet learned he obedience by the things which he suffered; 9 **And being made perfect, he became the author of eternal salvation unto all them that obey him; 10 Called of God an high priest after the order of Melchisedec.**

Jesus was unlike the high priests who were "taken from among men." Those priests had to offer sacrifices first for their own sins, then for the people's sins. Because Jesus was sent from Heaven and begotten of God, He had no sin. In his birth Jesus was made the "perfect" man (verse 9 above), and therefore became "the author of eternal salvation." When Jesus saves it is forever—we can never lose the salvation He gives us, because the salvation Jesus gives is by grace through faith, not of works, lest any man should boast (Ephesians 2:8-9).

> **Beware! Islamic deception follows:**

Hot Tip:
"And Peter said to them, 'Repent, and let each of you be baptized in the name of Jesus Christ for the forgiveness of your sins;...'" (Acts 2:38). It is most unlikely that apostle Peter would have disobeyed the specific command of Jesus Christ for

baptising in the three names and baptized them in the name of Jesus Christ, alone.

This verse is no problem for those who believe in the Trinity, for if "these three are one" (1 John 5:7), then to use the name of one would be equivalent to using the name of the three. Remember, Mat. 28:17 says, "baptizing them in the name [not names] of the Father, and of the Son, and of the Holy Ghost."

7.1.2 Is 1 John 5:7 genuine?

Question No.7
Apostle John in his first Epistle, chapter 5 and verse 7 wrote: "For there are three that bear record in heaven, the Father, the Word, and the Holy Ghost, and these three are one."; is this not a fair testimony to acknowledge the 'Doctrine of Trinity'?

> **Beware! Islamic deception follows:**

Answer No.7
1. The text quoted does appear in the Kings James Version but has been omitted by most of the editors of the recent versions e.g. Revised Standard Version, New American Standard Bible, New English Bible, Phillips Modern English Bible, because the quoted text does not appear in the older Greek manuscripts. 2. Renowned historian Edward Gibbon calls the addition a "Pious Fraud" in his famous history book 'Decline and Fall of Roman Empire'. 3. Peakes commentary on the subject reads; "The famous interpolation after "three witnesses" is not printed even in RSVn, and rightly. It cites the heavenly testimony of the Father, the logos, and the Holy Spirit, but is never used in the early trinitarian controversies. No respectable Greek MS contains it. Appearing first in a late 4th-cent. Latin text, it entered the Vulgate and finally the NT of

Erasmus."

We thank Meherally for admitting that 1 John 5:7 does appear in the King James Bible. The King James Version of the Bible is the very best English translation of the Divinely preserved original Bible texts (the Masoretic Hebrew Old Testament text, and the Textus Receptus Greek New Testament text).

The text supporting the Trinity in 1 John 5:7 has been omitted by the "more recent" translations, including the Revised Standard Version, New American Standard Bible, New English Bible, Phillips Modern English Bible, etc., because they are translated from corrupted texts (Codex Aleph and Codex B, also known as Codex Sinaiticus and Codex Vaticanus), which were purposely changed in order to try to oppose the genuine Christ of true Christianity. So, naturally these translations of corruptions are favored by Muslims, atheistic humanists, and other infidels who are desperately grasping at straws to justify their rebellion against God. However, one by one these phony bibles are exposed as corrupt, and thus lose popularity and go out of print. But the King James Bible (like other translations from the Divinely preserved original texts) abideth forever.

The Arabic Quran **in use today** may not be the original Quran since two caliphs burned many surahs that might have actually been the originals, nevertheless the Arabic Quran **in use today** has no counterfeits. The Hebrew and Greek texts of the Bible, however, have been counterfeited. Why is this? It is because the Quran is already a false book. Why counterfeit a counterfeit? Satan cannot make the Quran much more corrupt than it already is. But the Bible is God's revelation of the truth, and is therefore the most valuable book on the face of the earth. Therefore, Satan devotes his energy to counterfeiting the book with the most value. By producing corrupted Bible manuscripts and translations,

Satan is able to give uneducated Christians a dull sword with a changed message which cannot stand up against attacks from the heathen, but instead becomes a weapon for the heathen to use against Christianity.

But note carefully: Satan having produced corrupted manuscripts and translations of the Bible does not mean that the pure text of God's word no longer exists, as many of the heathen claim. To the contrary, the pure text of God's word is sharper than any twoedged sword, and will be preserved inerrant forever.

> Hebrews 4:12 For **the word of God** is quick, and powerful, and sharper than any twoedged sword, piercing even to the dividing asunder of soul and spirit, and of the joints and marrow, and is a discerner of the thoughts and intents of the heart.
>
> Matthew 5:18 For verily I say unto you, **Till heaven and earth pass, one jot or one tittle shall in no wise pass from the law, till all be fulfilled**.
>
> Psalms 12:6 The **words** of the LORD are **pure words**: as silver tried in a furnace of earth, purified seven times. 7 **Thou shalt keep them, O LORD, thou shalt preserve them from this generation for ever.**
>
> 1 Peter 1:24 For all flesh is as grass, and all the glory of man as the flower of grass. The grass withereth, and the flower thereof falleth away: 25 **But the word of the Lord endureth for ever.** And this is the word which by the gospel is preached unto you.

God would not be God if He could not preserve His word down through the centuries to this day. JEHOVAH, the God of the Bible, is certainly more powerful than Allah, the god of the Quran. JEHOVAH, the God of the Bible, could and did preserve His word—as the above verses say. Allah, the god of Islam, falsely claims to be the God of the Bible, and falsely claims to be the author of the "original" Bible. But this is obviously not true, for Islam teaches that the Injil[4] (Gospel) and

---

[4]Injil means gospel. Most Muslims incorrectly call the Bible of the Christians the "Injil." Injil

Torah were not preserved. If that were true (it isn't), and if Allah was truly their author (he isn't), then Allah obviously couldn't preserve his word. Islam says that the true Injil is the one quoted in the Quran. Yet there is no book in existence today that reads like the one supposedly quoted by the Quran. Either that book never actually existed (in which case Allah is either a liar or has never actually existed), or else that book was not preserved (in which case Allah is very weak. Why should we believe that Allah preserved the Quran if Allah was not able to preserve the Injil? The hadiths reveal that many copies of the early surahs were burned by the first few caliphs. Those burned copies may have been the originals, and the Quran today a "refined" one with some of the too obvious and hard to defend errors removed—still a false book, but more deceptive than before.

Beware! Islamic deception follows:

Hot Tip:
Notwithstanding the above rejections, the verse that follows the quoted text reads in KJV; "And there are three that bear witness in earth, the spirit, and the water, and the blood; and these three agree in one." (1John5:8). Are these three witnesses "co-equal"? Can blood be substituted with water? Can water be regarded as the same in any respect with the Spirit? Just as the

---

(Gospel) means "Good News." There are many teachings in the Bible that are not good news—for instance the teaching of the existence of an eternal fiery Hell where people who refuse to believe in Christ will be tormented for eternity. According to 1 Corinthians 15:1-4, the gospel is actually composed of only three teachings contained in the Bible: (1) that Christ died for our sins according to the scriptures; and (2) that he was buried, and (3) that he rose again the third day according to the scriptures. If we believe the gospel we are saved for eternity.

spirit, the blood and the water are three separate entities, so are the first three witnesses, namely; the Father, the Son (Word, Logos) and the Holy Spirit (Ghost).

No, the King James Bible does not say in 1 John 5:8 that the Spirit, the water, and the blood are "co-equal." The Spirit, the water, and the blood are **not** one, but merely "**agree in one.**" In contrast, 1 John 5:7 says that the Father, the Word, and the Holy Ghost "**are** one." This is a very important difference which Meherally conveniently ignores. Always examine the context. Here it is:

> 1 John 5:7 For there are **three** that bear record in heaven, the **Father**, the **Word**, and the **Holy Ghost**: and **these three are one.** 8 And there are **three** that bear witness in earth, the **Spirit**, and the **water**, and the **blood**: and these three **agree** in one. 9 If we receive the witness of men, **the witness of God** is greater: **for this is the witness of God** which he hath testified of **his Son.** 10 He that believeth on the **Son of God** hath the witness in himself: he that believeth not God hath made him a liar; because he believeth not the record that God gave of **his Son.** 11 And this is the record, that God hath given to us **eternal life**, and this life is in **his Son.** 12 **He that hath the Son hath life; and he that hath not the Son of God hath not life.** 13 These things have I written unto you that believe on the name of the **Son of God**; that ye may know that ye have **eternal life**, and that ye may believe on the name of the **Son of God**.

Also, note that **God** bears witness "of **his Son.**" This is yet another proof that Jesus is God's Son. Not only that, but verse 12 says that "**he that hath not the Son of God hath not life.**" This means that Muslims—who deny that God has a Son—are in a very dangerous situation; they have no life, being spiritually dead in trespasses and sins. Verse 10 says that they are calling God a liar. Can a person who calls God a liar get to Heaven? Of course not! See the deception and folly of Islam!

7.2 Does God's wrath abide on Muslims?

Question No.8 [from a Christian to Islamic teacher Meherally.]

Jesus said: "He who believes in the son has eternal life; but he who does not obey the son shall not see life, but the wrath of God abides on him." (John 3:36); are you not under the wrath of God for not being a follower of Christ - a Christian, by belief?

Beware! Islamic deception follows:

Answer No.8

It is an interesting question. In fact, we Muslims should be asking the question to you the followers of Christ. Do the vast majority of Christians truthfully believe Christ for what he said he was, and, truly understand his commands and obey them? We believe, most of the followers who claim to be Christians do not even understand the implications of calling their Leader or Lord; "Christ". (The readers will understand what I mean by the last sentence, once they go through the rest of the text). Here is the answer to your question. The above verse has two parts. 'Belief' and 'Obedience'. On the subject of Belief in Christ, Jesus asked his disciples; "But who do you say that I am? And Peter answered and said, "The Christ of God." (Luke 9:20). Peter did not say God or a god. We Muslims truly believe Jesus was "The Christ (al-Masih) of God". The expression "The Christ of God" literally means; "The one that was anointed by God himself". Please go back in time and think. God performed the ceremony of anointing (physically or spiritually) and for that reason, Jesus became "The Christ of God". Now may I please ask you a simple question. Who is greater and exalted; the one who anointed, or, the one who got anointed? Since God

anointed Jesus, God is the greater and exalted between the two, which we Muslims, do truly believe. But surprisingly, the followers who say Jesus is "Christ", don't.

First, note that the Christian asking Meherally this question is obviously very naive about the Bible. That is obvious because he or she quoted John 3:36 from the so-called New American Standard Bible, which is a corrupted bible, and not the standard for Christians at all. Look in the KJV of 1611 to find what that verse actually says:

> John 3:36 He that **believeth on the Son** hath everlasting life: and he that **believeth not the Son** shall not see life; **but the wrath of God abideth on him.**

The word "**obey**" is **not** found in this verse, but rather the word "**believeth.**" Unbelievers do not like the word "believeth," so they replace it with the word "obey" to try to defend their belief in salvation by works.

Second, John 3:36 plainly states that Jesus is "the Son." The context of the verse as well as its content lets us know whose Son He is. Just a few verses above this verse in the same chapter we read:

> John 3:16 For **God** so loved the world that he gave **his only begotten Son**, that whosoever believeth in him should not perish, but have everlasting life. 17 For **God** sent not **his Son** into the world to condemn the world; but that the world through him might be saved. 18 **He that believeth on him is not condemned: but he that believeth not is condemned already, because he hath not believed in the name of the only begotten Son of God.** 19 And this is the condemnation, that light is come into the world, and men loved darkness rather than light, because their deeds were evil. (John 3:16-19)

Note that the word "Christ" is not even used in John 3:36. Meherally simply cannot answer the question that was asked of him, so he tries to divert attention from the verse that so embarrasses him.

Third, since the word "obey" is not actually found in John 3:36, but was deceptively added by unbelievers, his answer to the question asked him is based on a false quotation, and is therefore invalid.

Fourth, Meherally either does not understand the doctrine of the Christ, or else purposely misrepresents it. John 1:41 informs us that Christ is the Greek word for the Hebrew word Messias (Messiah). The word Messiah is only found twice in the whole Old Testament, and only in Daniel chapter 9. Here is what that extremely important passage says:

> Daniel 9:24 Seventy weeks are determined upon thy people and upon thy holy city, to finish the transgression, and to make an end of sins, and to make reconciliation for iniquity, and to bring in everlasting righteousness, and to seal up the vision and prophecy, and to anoint **the most Holy**. 9:25 Know therefore and understand, that from the going forth of the commandment to restore and to build Jerusalem unto the **Messiah** the Prince shall be seven weeks, and threescore and two weeks: the street shall be built again, and the wall, even in troublous times. 9:26 **And after threescore and two weeks shall Messiah be cut off, but not for himself**.

Jesus is indeed the Messiah, the anointed of God. The Messiah is described as "the Prince" (Daniel 9:25). Most importantly, however, the Messiah is "the most Holy" (Dan. 9:24). There is none more holy than God, so the "**most Holy**" is **God** Himself. The Messiah was God Himself in a human body. Since Jesus is Messiah He is God. The commandment to restore and to build Jerusalem was given in Ezra 1:1-4, and was fulfilled by Jesus Christ exactly as prophesied (the Bible is always true, and everything it prophecies comes to pass without fail). He was "**cut off**, but not **for himself**" when He died on the cross for our sins.

> Hebrews 4:14 Seeing then that we have a great high priest, that is passed into the heavens, **Jesus the Son of God**, let us hold fast our profession. 15 For we have not an high priest which cannot be touched with the feeling of our infirmities; but was in all points tempted like as we are, **yet without sin**.

Poison must be mixed with good food or drink to deceive people into drinking it. In like manner, some truth had to be mixed into the Quran to deceive people into believing it. One such truth found in the Quran is its admission in surah 19:19 that Jesus was sinless:

> YUSUFALI: He said: "Nay, I am only a messenger from thy Lord, (to announce) to thee the gift of a **holy** son.

> PICKTHAL: He said: I am only a messenger of thy Lord, that I may bestow on thee a **faultless** son.

> SHAKIR: He said: I am only a messenger of your Lord: That I will give you a **pure** boy.

As God, Jesus could not die, but as a human He could and did die—not for any sins He committed (for He never sinned), but for your sins and mine. His death on the cross for our sins makes it possible for us to receive as a free gift "an end of sins," "reconciliation for iniquity," and "everlasting righteousness."

Meherally quoted Luke 9:20, so let's look at the context of that verse also.

> Luke 9:18 And it came to pass, as he was alone praying, his disciples were with him: and he asked them, saying, **Whom say the people that I am?** 19 They answering said, John the Baptist; but some say, Elias; and others say, that one of the old prophets is risen again. 20 He said unto them, **But whom say ye that I am?** Peter answering said, **The Christ of God**. 21 And he straitly charged them, and commanded them to tell no man that thing; 22 Saying, **The Son of man must suffer many things**, and be rejected of the elders and chief priests and scribes, **and be slain, and be raised the third day**.

Note verse 22 in which Jesus says he will die, and rise from the dead the third day—which Islam denies happened. This verse does not prove Islam, but rather disproves Islam.

97

So, yes, the wrath of God does abide on Muslims and upon all others who reject Jesus Christ as the Son of God. But by repenting of the sin of unbelief in turning from Islam to Christ, Muslims can appease that wrath, and receive the gift of eternal life. Jesus is the only way to Heaven.

> Psalms 2:12 Kiss **the Son**, lest he be angry, and ye perish from the way, when his wrath is kindled but a little. Blessed are all they that put their trust **in him**.

7.3 Is Jesus just God's servant?

Beware! Islamic deception follows:

HOT TIP:

"...Thy holy Servant Jesus, whom Thou didst anoint,..." (Acts 4:27 - New American Standard Bible). This leaves no room for doubt that Jesus was a 'Servant of God'. Besides, there are other verses which declare Jesus; God's Servant. ——————
Now let us go to the second part of the quoted verse; "obeying the Christ". Please read the following verse and ask yourself a question; have I obeyed? "Truly, truly, I say to you, he who hears my word, and believes Him who sent me, has eternal life, and does not come into judgement, but has passed out of death into life." John 5:24 Have I believed and placed my trust basically, fundamentally and predominately in Him or in Jesus?

As I have already pointed out, Meherally quoted John 3:36 from a phony bible. The word obey is not actually found in John 3:36. Acts 4:27 also has been corrupted in the New American Standard Version, as have a multitude of other verses. The only way that Meherally can prove his points is by either misquoting verses from the Bible, or else by quoting from a phony bible such as the

New American Standard Bible. Make him stay with the King James Version of 1611 and he is helpless. **What does this verse really say in the true Bible?** It says that Jesus is God's "holy **child**," **not** His holy servant.

> Acts 4:24 And when they heard that, they lifted up their voice to **God** with one accord, and said, Lord, thou art God, which hast made heaven, and earth, and the sea, and all that in them is: 25 Who by the mouth of thy servant David hast said, Why did the heathen rage, and the people imagine vain things? 26 The kings of the earth stood up, and the rulers were gathered together against the Lord, and against his Christ. 27 For of a truth against thy **holy child Jesus**, whom thou hast anointed, both Herod, and Pontius Pilate, with the Gentiles, and the people of Israel, were gathered together, 28 For to do whatsoever thy hand and thy counsel determined before to be done. 29 And now, Lord, behold their threatenings: and grant unto thy servants, that with all boldness they may speak thy word, 30 By stretching forth thine hand to heal; and that signs and wonders may be done by the name of **thy holy child Jesus**. 31 And when they had prayed, the place was shaken where they were assembled together; and they were all filled with the Holy Ghost, and they spake the word of God with boldness.

Now there **is** a passage in the true Bible that calls Jesus God's **servant**. Why does Meherally not quote that passage? Because that passage says that the Gentiles (non-Jews) would TRUST in the name of Jesus! To trust in Jesus is trusting in God, for Jesus IS God.

> Matthew 12:14 Then the Pharisees went out, and held a council against him, how they might destroy him. 15 But when **Jesus** knew it, he withdrew himself from thence: and great multitudes followed him, and he healed them all; 16 And charged them that they should not make him known: 17 That it might be fulfilled which was spoken by Esaias the prophet, saying, 18 Behold **my servant**, whom I have chosen; my beloved, in whom my soul is well pleased: I will put my spirit upon him, and he shall show judgment to the Gentiles. 19 He shall not strive, nor

cry; neither shall any man hear his voice in the streets. 20 A bruised reed shall he not break, and smoking flax shall he not quench, till he send forth judgment unto victory. 21 **And in his name shall the Gentiles trust**. (Mat:14-21)

For Jesus—God the Son—to be God the Father's servant is no problem since God is a Trinity—one God composed of three distinct Persons. Meherally only has problems understanding this because he insists on lowering God to be less than even a normal human. Does he not believe God to be impotent and barren—childless? A human is only one person so Meherally thinks God is also so limited. This low concept of God is a major defect of Islam.

7.4 Will Jesus be the judge on judgment day?

> **Beware! Islamic deception follows:**
>
> Hot Tip:
> Jesus said; "But I do not seek my glory; there is One who seeks and judges." John 8:51. Who is this "One", who is not Jesus? Have you basically, essentially and fundamentally glorified the "One" or Jesus? Please remember, the "One" will be the Judge on the Day of Judgement and not Jesus. If you disbelieve or disobey the above word of Jesus please read the verse quoted by you and then think about the "wrath of God".

Meherally means John 8:50, not 8:51. Meherally and his Muslim friends are the ones who should be thinking about the "wrath of God." First of all, this "one that seeketh and judgeth" is the **Father**, not the non-Father. The Son does not have to glorify Himself because the **Father** glorifies Him. In fact, the context of John 8:50 is

Jesus' defense of His Deity and Divine Sonship. Muslim teachers almost always try to deceive by taking verses out of context. So, when dealing with Muslims, always check the context. Here is John 8:12-59 in its context so you can see it for yourself:

John 8:12 Then spake **Jesus** again unto them, saying, **I am the light of the world**: he that followeth me shall not walk in darkness, but shall have the light of life. 13 The Pharisees therefore said unto him, Thou bearest record of thyself; thy record is not true. 14 Jesus answered and said unto them, Though I bear record of myself, yet my record is true: for I know whence I came, and whither I go; but ye cannot tell whence I come, and whither I go. 15 Ye judge after the flesh; I judge no man. 16 **And yet if I judge, my judgment is true**: for I am not alone, but I and the Father that sent me. 17 It is also written in your law, that the testimony of two men is true. 18 I am one that bear witness of myself, and the Father that sent me beareth witness of me. 19 Then said they unto him, Where is thy Father? Jesus answered, Ye neither know me, nor my Father: if ye had known me, ye should have known my Father also. 20 These words spake Jesus in the treasury, as he taught in the temple: and no man laid hands on him; for his hour was not yet come. 21 Then said Jesus again unto them, I go my way, and ye shall seek me, and shall die in your sins: whither I go, ye cannot come. 22 Then said the Jews, Will he kill himself? because he saith, Whither I go, ye cannot come. 23 And he said unto them, Ye are from beneath; **I am from above**: ye are of this world; I am not of this world. 24 I said therefore unto you, that ye shall die in your sins: for **if ye believe not that I am he, ye shall die in your sins**. 25 Then said they unto him, Who art thou? And Jesus saith unto them, Even the same that I said unto you from the beginning. 26 I have many things to say and to judge of you: but he that sent me is true; and I speak to the world those things which I have heard of him. 27 They understood not that he spake to them of the Father. 28 Then said Jesus unto them, When ye have lifted up the Son of man, then shall ye know that I am he, and that I do nothing of myself; but as my Father hath taught me, I speak these things. 29 And he that sent me is with me: the Father hath not left me alone; for I do always those things that please him. 30 As he spake these words, many believed on him. 31 **Then said Jesus to those Jews which believed on him, If ye continue in my word, then are ye my disciples indeed; 32 And ye shall know the truth, and the truth shall make you free**. 33 They answered him, We be Abraham's seed, and were never in bondage to any man: how sayest thou, Ye shall be made free? 34 Jesus answered them, Verily, verily, I say unto you, Whosoever committeth sin is the servant of sin. 35 And the servant abideth not in the house for ever: but the Son abideth ever. 36 **If the Son therefore shall make you free, ye shall be free indeed**. 37 I know that ye are Abraham's seed; but ye seek to kill me, because my word hath no place in you. 38 I speak that which I have seen with **my Father**: and ye do that which ye have seen with your father. 39 They answered and said unto him, Abraham is our father. Jesus saith unto them, If ye were Abraham's children, ye would do the works of Abraham. 40 But now ye seek to kill me, a man that hath told you the truth, which I have heard of God: this did not Abraham. 41 Ye do the deeds of your father. Then said they to him, We be not born of fornication; we have one Father, even God. 42 Jesus said unto them, **If God were your Father, ye would love me: for I proceeded forth and came from God; neither came I of myself, but he sent me. 43 Why do ye not understand my speech? even because ye cannot hear my word. 44 Ye are of your father the devil, and the lusts of your father ye will do. He was a murderer from the beginning, and abode not in the truth, because there is no truth in him. When he speaketh a lie, he speaketh of his own: for he is a liar, and the father of it. 45 And because I tell you the truth, ye believe me not. 46 Which of you convinceth me of sin? And if I say the truth, why do ye not believe me? 47 He that is of God heareth God's words: ye therefore hear them not, because ye are not of God.** 48 Then answered the Jews, and

said unto him, Say we not well that thou art a Samaritan, and hast a devil? 49 Jesus answered, I have not a devil; but I honour my Father, and ye do dishonour me. 50 And I seek not mine own glory: there is one that seeketh and judgeth. 51 Verily, verily, I say unto you, **If a man keep my saying, he shall never see death**. 52 Then said the Jews unto him, Now we know that thou hast a devil. Abraham is dead, and the prophets; and thou sayest, If a man keep my saying, he shall never taste of death. 53 Art thou greater than our father Abraham, which is dead? and the prophets are dead: whom makest thou thyself? 54 Jesus answered, If I honour myself, my honour is nothing: it is my Father that honoureth me; of whom ye say, that he is your God: 55 Yet ye have not known him; but I know him: and if I should say, I know him not, I shall be a liar like unto you: but I know him, and keep his saying. 56 **Your father Abraham rejoiced to see my day: and he saw it, and was glad.** 57 Then said the Jews unto him, Thou art not yet fifty years old, and hast thou seen Abraham? 58 Jesus said unto them, **Verily, verily, I say unto you, Before Abraham was, I am**. 59 Then took they up stones to cast at him: but Jesus hid himself, and went out of the temple, going through the midst of them, and so passed by.

Also, Meherally is wrong in saying, "Please remember, the "One" will be the Judge on the Day of Judgment and not Jesus." That "One" is the Father, and Meherally is saying that the Father will be the Judge on the Day of Judgment, and not Jesus. Just exactly the opposite is true:

John 5:22 **For the Father judgeth no man, but hath committed all judgment unto the Son**: 23 That all men should honour the Son, even as they honour the Father. **He that honoureth not the Son honoureth not the Father which hath sent him**. 24 Verily, verily, I say unto you, He that heareth my word, and believeth on him that sent me, hath everlasting life, and shall not come into condemnation; but is passed from death unto life. 25 Verily, verily, I say unto you, The hour is coming, and now is, when the dead shall hear the voice of the **Son** of God: and they that hear shall live. 26 For as the Father hath life in himself; so hath he given to the Son to have life in himself; 27 **And hath given him authority to execute judgment also, because he is the Son of man**.

When Jesus said in John 8:15 above, "I judge no man," He was referring to the fact that He had come to the world to save souls, not to condemn them.

John 3:17 **For God sent not his Son into the world to condemn the world; but that the world through him might be saved.** 18 He that believeth on him is not condemned: but **he that believeth not is condemned already, because he hath not believed in the name of the only begotten Son of God.** 19 And this is the condemnation, that light is come into the world, and men loved darkness rather than light, because their deeds were evil. 20 For every one that doeth evil hateth the light, neither cometh to the light, lest his deeds should be reproved. 21 But he that doeth truth cometh to the light, that his deeds may be made manifest, that they are wrought in God.

It was not necessary for Jesus to sit as judge, determining if men were sinners, and condemning them to some punishment if they were guilty. Why? Because the Bible had already clearly stated that "all have sinned, and come short of the glory of God" (Romans 3:23), and were therefore **already condemned** unless they have "believed in the name of the only begotten Son of God" (see John 3: 18 above). You don't have to wait until the judgment day to find out if you have lived good enough to go to Heaven. You haven't! And therefore **you are already condemned to Hell unless you believe that Jesus died on the cross for your sins, and was buried, and rose again the third day**, as the Scriptures clearly teach. Believing in Jesus is your only hope.

When Jesus was born of the virgin Mary, He came to save the world, not to judge it. But when he comes back the second time it will be different—he will come to judge in

righteousness. The Triune God will judge the world, not in the Person of the Father, but in the Person of the Son, whom He hath raised from the dead.

Acts 17:29 Forasmuch then as we are the offspring of God, we ought not to think that the Godhead is like unto gold, or silver, or stone, graven by art and man's device. 30 And the times of this ignorance God winked at; but now commandeth all men every where to repent: 31 **Because he hath appointed a day, in the which he will judge the world in righteousness by that man whom he hath ordained; whereof he hath given assurance unto all men, in that he hath raised him from the dead.**

Revelation 19:11 And I saw heaven opened, and behold a white horse; and he that sat upon him was called **Faithful and True**, and **in righteousness** he doth **judge** and make war. 12 His eyes were as a flame of fire, and on his head were many crowns; and he had a name written, that no man knew, but he himself. 13 And he was clothed with a vesture dipped in blood: and **his name is called The Word of God**. 14 And the armies which were in heaven followed him upon white horses, clothed in fine linen, white and clean. 15 And out of his mouth goeth a sharp sword, that with it he should smite the nations: and he shall rule them with a rod of iron: and he treadeth the winepress of the fierceness and wrath of Almighty God. 16 And he hath on his vesture and on his thigh a name written, **KING OF KINGS, AND LORD OF LORDS.** 17 And I saw an angel standing in the sun; and he cried with a loud voice, saying to all the fowls that fly in the midst of heaven, Come and gather yourselves together unto the supper of the great God; 18 That ye may eat the flesh of kings, and the flesh of captains, and the flesh of mighty men, and the flesh of horses, and of them that sit on them, and the flesh of all men, both free and bond, both small and great. 19 And I saw the beast, and the kings of the earth, and their armies, gathered together to make war against him that sat on the horse, and against his army. 20 **And the beast was taken, and with him the false prophet that wrought miracles before him,** with which he deceived them that had received the mark of the beast, and them that worshipped his image. These both were cast alive into a lake of fire burning with brimstone. 21 And the remnant were slain with the sword of him that sat upon the horse, which sword proceeded out of his mouth: and all the fowls were filled with their flesh.

Note in verse 13 above that this judge is called "the Word of God" ('O λόγος τοῦ Θεοῦ). "Word" being translated from the Greek word λόγος (Logos). This is the same Logos found in John 1:1, "and the Word (Logos) was God," and in John 1:14, "And the **Word** was made **flesh**, and **dwelt among us**, (and we beheld his glory, the glory as of **the only begotten of the Father**,) full of grace and truth." In verse 16 above this Word is revealed to be a person who is "**KING OF KINGS, AND LORD OF LORDS.**" This is the true Jesus, who will judge you someday. Are you prepared to meet Him?

Islam's denial that Jesus will be the final judge of the world is another example of Islam not glorifying Jesus. Islam's claim to glorify Jesus is just a lie. Jesus said, "He that honoureth not the Son honoureth not the Father which hath sent him" (John 5:23). Muhammad did not honor God the Son, and so he didn't honor God the Father either. And that means that he didn't honor God at all.

7.5 Does Genesis 1:26 prove the Trinity?

Question No.9 [from a Christian to Islamic teacher Meherally.]

In the Book of Genesis 1:26, we read; "And God said, Let us make man in our image, after our likeness..."; does not the use of terms "us" and "our" prove that the God which created man was not a singular entity, furthermore, does it not support the Johnannine concept (John 1:3); all things came into being through Jesus?

Beware! Islamic deception follows:

Answer No.9

1. Below is an extract from a commentary for the above verse, written by the editors of King James Version (The Hebrew-Greek Key Study Bible, 6th edition): "The Hebrew word for God is 'Elohim' (430), a plural noun. In Genesis 1:1, it is used in grammatical agreement with a singular verb 'bara' (1254), created. When plural pronouns are used, "Let us make man in our image after our likeness," does it denote a plural of number or the concept of excellence or majesty which may be indicated in such a way in Hebrew? Could God be speaking to angels, the earth, or nature thus denoting Himself in relation to one of these? Or is this a germinal hint of a distinction in the divine personality? One cannot be certain." Having written "One cannot be certain", the editors try to advocate the theory of Jesus, as the "essential (internal) unity of Godhead." 2. The response to your question, as well as, to the commentators remark; "One cannot be certain", lies not very far, but in the next verse (Genesis 1:27), which reads; "And God created man in His own image,..." This statement tells us that the actual act of creation when performed, was performed by "Him" and in "His" image and not by "Us" in "Our" image.

Hot Tip:

As a closing conclusive argument, here is a statement of truth from Jesus himself; "And he (Jesus) answered and said unto them, 'Have you not read, that He which made them at the beginning made them male and female." (Matthew 19:4). This statement by Jesus also negates the so called Johannine concept put forward by you (NOT by apostle John); "all things came into being through Jesus."

WARNING: note the deception. The editors of the The *Hebrew-Greek Key Study Bible* were **not** the editors of the King James Version of the Bible, but only of the **notes** found in that particular study Bible. So again Meherally lies to deceive. Those editors were obviously pagans like Meherally, grasping at straws for some way to discredit the basic doctrines of the Bible. Their opinions have no more authority than Meherally's opinion—which is none. However, let us answer the questions raised in these notes:

1. **Question:** "'Let us make man in our image after our likeness,' does it denote a plural of number or the concept of excellence or majesty which may be indicated in such a way in Hebrew?" **Answer:** It denotes a plural of number. There is only one God, and He is three persons.

2. **Question:** "Could God be speaking to angels, the earth, or nature thus denoting Himself in relation to one of these?" **Answer:** no. The angles, the earth, and nature are obviously not of the same image as God, and they did not help God create humans. The idea that God and the Creation are one and the same is called "pantheism," and is the basis of all idolatry. In spite of what they say, Muslims **are** idolaters for they bow down to and kiss the Black Stone—an idol embedded in the wall of the Ka'abah. Their actions (kissing a rock) speak louder than their words (their denial that they are worshiping an idol).

3. **Question:** "Or is this a germinal hint of a distinction in the divine personality?" **Answer:** It is more than a hint. It is a clear reference to God's triune nature.

Hotter Tip than Meherally's Hot Tips:

The Author of Genesis 1:26 (God himself) did not in the very next verse forget that He had just said "Let **us** create man in our image, after our likeness..." To think that God forgot is truly naive. When referring to God, the Bible always uses singular pronouns "he," "him," "his," for there is only **one** true and living God. But when referring to God's **persons**, plural pronouns are used, for the **one** God is **three** persons. The three persons of the Godhead are **not** three separate Gods, but are the three distinct persons of the one God. Muslim teachers say that Christians believe in three separate Gods, but that is just another lie of Islam, and they know it.

By the way, in surah 56:57 of the Quran, Allah states: "It is **We** Who have Created you." The use of "We" instead of "I" in this verse is probably a result of the author of the Quran trying to make the Quran read similar to the Bible in Genesis 1:26, to make the Quran sound more spiritual. But this causes a problem for Islam. Since Allah is not a trinity like the true God, the use of "We" implies that Allah was not able to create man by himself, but needed help from some other being or beings. The Allah of the Quran also cannot have a son for he is impotent. There seems to be many things that the true God can do, that Allah cannot do! The Bible tells us that Lucifer made himself into Satan by sinfully saying in his heart: "I will ascend into heaven, I will exalt my throne above the stars of God: I will sit also upon the mount of the congregation, in the sides of the north: I will ascend above the heights of the clouds; **I will be like the most High**" (Isaiah 14:13-14). Lucifer was an angel, and Jesus taught in Mark 12:18 that angels cannot marry. Angels cannot have children.

Mark 12:18 Then come unto him the Sadducees, which say there is no resurrection; and they asked him, saying, 19 Master, Moses wrote unto us, If a man's brother die, and leave his wife behind him, and leave no children, that his brother should take his wife, and raise up seed unto his brother. 20 Now there were seven brethren: and the first took a wife, and dying left no seed. 21 And the second took her, and died, neither left he any seed: and the third likewise. 22 And the seven had her, and left no seed: last of all the woman died also. 23 In the resurrection therefore, when they shall rise, whose wife shall she be of them? for the seven had her to wife. 24 And Jesus answering said unto them, Do ye not therefore err, because ye know not the scriptures, neither the power of God? 25 **For when they shall rise from the dead, they neither marry, nor are given in marriage; but are as the angels which are in heaven**.

There is the true omnipotent God who has a Son, and then there is a rebellious, fallen, impotent angel who wants to be God, but is unable to have a son. Whom do you serve?

7.6 Does John 20:28 prove Jesus is God?

An any sincere man who has ever read the Bible carefully will acknowledge, John 20:28 does prove that Jesus is God. Seeing the absurd arguments Christ rejecters use to explain away this verse is actually a little funny sometimes.

Question No.10 [from a Christian to Islamic teacher Meherally.]

In the Gospel of John, we find that eight days after his resurrection, Jesus stood before his disciples and asked the unbelieving Thomas to feel his hands and side, to verify the nail marks and spear scar. After seeing the hands and the side, Thomas said to Jesus; "My Lord and my God." If Jesus was not God, he would have certainly reprimanded Thomas, but he did no such thing, does this not prove, 'Jesus was God'?

Beware! Islamic deception follows:

Answer No.10

Please allow me quote from the 'New American Standard Bible' the entire text as it appears in Ch.20:27-28 from John's Gospel: "Then he (Jesus) said to Thomas, "Reach here your finger, and see my hands, and reach here your hand, and put it into my side; and be not unbelieving, but believing." Thomas answered and said to him, "My Lord and my God!" 1. Please observe the mark of exclamation (!) at the end of the phrase. (Note: K.J.V. has removed the exclamation mark). 2. Please observe there was no question asked in the entire narration. Hence, the text which reads "Thomas answered" is inaccurate. 3. The last phrase "My Lord and my God!" was not an *answer* but an outburst of *exclamation* by Thomas, having seen something inexplicable and baffling. Often, we too cry out; "O' my God!" when we see something totally bizarre or grotesque. 4. To prove that the above explanation is not my concocted theory, below are the texts from two reputed versions of the Bible that support this theory. a. In the 'New English Bible' it reads: Thomas said, "My Lord and my God!" b. In the 'Phillips Modern English Bible' it reads: "My Lord and my God!" cried Thomas.

The KJV did not remove the exclamation point, for there was no exclamation point to remove. Rather unbelievers have added an exclamation point to vainly try to change the meaning of a verse they don't like. Also, a question is clearly implied by the context—always examine the context. The implied question was, Will you believe now that you have seen the wounds in my hands and side, Thomas?

So again Meherally must resort to a phony, corrupted Bible to prove his point. Using that tactic, we could make our own version of the Quran, and use it prove that the Quran teaches that Jesus is God. But then we would be dishonest, just as Meherally is being dishonest. The fact is that in the true Bible there is no exclamation point in John 20:27-28, (but even if there were one, it would not really prove Meherally's point). Here are those verses in their context:

> John 20:24 But Thomas, one of the twelve, called Didymus, was not with them when Jesus came. 25 The other disciples therefore said unto him, We have seen the Lord. But he said unto them, Except I shall see in his hands the print of the nails, and put my finger into the print of the nails, and thrust my hand into his side, I will not believe. 26 And after eight days again his disciples were within, and Thomas with them: then came Jesus, the doors being shut, and stood in the midst, and said, Peace be unto you. 27 Then saith he to Thomas, Reach hither thy finger, and behold my hands; and reach hither thy hand, and thrust it into my side: and be not faithless, but believing. 28 And Thomas answered and said unto him, **My Lord and my God.** 29 Jesus saith unto him, Thomas, because thou hast seen me, thou hast believed: blessed are they that have not seen, and yet have believed. 30 And many other signs truly did Jesus in the presence of his disciples, which are not written in this book: 31 But these are written, that ye might believe that Jesus is the Christ, the **Son of God**; and that believing ye might have life through his name.

There is no exclamation point, and the context shows without any shadow of doubt that Thomas was acknowledging Jesus as God. Jesus had just told Thomas to "be not faithless, but believing" (verse 27). Shortly before that Jesus had walked into a room in which the doors were shut (verse 26). Shortly before that, Jesus had risen from the dead as He promised He would do. It was getting pretty obvious that He was God.

Meherally and the heretics who mistranslated the perverted versions of the Bible he quotes are implying that Thomas actually took God's name in vain, yet received no rebuke from the Lord Jesus Christ for doing so. There is no way that could be true!

Note also that verse 31 proves again that Jesus is the **Son** of God as well as God. I keep pointing out verses like this because they disprove one of the major lies of Islam, which is Islam's claim that the Bible doesn't teach that God has a Son.

One of the funniest things a Christian encounters when dealing with Muslims is that they won't accept that Christians believe what they believe. They will make silly statements like, "You don't believe that, you believe what my Muslim teachers says you believe." And no matter what you say you can't convince them otherwise. Our experience is that students from many Muslim countries who are studying at U.S. universities are not allowed by their governments to be alone. They must be with another Muslim at all times, so that they are never free to think. That is why you always get such silly logic from them. They dare not show even the slightest doubt of Islam, for fear of being reported. They are enslaved, even while in the USA. The idea that Christians believe in and worship three gods is one of those made-up beliefs Muslim teachers claim that Christians believe. One of the main purposes of this book is to show the reader what the Bible actually teaches Christians to believe, so that the reader can see how Muslim teachers lie and deceive even their Muslim followers.

Beware! Islamic deception follows:

HOT TIP:
Apostle John writes, immediately after the discourse between Jesus and Thomas; "Many other signs therefore Jesus also performed in the presence of the disciples, which are not written in this book; but these have been written that you may believe that Jesus is the Christ..." If John had recognized the answer by Thomas to be a testimony for the 'Deity of Jesus' and the observed silence by Jesus to be his acquiesce to such a testimony, then John would have

written "Jesus is the God" and not "Jesus is the Christ..."

HOTTER TIP! Meherally does not understand the importance of the Christ. Only God in human flesh could be the Christ. The word Christ is the Greek translation of the Hebrew word Messias (spelled Messiah in the Old Testament).

> One of the two which heard John speak, and followed him, was Andrew, Simon Peter's brother. 41 He first findeth his own brother Simon, and saith unto him, **We have found the Messias, which is, being interpreted, the Christ.** 42 And he brought him to Jesus. (John 1:40-42)

The Messiah was the anointed Savior who would be "cut off" (given capital punishment), "but not for himself." In other words, He would not die for any sins that He had committed for he was totally without sin, but he would die for the sins of all the people on earth.

> And after threescore and two weeks shall **Messiah be cut off, but not for himself**: and the people of the prince that shall come shall destroy the city and the sanctuary; and the end thereof shall be with a flood, and unto the end of the war desolations are determined. (Dan. 9:26)

This prophesy was fulfilled by Jesus.

> For I delivered unto you first of all that which I also received, how that **Christ died for our sins according to the scriptures**; 4 And that he was **buried**, and that he **rose again the third day** according to the scriptures. (1 Cor. 15:3-4)

Jesus was able to die for our sins because He never sinned.

> Seeing then that we have a great high priest, that is passed into the heavens, **Jesus the Son of God**, let us hold fast our profession. 15 For we have not an high priest which cannot be touched with the feeling of our infirmities; **but was in all points tempted like as we are, yet without sin**. 16 Let us therefore come boldly unto the throne of grace, that we may obtain mercy, and find grace to help in time of need. (Heb. 4:14-16)

NOTICE THAT MEHERALLY DOES NOT QUOTE THE WHOLE VERSE. WHY? Below is the whole verse:

> And many other signs truly did Jesus in the presence of his disciples, which are not written in this book: 31 But these are written, that ye might believe that Jesus is the Christ, **the Son of God**; and that **believing ye might have life through his name**. (John 20:30-31)

Note that this verse says that Jesus is the Son of God, and that if you believe in Jesus you will have life through his name! Since Meherally uses this verse as a proof text, he must realize that it is true. So his deception must be on purpose.

7.7 Did Jesus accept worship as being God?

Question No.11 [from a Christian to Islamic teacher Meherally.]

Apostle Matthew records that Jesus was worshipped by Magi that came from the East (2:11); by the boat people (14:33); by Mary Magdalene and the other Mary (28:9); and also by his disciples on a mountain in Galilee (28:17). Since worshipping any one other than God is a fundamental sin, why did not Jesus stop these people from worshipping him, unless he was God himself?

Beware! Islamic deception follows:

Answer No.11 1. For your information, none of the above worshipped Jesus. Nor, did apostle Matthew record it so. According to the lexical aids to the Bible, the proper Greek word for 'worship' is 'se-bomai' (4576) from the root 'seb'. That word 'sebomai' is used by apostle Matthew in 15:9 where Jesus said; "But in vain do they worship me,..." The Greek word used by the apostle in the above quotes is 'prosekunesan' and not 'sebomai'. 'Pros-ekunesan' comes from 'proskuneo' (4352), which literally means bow, crouch, crawl, kneel or prostrate. If the apostle wanted to convey; 'Jesus was worshipped', he would have used the word 'sebomai' which he did not. 2. To prove the point fur-ther, in 'New English Bible' the transla-tions of the quoted verses read; 'bowed to the ground' in (2:11); 'fell at his feet' in (14:33); 'falling prostrate before him' in (28:9), and 'fell prostrate before him' in (28:17). 3. The question of Jesus stopping them for worshipping, therefore does not arise, because they simply bowed or pros-trated to him.

Again, Meherally either does not know Greek at all, or else he is intentionally try-ing to deceive his readers—or both. The Greek word προσεκύνησαν (prosekunesan) **does** mean worship. Below it is clearly used to refer to worship toward God.

> Revelation 7:11 And all the angels stood round about the throne, and about the elders and the four beasts, and **fell before the throne on their faces**, and **worshipped** [prosekunesan] God, 12 Saying, Amen: Blessing, and glory, and wisdom, and thanksgiving, and honour, and power, and might, be unto our God for ever and ever. Amen.

Note that the above verse shows that they fell prostrate before Him (that is obviously what "fell before the throne on their faces" means), **and** they **worshipped** (prosekunesan) God. It would make no sense to say, "They fell prostrate before God, and they fell prostrate before God."

As already pointed out, the so-called New English Bible is a phony Bible purposely cor-rupted by enemies of Christianity, with many verses mistranslated to deny the Bible's core teachings. So, naturally, an enemy of Christ would choose to use the New English Bible that helps him defend his heresies, rather than the King James Bible which proves him a liar. In the English language knowledgeable Christians use only the King James Version of the Bible.

Beware! Islamic deception follows:

HOT TIP:
Apostle Mark records in 10:17-18; "And as he (Jesus) was setting out on a journey, a man ran up to him and knelt before him and began asking him, "Good Teacher, what shall I do to inherit the eternal life?" And Jesus said to him, "Why do you call me good? No one is good except God alone." It sounds inharmonious and inconsistent that a person who even refuses to be called "good" could have allowed any one to wor-ship him. Since, no one is good except "God alone", should not Christians be wor-shipping directly to that solitary God to whom Jesus himself prayed more than a dozen times, according to the Gospels?

Jesus was not refusing to be called good. Meherally totally misses the point Jesus was making. Jesus was telling this man that by admitting that Jesus was good, he was ad-mitting that Jesus is God. Among ordinary humans there is not one that is good in God's judgment.

> Romans 3:10-12 As it is written, There is **none** righteous, **no, not one**: 11 There is **none** that understandeth, there is **none** that seeketh after God. 12 They are **all** gone out of the way, they are together become unprofitable; there is **none** that doeth good, **no, not one**.

This means Muhammad was not good, and it means that you and I are not good. Because of this we cannot save ourselves from our own sins by good works.

Ephesians 2:8-9 For by **grace** are ye saved through **faith**; and that not of yourselves: it is the gift of God: 9 **Not of works**, lest any man should boast.

Among humans, only Jesus is good because only He is God. The fact that Jesus "was in all points tempted like as we are, **yet without sin**" proves that He is God. No other human being has ever lived without sin. Jesus was able to live the impossible sinless life because He is omnipotent God as well as human. Because Jesus never sinned, He was able to die on the cross for our sins so that we can be reconciled to God.

Hebrews 4:14 Seeing then that we have a great high priest, that is passed into the heavens, **Jesus the Son of God**, let us hold fast our profession. 15 For we have not an high priest which cannot be touched with the feeling of our infirmities; but was in all points tempted like as we are, **yet without sin**. 16 Let us therefore come boldly unto the throne of grace, that we may obtain mercy, and find grace to help in time of need.

1 Timothy 1:15 This is a faithful saying, and worthy of all acceptation, that **Christ Jesus** came into the world to save **sinners**; of whom I am chief.

Jesus lived his whole life without sin. That is power that only God possesses.

Beware! Islamic deception follows:

Note: The following is written in the language that is intended as an invitation (Daw'ah) to Christians, from their biblical perspective.

A question from a Christian:

Question No.12 [from a Christian to Islamic teacher Meherally.]
When prophet Moses asked God; What was His name? What shall he say to his people? From behind the Burning Bush God replied; "I AM THAT I AM." God also asked Moses to say to the sons of Israel: "I AM hath sent me unto you." Exodus 3:14. When confronted by Jews; "Jesus said unto them, 'Verily, verily, I say unto you, Before Abraham was, I am.'" (John 8:58 K.J.V.). Jesus also said; "I said therefore unto you, that ye shall die in your sins: for if ye believe not that I am (he), ye shall die in your sins." (John 8:24, K.J.V.). Does that not prove, Jesus existed before his birth; he was the One who spoke to Moses from behind the Burning Bush; and if you do not believe that, you will die in your sins?

Beware! Islamic deception follows:

Note: The word 'he' in the verse above as well as in the Hot Tip below, appear in the italic types in King James Version (K.J.V.). Since I cannot use italics on e-mail, I have placed the word 'he' within parenthesis.
Answer No.12
Your question is based upon a simple conjecture. Even the editors of K.J.V. insinuate that fact. Under the foot note of Exodus 3:14 the editors write; "Jesus probably alluded to this name of God in John 8:58, 'Before Abraham was, I AM." The use of phrase "probably alluded" clearly indicates it is not an established reality. My dear friend, a surmise can never take place of (replace) an acknowledged statement. This is what Jesus said; "...I am (he), and that I do nothing of myself; but as my Father hath taught me, I speak these things." (John 8:28). God of Moses that claimed "I AM THAT I AM" had no instructor or tutor, and, needed no tutoring. If God had an instructor or an educator, then what would you call that entity? God's mentor or boss?? As for the existence of Jesus before his birth, please remember Jesus

was anointed by God before he was born. Hence, he was called Christ (Messiah). Besides Jesus, there were others who were either anointed, consecrated or made holy, before their births. (see Ps. 89:20, Is. 45:1, 61:1; 1 Sam. 24:6). God did take a solemn covenant from Novah, Abraham, Moses, Jesus - son of Mary, and Muhammad before they were sent, reveals the Qur'an. Bible records, God came to prophet Jeremiah and said to him; "Before I formed you in the womb I knew you, and before you were born I consecrated you; I have appointed you a prophet to the nations." Jeremiah 1:5. I have question for you. How would you explain this ensuing statement? Jesus said to Jews; "Your father Abraham rejoiced to see my day, and he saw it, and was glad." (John 8:56)

That Jesus is the eternal God—without beginning—is not conjecture. Nor is it conjecture that John 8:58 shows that Jesus is the JEHOVAH God that spoke to Moses from the burning bush. It is not ordinary speech to say, "Before Abraham was, I AM." Jesus knew that by saying those words He was telling the world that He is God—just as Him saying that He is God's Son made Him equal to God. The Jews of that time, believing like the Muslims do today, clearly understood this, and so sought to kill Jesus.

> John 5:18 Therefore the Jews sought the more to kill him, because he not only had broken the sabbath, but said also that **God** was his Father, **making himself equal with God**.

God the Father has also declared Jesus to be God.

> Hebrews 1:1-8 God, who at sundry times and in divers manners spake in time past unto the fathers by the prophets, 2 Hath in these last days spoken unto us by **his Son**, whom he hath appointed heir of all things, by whom also he made the worlds; 3 Who being the brightness of his glory, and the express image of his person, and upholding all things by the word of

his power, when he had by himself purged our sins, sat down on the right hand of the Majesty on high; 4 Being made so much better than the angels, as he hath by inheritance obtained a more excellent name than they. 5 For unto which of the angels said he at any time, **Thou art my Son, this day have I begotten thee**? And again, I will be to him a **Father**, and he shall be to me a **Son**? 6 And again, when he bringeth in the **firstbegotten** into the world, he saith, And let all the angels of God worship him. 7 And of the angels he saith, Who maketh his angels spirits, and his ministers a flame of fire. 8 **But unto the Son he saith, Thy throne, O God**, is for ever and ever: a sceptre of righteousness is the sceptre of thy kingdom.

Meherally said: "I have question for you. How would you explain this ensuing statement? Jesus said to Jews; "Your father Abraham rejoiced to see my day, and he saw it, and was glad." (John 8:56). Here is the answer to Meherally's question: Jesus is JEHOVAH God—the one and only true God—, and He was in existence during Abraham's day. He was, in fact, in existence BEFORE Abraham. Note the context of John 8:56:

> John 8: 42-59 Jesus said unto them, **If God were your Father, ye would love me**: for I proceeded forth and came from God; neither came I of myself, but he sent me. 43 Why do ye not understand my speech? even because ye cannot hear my word. 44 Ye are of your father the devil, and the lusts of your father ye will do. He was a murderer from the beginning, and abode not in the truth, because there is no truth in him. When he speaketh a lie, he speaketh of his own: for he is a liar, and the father of it. 45 And because I tell you the truth, ye believe me not. 46 **Which of you convinceth me of sin?** And if I say the truth, why do ye not believe me? 47 He that is of God heareth God's words: ye therefore hear them not, because ye are not of God. 48 Then answered the Jews, and said unto him, Say we not well that thou art a Samaritan, and hast a devil? 49 Jesus answered, I have not a devil; but I honour **my Father**, and ye do dishonour me. 50 And I seek not mine own glory: there is

109

one that seeketh and judgeth. 51 **Verily, verily, I say unto you, If a man keep my saying, he shall never see death**. 52 Then said the Jews unto him, Now we know that thou hast a devil. Abraham is dead, and the prophets; and thou sayest, If a man keep my saying, he shall never taste of death. 53 Art thou greater than our father Abraham, which is dead? and the prophets are dead: whom makest thou thyself? 54 Jesus answered, If I honour myself, my honour is nothing: it is my Father that honoureth me; of whom ye say, that he is your God: 55 Yet ye have not known him; but I know him: and if I should say, I know him not, I shall be a liar like unto you: but I know him, and keep his saying. 56 **Your father Abraham rejoiced to see my day: and he saw it, and was glad**. 57 Then said the Jews unto him, Thou art not yet fifty years old, and hast thou seen Abraham? 58 Jesus said unto them, Verily, verily, I say unto you, **Before Abraham was, I am**. 59 Then took they up stones to cast at him: but Jesus hid himself, and went out of the temple, going through the midst of them, and so passed by.

Beware! Islamic deception follows:

HOT TIP:
When Jews were doubtful about the identity of a particular blind beggar who had been healed by Jesus, the blind beggar - who was no more blind, kept saying; "I am (he)" (John 9:9, K.J.V.). Does that make the blind beggar, God! Further more, the beggar when questioned about Jesus who had healed him, replied to Jews; "And he said, "He is a prophet." (John 9:17).

The typical Muslim teacher takes things out of context to try to deceive the unlearned. The once blind beggar was merely answering a question:

> The neighbours therefore, and they which before had seen him that he was blind, said, **Is not this he that sat and begged?** 9 Some said, This is he: others said, He is like him: but he said, I am *he*. (John 9:8-9)

The blind beggar's statement has nothing in common with the words of Christ, as the context clearly shows. Jesus' words were not in response to a question. Rather, Jesus was clearly stating that He is God—the Almighty I AM that talked with Moses. The beggar did not say, "**Before Abraham was, I am**," because the beggar was not before Abraham. By stating that He existed before Abraham, Jesus was making exceedingly clear that He is God.

Concerning the blind beggar's statement that Jesus was a prophet, it was a true statement—Jesus is **the prophet like unto Moses** which was prophesied to come. Jesus is also God's Son, the Holy One, the Just, the Prince of life, the Christ who died for our sins and rose from the dead, the Savior that can blot out your sins, the One that all the true prophets have prophesied about since the world began, the One you must believe in or be destroyed, and the One God sent to bless you by turning you from your iniquities, as the following Scripture passage shows:

> The **God of Abraham**, and of Isaac, and of Jacob, the God of our fathers, **hath glorified his Son Jesus**; whom ye delivered up, and denied him in the presence of Pilate, when he was determined to let him go. 14 But ye denied the **Holy One and the Just**, and desired a murderer to be granted unto you; 15 And killed the **Prince of life, whom God hath raised from the dead**; whereof we are witnesses. 16 And his name through faith in his name hath made this man strong, whom ye see and know: yea, the faith which is by him hath given him this perfect soundness in the presence of you all. 17 And now, brethren, I wot that through ignorance ye did it, as did also your rulers. 18 But those things, which **God before had shewed by the mouth of all his prophets, that Christ should suffer, he hath so fulfilled**. 19 Repent ye therefore, and be converted, that your sins may be blotted out, when the times of refreshing shall come from the presence of the Lord; 20 And he shall send Jesus Christ, which before was preached unto you: 21 Whom the heaven must receive un-

til the times of restitution of all things, which God hath spoken by the mouth of all his holy prophets since the world began. 22 **For Moses truly said unto the fathers, A prophet shall the Lord your God raise up unto you of your brethren, like unto me; him shall ye hear in all things whatsoever he shall say unto you. 23 And it shall come to pass, that every soul, which will not hear that prophet, shall be destroyed from among the people.** 24 Yea, and all the prophets from Samuel and those that follow after, as many as have spoken, have likewise foretold of these days. 25 Ye are the children of the prophets, and of the covenant which God made with our fathers, saying unto Abraham, And in thy seed shall all the kindreds of the earth be blessed. 26 Unto you first **God, having raised up his Son Jesus, sent him to bless you, in turning away every one of you from his iniquities.** (Acts 3:13-26)

⇨ Notice in verse 13 above that the God of Abraham, Isaac, and Jacob had a Son. So Allah was not their God.

⇨ Notice in verse 14 that Jesus is called the Holy One and the Just—terms that were used only of God in the Old Testament.

⇨ Notice in verse 15 that Jesus is called the Prince of life, and that He was killed—the Just died for the unjust.

⇨ Notice in verse 15 that God raised Jesus from the dead. This means He first had to be buried.

⇨ Notice that the context of verses 22-23 show without any shadow of doubt that Jesus—not Muhammad—is that prophet like unto Moses. This fact is covered in depth in chapter 13.

⇨ Notice in verse 26 that Jesus is again called God's Son.

Islam lies about all these things. Why would anyone want to follow such a purposely deceptive religion?

7.8 What about the last 12 verses of Mark?

Question No.13 [from a Christian to Islamic teacher Meherally.]

Apostle Mark records in 16:19; "...He (Jesus) was received up into heaven, and sat down at the right hand of God." The question is, who can have such an unparalleled privilege and distinction, besides his own begotten Son? Is there anyone else who has been elevated to that station, in any other scripture?

Beware! Islamic deception follows:

Answer No.13
1. Are you aware of the fact that there are two versions of Mark's Gospel? One is called the shorter version and other, the longer version. The shorter version, which ends at verse 8, does not contain the above verse. 2. One of the two great achievements of an eminent biblical critic of the nineteenth century, Lobegott Friedrich Konstantin Von Tischendorf, was the historical discovery of the oldest known Bible manuscript 'Codex Sinaiticus' from St. Catherine's Monastery in Mt. Sinai. The most damaging piece of evidence that Tischendorf discovered in this 5th century document was that the gospel of Mark ended at 16:8. In other words, the last 12 verses (Mark 16:9 to 20) were "injected" sometime after the 5th century. Clement of Alexandria and Origen never quoted these verses. Later on, it was also discovered that the said 12 verses, wherein lies the various accounts of "Resurrected Jesus", do not appear in codices Syriacus, Vaticanus and Bobiensis.

While reading the rest of Meherally's argument, note that he doesn't answer the question, but instead tries to discredit the Bible verses that prove him wrong. In actual fact, the manuscripts Meherally says discredit the Bible **actually prove Islam wrong,** as will be explained below. But first things first. Meherally is just trying to distract us from the fact of Jesus' exalted position in Heaven. **The question that was asked is, who can have the unparalleled privilege and distinction of sitting at God's right hand, besides God's own begotten Son?** Meherally doesn't want to acknowledge the exaltation of Jesus in the Bible, because he knows it proves Islam wrong, so he tries to distract us by attacking the credibility of the verse that was quoted in the book of Mark. But Meherally knows that **even without the book of Mark there are many verses which tell us that Jesus is exalted by God's right hand, or standing or sitting at the right hand of God. Here are a few:**

> Acts 2:32 This **Jesus** hath God raised up, whereof we all are witnesses. 33 Therefore **being by the right hand of God exalted,** and having received of the Father the promise of the Holy Ghost, he hath shed forth this, which ye now see and hear. 34 For David is not ascended into the heavens: but he saith himself, **The LORD said unto my Lord, Sit thou on my right hand,** 35 **Until I make thy foes thy footstool.** 36 Therefore let all the house of Israel know assuredly, that **God hath made that same Jesus, whom ye have crucified, both Lord and Christ.**

> Acts 5:30 The God of our fathers raised up **Jesus,** whom ye slew and hanged on a tree. 31 **Him hath God exalted with his right hand** to be a Prince and a Saviour, for to give repentance to Israel, and forgiveness of sins.

> Acts 7:55 But he, being full of the Holy Ghost, looked up stedfastly into heaven, and saw the glory of God, **and Jesus standing on the right hand of God,** 56 And said, Behold, I see the heavens opened, **and the Son of man standing on the right hand of God.**

> Romans 8:34 Who is he that condemneth? It is Christ that died, yea rather, that is risen again, **who is even at the right hand of God,** who also maketh intercession for us.

> Colossians 3:1 If ye then be risen with Christ, seek those things which are above, **where Christ sitteth on the right hand of God.** 2 Set your affection on things above, not on things on the earth. 3 For ye are dead, and your life is hid with Christ in God.

> Hebrew 10:10 By the which will we are sanctified through the offering of the body of **Jesus Christ** once for all. 11 And every priest standeth daily ministering and offering oftentimes the same sacrifices, which can never take away sins: 12 But this man, after he had offered one sacrifice for sins for ever, **sat down on the right hand of God;** 13 **From henceforth expecting till his enemies be made his footstool.** 14 For by one offering he hath perfected for ever them that are sanctified.

> Hebrews 12:2 Looking unto Jesus the author and finisher of our faith; who for the joy that was set before him endured the cross, despising the shame, **and is set down at the right hand of the throne of God.**

> 1 Peter 3:21 The like figure whereunto even baptism doth also now save us (not the putting away of the filth of the flesh, but the answer of a good conscience toward God,) by the resurrection of Jesus Christ: 22 Who is gone into heaven, **and is on the right hand of God; angels and authorities and powers being made subject unto him.**

Jesus is, indeed, the Son of God, and is, in fact, God the Son. Angels and authorities and powers are subject unto Jesus, and someday all His enemies will be made His footstool.

Now, let's consider the rest of Meherally's argument.

| Beware! Islamic deception follows: |

Today, in many of the revised versions of the Bible, the said twelve verses appear within parentheses. Tischendorf also discovered that John's gospel was heavily reworked. For example, verses starting from John 7:53 to 8:11 are not to be found in codices Sinaiticus or Vaticanus. Similarly, a verse from the gospel of Luke that speaks of Peter running to the tomb, stooping and looking in and finding it empty and marvelling at what had happened is not to be found in the ancient manuscripts. (For detailed information please read 'Secrets of Mount Sinai' by James Bentley, Orbis, London, 1985). 3. Peake's Commentary on the Bible records; "It is now generally agreed that 9-20 are not an original part of Mk. They are not found in the oldest MSS, and indeed were apparently not in the copies used by Mt. and Lk. A 10th-cent. Armenian MS ascribes the passage to Aristion, the presbyter mentioned by Papias (ap.Eus.HE III, xxxix, 15)."

We will now examine the old Bible manuscripts which Meherally claims discredit the last twelve verses of the book of Mark. Meherally admits they are very old— several hundred years older than the Quran. So, why don't they contain the verses supposedly quoted in the Quran? Answer to the question: because the Quran is not inspired of God, but was made up in the demon possessed mind of Muhammad.

It is true that Sinaiticus and Vaticanus have shortened versions of Mark, but the Sinaiticus and Vaticanus are probably the two most corrupted New Testament manuscripts ever, having been altered in thousands of other places also. As Greek scholar, Dr. D.A. Waite states on page 227 of his book DEFENDING THE KING JAMES BIBLE, "in practically every other Greek manuscript of the Gospel of Mark, the verses [16:9-20] do appear without question of any kind!" For a book-length defense of these verses see *THE LAST TWELVE VERSES OF MARK* by Dean John William Burgon, one of the greatest language and Bible scholars of all time.[5] A good summary of the evidence that Mark 16:9-20

___
[5]http://www.amazon.com/Last-Twelve-Verses-Mark/dp/1589600142

was in the original manuscript is given by Kyle Pope:

There are over 5000 manuscripts of the Greek New Testament which have been preserved. It is often falsely asserted that Sinaiticus and Vaticanus are the "oldest manuscripts" of the New Testament. That is not true. There are many fragmentary papyri which predate both texts. One of the most significant of these is the Chester Beatty Papyri (P45). It is a second or third century manuscript of the Gospels and Acts. Unfortunately, this ancient papyri is damaged before the text of Mark 4 and after Mark 12. That means it can't help us with regard to Mark's ending. However, the majority of manuscripts which have survived include Mark 16:9-20. Some of these are only slightly younger than Vaticanus and Sinaiticus. For example, Codex Alexandrinus, a fifth century text presented to Charles I in 1627 by Cyril Lucar, the archbishop of Constantinople has the text. Codex Bezae (5th-6th century), acquired by the Reformer Theodore Beza from a French monastery and given to the Cambridge library in 1581 has the passage in both Greek and Latin. The text is also in Codex Ephraemi Rescriptus (5th century) and Codex Washingtonensis (4th-5th century)....

Just as the majority of Greek manuscripts preserve Mark 16:9-20, so the majority of ancient translations do as well. These include the Syriac Peshitta (2nd-3rd century); the Sahidic Coptic (2nd-3rd century); the majority of the Old Latin translations (2nd-4th century); Latin Vulgate (4th-5th century); the Gothic (4th century)—although it is damaged in the middle of verse 12; many Armenian manuscripts (5th century) and Ethiopic manuscripts (5th century). To question the originality and inspiration of Mark 16:9-20 we must disregard the efforts of centuries of scholars and translators....

Overwhelmingly the evidence from the testimony of ancient writers falls in support of the antiquity and originality of the passage. **Not only do contemporaries of Jerome and Eusebius use the verses as authoritative but writers which predate Sinaiticus, Vaticanus, and the translations quote the pas-**

sage! The earliest undisputed example of this is found in the second century writings of Irenaeus. In his work Against Heresies, he writes, "at the end of the Gospel, Mark says: 'So then, after the Lord Jesus had spoken to them, He was received up into heaven, and sat at the right hand of God'" (III.10.5). Here Irenaeus not only quotes verse 19, but claims that this comes at the end of the Gospel. How can we question the antiquity and originality of this text if someone barely a generation after the composition of the New Testament quotes it? ("Is Mark 16:9-20 Inspired?" *Biblical Insights* 9.8 (August 2009): 22-23)[6]

While discussing the omission of Mark 16:9-20 in Codex Alpeh and Codex B, Martian A. Shue points out the following facts that will shock most Christians who have been persuaded to use the new perverted translations rather than the King James Bible.

It should also be noted that Codex Vaticanus also leaves out Gen. 1-46, Ps. 105-137, Heb. 9:14-13:25, and all of I and II Timothy, Titus, Philemon, and Revelation. So if we go by their reasoning then we should likewise omit all of the above from our Bibles as well. Codex Sinaiticus has its omissions as well but what I would like to point out about it is that it contains "The Epistle of Barnabas" and "The Shepherd of Hermas" as part of the New Testament. What will they do next add "The Epistle of Barnabas" and "The Shepherd of Hermas" to our Bibles?[7]

It also needs to be pointed out that there is not a single extant manuscript known that agrees with the text of the Nestle-Aland Greek New Testament used by the United Bible Societies. The Nestle-Aland text is basically the Westcott and Hort text with even more errors added. The Westcott and Hort text was a combining of the errors found in Codex Aleph and Codex B to produce a new text altogether—that did not exist until Westcott and Hort compiled it.

So, for the sake of Christians reading this book, I will state again that the promoters of that corrupt text are traitors and saboteurs of the Christian faith. In all reality, they are worse even than Judas Iscariot. Translations from their corrupt text are being used by Muslim teachers—Meherally is an example—to deceptively convert people to Islam.

Beware! Islamic deception follows:

HOT TIP:
The Book of Revelation (symbolic and obscure writings of uncertain authorship), records in 3:21 that Jesus sat down with his Father on his Father's throne. You write, based upon injected verse; Jesus sat down at the right hand side of God. Which one do you believe?

Why obviously both verses are true! Jesus sat down at the right hand of God His Father on His Father's throne. There is nothing hard to understand about that.

Muslim teachers only claim to accept the Bible as God's word in order the gain your confidence to deceive you. In fact, they do not believe the Bible. Macksood Aftab, managing editor of *The Islamic Herald*, admitted this in an article quoted on the Answering-Christianity.com web site:

In fact, the original Bible or New Testament (the very first one) did not correspond to the Injil, Taurat, or Zabur in the first place. It doesn't matter how unreliably it was transmitted; the Bible does not correspond to the Quranic Injil.

It is not that the Christians have changed the original, but rather they have the wrong book, altogether. The words of Christ are possibly the closest thing to the Injil, but if some of them don't agree with the Noble Quran, then

---

[6]http://ancientroadpublications.com/ Studies/BiblicalStudies/Mark16.html

[7]http://www.avdefense.webs.com/mark16. html

we don't take them. The recently discovered Gospel of Thomas, which is nothing but a list of sayings of Jesus, is even closer to the Islamic concept of Injil. Therefore, it should be kept in mind in discussion with Christians that the Bible has not been changed, but rather the original documents chosen as the word of God were incorrect.[8]

Aftab correctly states that the Injil of the Quran is a completely different book than the New Testament used by Christians. Note also that Aftab says, "The words of Christ are possibly the closest thing to the Injil, but if some of them don't agree with the Noble Quran, then we don't take them." Muslim teachers quote the Bible only to deceive. They use verses out of context to deceive you, but when you show Bible verses in context that disprove Islam, they dishonestoy reject them as being added by men.

There are no ancient Bible manuscripts to be found that read like the quotes in the Quran. Even the most corrupt manuscripts, like Aleph and B, are not that corrupt. In vivid contrast, the words of JEHOVAH, the true God, are preserved forever:

> Psalms 12:6 The **words** of the LORD are **pure words**: as silver tried in a furnace of earth, purified seven times. 7 Thou shalt **keep** them, O LORD, thou shalt **preserve** them **from this generation for ever**.

You can read those pure preserved words in the Masoretic Hebrew Old Testament and in the Textus Receptus Greek New Testament. And you can read an accurate translation of those words in the King James Bible of 1611.

Figure 7.1: *The ending of Mark and beginning of Luke in the corrupted Codex Sinaiticus (Codex Alpeh). Note the blank space between the two, indicating that the scribe was reserving a space for Mark 16:9-20, which he knew should be included.*

---

[8]http://www.answering-christianity.com/warning.htm

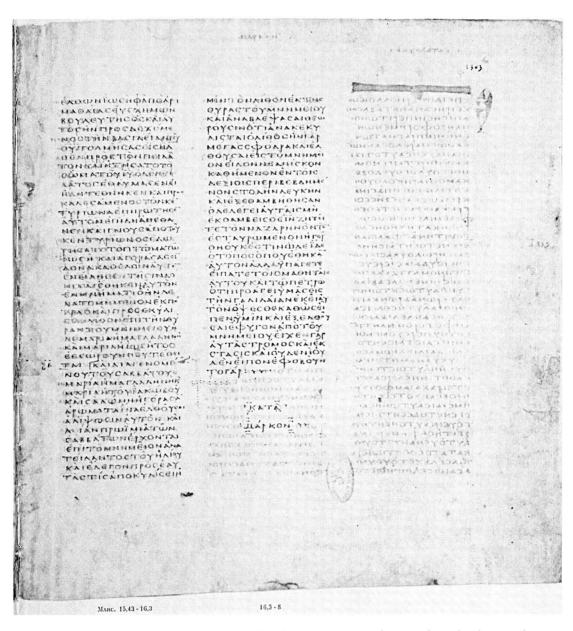

Figure 7.2: *The end of Mark in the corrupted Codex Vaticanus (Codex B). The only place in the entire manuscript where an entire columns is left vacant. It is evident that the scribe left this blank space in case it was decided later to include Mark 16:9-20.*

Chapter 8

Deceptive Muslim Answers To Christian's Questions 14–15

8.1 Is Romans 10:9-10 true?

Question No.14 [from a Christian to Islamic teacher Meherally.]

In the Epistle of Paul to Romans, it reads; "that if you confess with your mouth Jesus as Lord, and believe in your heart that God raised him from the dead, you shall be saved; for with the heart man believes, resulting in righteousness, and with the mouth he confesses, resulting in salvation." (Roman 10:9-10, NASB). The salvation is assured to us Christians who confess with our mouth and heart; Jesus Christ to be our Lord. What do Muslims have for their salvation?

Beware! Islamic deception follows:

This is a preferred verse with the evangelic missionaries. It is one of the bases of the Christianity propagated by Paul and needs to be addressed in detail and from various perspectives.
1. This is a quotation from one of the Epistles (letters) written by Paul. While reading a passage from an Epistle one has to bear in mind that these letters when written by the author, were a sort of discourse containing religious instructions and admonitions, and, were not intended to form a part and parcel of the canonical Scripture.

Romans 10:9-10 is indeed an important passage of Scripture. Meherally is correct in saying that this passage "needs to be addressed in detail and from various perspectives." This passage of Scripture is devastating to Islam.

But since Meherally is saying that none of the epistles are actually Scripture, let's consider the Quran for a moment. The Quran supposedly quotes from the Bible in scores of places, yet there is no Bible to be found anywhere that reads like the quotations found in the Quran. Even the most corrupted Bible manuscripts are different from the supposedly quoted verses in the Quran. So it is obvious that the so-called Bible quotations in the Quran are phony quotations. They are based on the vain imagination of Muhammad or whoever it was that actually wrote the Quran. The authorship of the entire Quran is therefore highly questionable. So, while Meherally vainly searches for a manuscript to support his false book, let us examine the deception is the rest of his argument.

┌─────────────────────────────────────┐
│ **Beware! Islamic deception follows:** │
└─────────────────────────────────────┘

2. To substantiate the above claim, please read 1 Corin 7:25-26 and 7:40. Here Paul writes; "I give an opinion"; "in my opinion" and "I think" (twice). Whereas, Jesus - the prophet of God, admitted; "...and I do nothing on my own initiative, but I speak these things as the Father taught me." (John 8:28). One has to differentiate "my opinion" and "my thought" from the "inspired" or the divinely "tutored" document.

3. In 2 Corin 12:16, Paul - a zealous persecutor of the disciples that overnight became a fervent propagator of 'Christianity', makes a perplexing statement; "...crafty fellow that I am, I took you in by deceit." Jesus was a righteous prophet propagating the 'Kingdom of God'. His mission was, alike every other Jewish prophet, to glorify God alone.

4. Imagine, you are at a crossroad. There are three signs. Paul transcribes; Take the Left turn to reach the Destination. Jesus transcribes; Take the Right turn. The Old Testaments transcribes; Take the Right turn. Which way should you be headed if you wish to reach the Destination with certainty? Please bear this viewpoint in mind, while comparing various passages from the Bible.

5. Now let us go to Roman 10:9-10, the verses quoted by you in the above question. Please continue reading the succeeding verses, which say; "For the Scripture says, 'Whoever believes in Him will not be disappointed.' For there is no distinction between Jew and Greek; for the same Lord is Lord of all, abounding in riches for ^^^^^^^^^^^^^^^^^^^^^^^^^^^^ all who call upon Him; for 'Whoever will call upon the name of the Lord will be saved." (Ro-

man 10:11-13). Note: The editors of the New Testament have created confusion by translating the Greek word 'Theos' (meaning, God) as "Lord". And, the Greek word 'Kurios' (meaning, Master, Owner, Head of a house) as "Lord", as well. For those who consider Jesus to be God, it may not make any difference, but for the rest it does.

6. To resolve the dilemma as to who is this "the same Lord" who is the Lord of Jews, of Greeks and of all; let us go to verses 3:29-30 in the same Epistle. It reads; "Or is God the God of Jews only? Is He not the God of Gentiles also? Yes, of Gentiles also-if indeed God is one- and He will justify the circumcised by faith and the uncircumcised through faith." Jews never accepted Jesus as their Prophet or Messiah, leave alone accepting him as their Lord (Master) or as their Lord (God). So, "Lord Jesus" is out of the picture, leaving "Lord the God" to be the "one God" of all.

7. To answer your specific question, the verse above reads; "Whoever will call upon the name of the Lord (Lord of all) will be saved." We Muslims call upon the name of that Almighty God, the God of all, who pronounced His Commands to Adam, Noah, Abraham, Ishmael, Isaac, Jacob, Moses, David, Solomon, Jesus, Muhammad and many others (peace be upon all the prophets).

8. BTW, the verses that you have originally quoted has one very portentous underlying theme which you probably might have over looked. It says; "and (if you) believe in your heart that God raised him from the dead, you shall be saved." This sentence conveys there were two separate entities: a. One called Jesus, who was dead and lying motionless in a tomb. b. One called God, who was alive and able to perform acts. The entity (b) raised the entity (a) that was in an agony. "And God raised him up again, putting an end to the agony of death..." Acts 2:24. I hope you will hence-

forth recognize "the dead" and "the alive" to be two distinct entities and "un-equal", whenever you think of the "Risen Jesus".

9. Would it not be an unfair practise on part of the Almighty God to have sent His son as a "Saviour to all" thousands of years after Adam. Did not that deprive those born before the Christian Era of "the easy way out" to the Salvation? God cannot be unfair. He is a Righteous God. May be the entire concept is an Innovation.

10. Tom Harpur, a former professor of New Testament and an Anglican Minister writes; "Perhaps I am lacking in piety or some basic instinct, but I know I am not alone in finding the idea of Jesus' death as atonement for the sins of all humanity on one level bewildering and on the other morally repugnant. Jesus never to my knowledge said anything to indicate that forgiveness from God could only be granted 'after' or 'because of' the cross." (For Christ's Sake, p.75).

Meherally is extremely deceptive in his comments about Romans 10: 9-10. First of all, note that Meherally does not quote from the true Bible. Possibly he is not quoting at all (note that he doesn't say what version he is using), but is merely "wresting" the Scriptures. According to the *Oxford English Dictionary*, the word wrest means: "To strain or overstrain the meaning or bearing of (a writing, passage, word, etc.); to deflect or turn from the true or proper signification; to twist, pervert.... To derive or deduce (a name, etc.) irregularly from something; to change improperly.... To turn or deflect (a matter, etc.); to divert to (unto, †into) some different (esp. undue or improper) purpose, end, etc.); to distort or pervert.... To deflect (the law, etc.) from its proper course or interpretation; to turn from the right application; to misapply, pervert." The Apostle Peter spoke of men who would wrest the Scriptures:

2 Peter 3:15 And account that the longsuffering of our Lord is salvation; even as our

beloved brother **Paul** also according to the wisdom given unto him hath written unto you; 16 As also in all his epistles, speaking in them of these things; in which are some things **hard to be understood, which they that are unlearned and unstable wrest, as they do also the other scriptures, unto their own destruction**.

Second, Meherally's claim that "Theos" is translated as Lord in the New Testament is simply another lie. There is not a single place in the New Testament where the Greek word "Theos" is translated "Lord" in the King James Bible, which is the only trustworthy translation in English.

Third, Meherally is constantly talking about the "editors" of the New Testament? To whom is he referring? Some Muslims could print an edition of the Bible, and they could then claim to be the editors. They might have only a third grade education, and know nothing about the Bible, but they could claim to be editors! What value would their comments have? None!

Fourth, Meherally quotes such heretics as Tom Harpur as though their words have great authority. But as has already been pointed out, Harpur does not believe Jesus ever existed. The Quran, in it's attempt to counterfeit and replace God's word, MUST deal with Jesus (as must all false religions), and, therefore, by quoting Harpur, Meherally disproves his own religious book!

Now let us consider Meherally's **crafty** and **deceptive** arguments. I'll not follow Meherally's ten points above, but rather will expose eight of the false arguments found in those ten points.

8.1.1 Exposing deception #1

Is it true that Paul's writings "were not intended to form a part and parcel of the canonical Scripture," because in "1 Corin 7:25-26 and 7:40...Paul writes; 'I give an opinion'; 'in my opinion' and 'I think' (twice)?" No, that is not true. Here is the complete context of those verses so you can see for yourself:

> 1 Corinthians 7: 25 Now concerning virgins **I have no commandment of the Lord**: yet **I give my judgment, as one that hath obtained mercy of the Lord to be faithful**. 26 I suppose therefore that this is good for the present distress, I say, that it is good for a man so to be. 27 Art thou bound unto a wife? seek not to be loosed. Art thou loosed from a wife? seek not a wife. 28 But and if thou marry, thou hast not sinned; and if a virgin marry, she hath not sinned. Nevertheless such shall have trouble in the flesh: but I spare you. 29 But this I say, brethren, the time is short: it remaineth, that both they that have wives be as though they had none; 30 And they that weep, as though they wept not; and they that rejoice, as though they rejoiced not; and they that buy, as though they possessed not; 31 And they that use this world, as not abusing it: for the fashion of this world passeth away. 32 But I would have you without carefulness. He that is unmarried careth for the things that belong to the Lord, how he may please the Lord: 33 But he that is married careth for the things that are of the world, how he may please his wife. 34 There is difference also between a wife and a virgin. The unmarried woman careth for the things of the Lord, that she may be holy both in body and in spirit: but she that is married careth for the things of the world, how she may please her husband. 35 And this I speak for your own profit; not that I may cast a snare upon you, but for that which is comely, and that ye may attend upon the Lord without distraction. 36 But if any man think that he behaveth himself uncomely toward his virgin, if she pass the flower of her age, and need so require, let him do what he will, he sinneth not: let them marry. 37 Nevertheless he that standeth stedfast in his heart, having no necessity, but hath power over his own will, and hath so decreed in his heart that he will keep his virgin, doeth well. 38 So then he that giveth her in marriage doeth well; but he that giveth her not in marriage doeth better. 39 The wife is bound by the law as long as her husband liveth; but if her husband be dead, she is at liberty to be married to whom she will; only in the Lord. 40 But she is happier if she so abide, after my judgment: **and I think also that I have the Spirit of God**.

Note that not even once does Paul write "I give an opinion," or "in my opinion." And he does not **twice** say "I think." He does once say, "But she is happier if she so abide, after my judgment: and I think also that I have the Spirit of God.." In other words, since the Lord Jesus Christ said nothing about this subject during His earthly ministry, Paul gave his authoritative judgment concerning the subject as an Apostle moved by the Holy Spirit to pen the inspired words of Scripture.

To make this crystal clear, Paul said later in this same epistle:

> 1 Corinthians 14:37 **If any man think himself to be a prophet, or spiritual**, let him **acknowledge** that the things that **I write** unto you are **the commandments of the Lord**.

So, when a Muslim teacher such as Meherally refuses to acknowledge Paul's writings to be "the commandments of the Lord," he exposes himself as not being a true prophet and not being spiritual.

Note also that the Apostle Peter considered Paul's writings "**scripture**," and said that the persons that **wrested** Paul's writing would do so "**unto their own destruction**." Muslim teachers such as Meherally should take warning from the following verses which describe such Scripture wresters as "unlearned" and "unstable":

> 2 Peter 3: 15 And account that the longsuffering of our Lord is salvation; even as our beloved brother **Paul** also according to the wisdom given unto him hath written unto you; 16 As also **in all his epistles**, speaking in them of these things; in which are some things hard to be understood, **which they that are unlearned and unstable wrest, as they do also the other scriptures, unto their own destruction**.

Muslim teachers who wrest the Scriptures **are in fact** "unlearned" and "unstable." They have not learned common decency, or honesty, or the appreciation of life and peace. And note how emotionally unstable they are—in most pictures of them they are jabbing their fists into the air and screaming and cursing. **That** is why people fear them—not because they are on God's side, but because they are on Satan's side and so easily loose control of their emotions, and start spewing out threats and violence.

Since Muhammad also refused to acknowledge that the things Paul wrote "are the commandments of the Lord," it is obvious that Muhammad was not a prophet of God, nor was he spiritual.

The apostle Peter explained how the real Scriptures were received from God:

> 2 Peter 1: 16 **For we have not followed cunningly devised fables**, when we made known unto you the power and coming of our Lord Jesus Christ, but were eyewitnesses of his majesty. 17 For he received from **God the Father** honour and glory, when there came such a voice to him from the excellent glory, This is **my beloved Son**, in whom I am well pleased. 18 And this voice which came from heaven we heard, when we were with him in the holy mount. 19 We have also **a more sure word of prophecy**; whereunto ye do well that ye take heed, as unto a light that shineth in a dark place, until the day dawn, and the day star arise in your hearts: 20 Knowing this first, that **no prophecy of the scripture is of any private interpretation**. 21 For the prophecy came not in old time by the will of man: **but holy men of God spake as they were moved by the Holy Ghost**.

When the true Scriptures were given, there was no fear of demonic possession as there was with Muhammad, there was no foaming at the face or roaring like a camel. The friends of the prophets God used to give us the Bible did not think that they had the evil eye. But here is what Islamic history tells us about Muhammad:

> Mizanu'l Haqq, (page 345). Ibn Ishaq says that, before the Revelation first began to descend

upon him, **Mohammed's friends feared that he was suffering from the evil eye**: and that, when it came upon him, almost the same illness attacked him again. In tradition it is stated that he **(Mohammed) said: 'I fear lest I should become a magician, lest one should proclaim me a follower of the Jinn (spirit)', and again: 'I fear lest there should be madness' (or demonic possession) 'in me.'** After an accession of shivering and shutting his eyes, there used to come over him what resembled a swoon, **his face would foam and he would roar like a young camel.**[1]

Considering all the contradictions and errors[2] in the Quran, and considering that Muhammad feared he was possessed of a demon, and his friends thought he suffered from the evil eye, and that he foamed at the face, and roared like a camel while supposedly receiving revelation, it seems more logical to believe that Muhammad really was demon possessed, and that the Quran is from Satan, than to believe that the Quran is from God.

8.1.2 Exposing deception #2

Is it true that in 2 Corinthians 12:16, "Paul...makes a perplexing statement; '...crafty fellow that I am, I took you in by deceit.'"? **No, that is not true.** Again Meherally wrests the Scriptures. Here is that verse in its context so you can see for yourself how Meherally wrests the words to try to deceive you:

> 2 Corinthians 12:14 Behold, the third time I am ready to come to you; and I will not be burdensome to you: for I seek not yours, but you: for the children ought not to lay up for the parents, but the parents for the children. 15 And I will

---

[1]For more information concerning the Quran, read: http://www.answering-islam.org/Nehls/Ask/revealed.html

[2]A long documentation of contradictions and errors in the Quran is available here: http://www.answering-islam.org/Nehls/Ask/contra.html

very gladly spend and be spent for you; though the more abundantly I love you, the less I be loved. 16 But be it so, I did not burden you: nevertheless, **being crafty, I caught you with guile**. 17 Did I make a gain of you by any of them whom I sent unto you? 18 I desired Titus, and with him I sent a brother. Did Titus make a gain of you? walked we not in the same spirit? walked we not in the same steps? 19 Again, think ye that we excuse ourselves unto you? we speak before God in Christ: but we do all things, dearly beloved, for your edifying. 20 For I fear, lest, when I come, I shall not find you such as I would, and that I shall be found unto you such as ye would not: lest there be debates, envyings, wraths, strifes, backbitings, whisperings, swellings, tumults: 21 And lest, when I come again, my God will humble me among you, and that I shall bewail many **which have sinned already, and have not repented of the uncleanness and fornication and lasciviousness which they have committed**.

Note that Paul did **not** say, "I took you in by deceit." That implies that he was being deceitful. Rather he said, "Being crafty, I caught you with guile." In other words Paul was clever, and caught them in their deceit (guile). The word "crafty" means "Skilful, dexterous, clever, ingenious. a. Of persons or their faculties, etc." (Oxford English Dictionary). Although craftiness can be used to do evil, it can also be used to do good. In this case, **Paul** did not sin. Rather he caught **them** in sin. Not only this, the context (verse 14) of this Scripture shows that Paul was not trying to get material gain from the church at Corinth. In fact, he had refused to accept anything from them. He was honest in all his dealings with them. He was not seeking to be helped by them, but rather to help them.

So, Meherally's insinuation that Paul is dishonest and not trustworthy is simply his attempt to try to discredit the verbally inspired and divinely preserved words of God. The fact is that the writings of the Apostle Paul are of equal authority with all the other parts of the Bible, and does not contradict them, but rather compliments and harmonizes with them.

8.1.3 Exposing deception #3

Is it true that Theos is mistranslated as Lord in Romans 10:13?

No. As I have already pointed out, that is simply a lie. Check it out for yourself. The Greek word Θεὸς (Theos) does not even appear in that verse of the Greek New Testament. The word which does appear is Κυρίου (Kurion) which always means "Lord." So, I repeat that MEHERALLY SIMPLY LIED ABOUT THIS. Why does he lie? Because this verse proves Islam to be untrue. Meherally knows this, but the truth doesn't matter to him. All that matters to him is deceiving you!

8.1.4 Exposing deception #4

Is it true that "Muslims call upon the name of that Almighty God, the God of all, who pronounced His Commands to Adam, Noah, Abraham, Ishmael, Isaac, Jacob, Moses, David, Solomon, Jesus, Muhammad and many others (peace be upon all the prophets)"?

No, that also is not true. Muslims do not call upon the name of the "Almighty God." The name of the Almighty God is **JEHOVAH** in the Old Testament, and in the New Testament He is called "Jesus" and "Emmanuel."

> Isaiah 12:2 Behold, God is my salvation; I will trust, and not be afraid: for the **LORD JEHOVAH** is my strength and my song; he also is become my salvation.

> Matthew 1:21 And she shall bring forth **a son**, and thou shalt call his name **JESUS**: for he shall save his people from their sins. 22 Now all this was done, that it might be fulfilled which was spoken of the Lord by the prophet, saying, 23 Behold, **a virgin** shall be with child, and

shall bring forth **a son**, and they shall call his name **Emmanuel**, which being interpreted is, **God with us**. 24 Then Joseph being raised from sleep did as the angel of the Lord had bidden him, and took unto him his wife: 25 And knew her not till she had brought forth her firstborn son: **and he called his name JESUS**.

Muslims do not worship the **Almighty** God, rather they worship the **impotent** Allah—the god that cannot have a son—the powerless god of the God-rejecters of this lost world— the god that cannot save them, but rather orders them to save themselves by doing "good works" such as giving alms to the poor, fasting (through the daylight hours only—but feasting at night) for one month each year, making the pilgrimage to Mecca at least once before dying, or by committing a suicide bombing. Allah is the god of death—the god that is, in fact, a fallen angel (this will be explained in detail in chapter 12).

Does "Allah" mean "God"? Listen to what one Muslim website says:

THE MEANING OF: LA ILAHA ILL ALLAH

Let us start by looking at the literal translation of the words LA ILAHA ILL ALLAH.

LA means NO

ILAHA means GOD

ILL means ONLY or BUT

ALLAH means ALLAH

Most of the Muslims even today substitute the word GOD for the Name ALLAH. They go so far as translating the words LA ILAHA ILL ALLAH

to mean There is no god but God. **This latter translation is incorrect. IT DOES NOT MAKE SENSE!** Is Allah a God? No! Is the short and simple answer. Allah is not a God with a capital G or little g . The first Kalima (Testification) says clearly LA ILAHA (NO GOD!) ILL ALLAH (Only ALLAH). The biggest misunderstanding has started from the Translations of the Holy Quran. The translators freely substituted the word GOD where ever the name ALLAH is mentioned. It is, as if they are apologising on Allah's behalf and, in their minds, correcting the words of the Holy Quran. To compound the problem, the translators use outdated English which is neither spoken nor read by the majority of the population. It is this misrepresentation that has caused the confusion. Today so many Muslims who do not understand Arabic believe Allah and God is one and the same because they can only understand the (incorrect) English translation. This is a major downfall. Have you ever really considered why the Kalima started with a Negative word NO followed by GOD? It was to stop the people worshipping gods in the form of statues or in the form of pictures, or in the form of mental images. It was to stop people worshipping a god or gods sitting on a throne. If Allah is a god then the Kalima might have started with YES there is a God, or Allah is the only God, but it does not. The Kalima starts with NO god.

The name Allah cannot be converted to the English word God.

Could a Muslim make it any clearer than that? Allah cannot be properly translated as "God," but is the proper name of the Muslim's god.

8.1.5 Exposing deception #5

Is it true that the fact that Jesus died, was buried, and rose again proves that Jesus was not God?[3]

---

[3]Meherally, of course, didn't word this question so directly, but was very deceptive (see his point 8 under section 8.1 on page 118). He first quoted Ro-

No, of course not. In fact, it proves just the opposite. It proves that Jesus is both Human and God. Muslim readers should note this well: your teachers have lied to you about what Christianity teaches. It is not true that Christians worship three gods. Christians worship only one God who is three Persons.

> 1 Timothy 2: 3 For this is good and acceptable in the sight of God our Saviour; 4 Who will have all men to be saved, and to come unto the knowledge of the truth. 5 **For there is one God**, and one mediator between God and men, the man Christ Jesus; 6 Who gave himself a ransom for all, to be testified in due time.

> Ephesians 4:4 There is one body, and one Spirit, even as ye are called in one hope of your calling; 5 One Lord, one faith, one baptism, 6 **One God and Father of all**, who is above all, and through all, and in you all.

> Gal. 3:20 Now a mediator is not a mediator of one, but **God is one**.

> 1 John 5: 7 For there are three that bear record in heaven, **the Father, the Word, and the Holy Ghost: and these three are one**.

Islam redefines God to lower Him to the level of a man by saying that God is only one person as a man or angel is only one person. Some Muslims seem to lower God even further than that by stressing that God is not knowable, implying that God is not a person at all, but just an impersonal force like gravity. That is a major flaw in Islam. Allah, the impotent god, is only one person or none, but the true God is three persons. Allah is one

---

mans 10:9: "... if you believe in your heart that God raised him from the dead..." He goes on to try to say that God and Jesus are two separate entities. Then he sums it all up by saying, "I hope you will henceforth recognize 'the dead' and 'the alive' to be two distinct entities and 'un-equal,' whenever you think of the 'Risen Jesus.'" Remember that Meherally actually doesn't believe that Jesus died, or was buried, or rose again. So, he is trying to use a verse he believes to be untrue as though he believes it to be true to prove his point. Sly like a snake!

person like a man or angel is only one person (or is not a person at all like dead matter is not a person), but the true God is not like a man and is not like the matter He created. He is infinitely higher than man. Do not try to lower God to be like a man or an angel or the universe.

> 2 Samuel 7:22 Wherefore thou art great, O LORD God: for **there is none like thee**, neither is there any God beside thee, according to all that we have heard with our ears.

> 1 Chronicles 17:20 O LORD, **there is none like thee**, **neither is there any God beside thee**, according to all that we have heard with our ears.

> Isaiah 46: 5 **To whom will ye liken me, and make me equal, and compare me, that we may be like?** 6 They lavish gold out of the bag, and weigh silver in the balance, and hire a goldsmith; and he maketh it a god: they fall down, yea, they worship. 7 They bear him upon the shoulder, they carry him, and set him in his place, and he standeth; from his place shall he not remove: yea, one shall cry unto him, yet can he not answer, nor save him out of his trouble. 8 Remember this, and shew yourselves men: bring it again to mind, O ye transgressors. 9 Remember the former things of old: for I am God, and there is none else; **I am God, and there is none like me**, 10 Declaring the end from the beginning, and from ancient times the things that are not yet done, saying, My counsel shall stand, and I will do all my pleasure: 11 Calling a ravenous bird from the east, the man that executeth my counsel from a far country: yea, I have spoken it, I will also bring it to pass; I have purposed it, I will also do it. 12 Hearken unto me, ye stouthearted, that are far from righteousness: 13 I bring near my righteousness; it shall not be far off, and my salvation shall not tarry: and I will place salvation in Zion for Israel my glory.

Jesus is both God and Man. The God who cannot die became a human through the miracle of the virgin birth, so that as a man He could die for our sins. Because Jesus is the omnipresent God, He is everywhere—all of

Him is in every point of the universe. When Jesus was talking to Nicodemus, He said, "And no man hath ascended up to heaven, but he that came down from heaven, even the Son of man **which is in heaven**" (John 3:13). Thus we see that as Jesus was talking to Nicodemus here on earth, He was at the same moment present also in Heaven. Jesus is both omnipresent God and Man, and therefore He is able to be our Savior.

8.1.6 Exposing deception #6

Meherally asked, "Would it not be an unfair practise on part of the Almighty God to have sent His son as a 'Saviour to all' thousands of years after Adam. Did not that deprive those born before the Christian Era of 'the easy way out' to the Salvation?"

By asking this question, Meherally again shows a great ignorance or disregard of what the Bible teaches about salvation. God's plan of salvation has always been the same, and will always be the same. Jesus is—and always has been—and always will be—the only way of salvation. Jesus is—and always has been, and always will be—the only way to God.

> John 14:6 Jesus saith unto him, **I am the way, the truth, and the life: no man cometh unto the Father, but by me**.

> Acts 4:8 Then Peter, filled with the Holy Ghost, said unto them, Ye rulers of the people, and elders of Israel, 9 If we this day be examined of the good deed done to the impotent man, by what means he is made whole; 10 Be it known unto you all, and to all the people of Israel, that **by the name of Jesus Christ of Nazareth, whom ye crucified, whom God raised from the dead**, even by him doth this man stand here before you whole. 11 This is the stone which was set at nought of you builders, which is become the head of the corner. 12 **Neither is there salvation in any other: for there is none other name under heaven given among men, whereby we must be saved**.

The whole Old Testament prophesied of Jesus Christ. Moses wrote about Jesus in the book of Genesis. The prophets wrote about Jesus. The Psalms speak of Jesus. Jesus is the central theme of the Bible.

> Luke 24: 36 And as they thus spake, Jesus himself stood in the midst of them, and saith unto them, Peace be unto you. 37 But they were terrified and affrighted, and supposed that they had seen a spirit. 38 And he said unto them, Why are ye troubled? and why do thoughts arise in your hearts? 39 Behold my hands and my feet, that it is I myself: handle me, and see; for a spirit hath not flesh and bones, as ye see me have. 40 And when he had thus spoken, he shewed them his hands and his feet. 41 And while they yet believed not for joy, and wondered, he said unto them, Have ye here any meat? 42 And they gave him a piece of a broiled fish, and of an honeycomb. 43 And he took it, and did eat before them. 44 And he said unto them, **These are the words which I spake unto you, while I was yet with you, that all things must be fulfilled, which were written in the law of Moses, and in the prophets, and in the psalms, concerning me. 45 Then opened he their understanding, that they might understand the scriptures, 46 And said unto them, Thus it is written, and thus it behoved Christ to suffer, and to rise from the dead the third day: 47 And that repentance and remission of sins should be preached in his name among all nations, beginning at Jerusalem.** 48 And ye are witnesses of these things. 49 And, behold, I send the promise of my Father upon you: but tarry ye in the city of Jerusalem, until ye be endued with power from on high. 50 And he led them out as far as to Bethany, and he lifted up his hands, and blessed them. 51 And it came to pass, while he blessed them, he was parted from them, and carried up into heaven. 52 **And they worshipped him**, and returned to Jerusalem with great joy: 53 And were continually in the temple, praising and blessing God. Amen.

Notice the above verse 44 carefully—Jesus said in that verse that the Old Testament

125

spoke of Him. That is what Jesus, Himself, said.

So, Jesus is the same Saviour God in the New Testament as He was in the Old Testament. Jesus saved the Old Testament believers by grace through faith, and Jesus saves New Testament believers by grace through faith.

> Ephesians 2: 8 For by **grace** are ye saved through **faith**; and that not of yourselves: it is the gift of God: 9 **Not of works**, lest any man should boast.

> Romans 4:1 What shall we say then that Abraham our father, as pertaining to the flesh, hath found? 2 For if Abraham were justified by works, he hath whereof to glory; but not before God. 3 For what saith the scripture? Abraham **believed God, and it was counted unto him for righteousness**. 4 Now to him that worketh is the reward not reckoned of grace, but of debt. 5 **But to him that worketh not, but believeth on him that justifieth the ungodly, his faith is counted for righteousness.** 6 Even as David also describeth the blessedness of the man, unto whom God imputeth righteousness **without works**, 7 Saying, Blessed are they whose iniquities are forgiven, and whose sins are covered. 8 Blessed is the man to whom the Lord will not impute sin.

Meherally is correct in calling this "'the easy way out' to the Salvation." This is, in fact, the ONLY way to salvation. Since salvation is "not of works" it **is** easy, and thank God it is easy, for otherwise we all would be damned to Hell.

On the other hand, Islam is the hard way of salvation—so hard that it is impossible to get to Heaven the Islam way.

> 2 Cor 11:14 And no marvel; for Satan himself is transformed into an angel of light. Therefore it is no great thing if his ministers also be transformed as the ministers of righteousness; whose end shall be according to their works.

8.1.7 Exposing deception #7

Is the idea of Jesus' death as atonement for the sins of all humanity...morally repugnant, as Meherally and Harpur argue? To wicked, proud-hearted men it is repugnant because it declares men to be sinners unable to save themselves. The only way of salvation is for men to humble themselves before the true God and let Him save them. Proud, arrogant men who consciously or unconsciously think that they have god-like power to save their own selves will be cast into Hell.

But the idea of Jesus' death as atonement for the sins of all humanity is not repugnant to God, for it is God's idea—it is God's only plan to save the world.

> Romans 5:10 For if, **when we were enemies, we were reconciled to God by the death of his Son**, much more, being reconciled, we shall be saved by his life. 11 And not only so, but we also joy in God through our Lord Jesus Christ, by whom we have now received the **atonement**. 12 Wherefore, as by one man sin entered into the world, and death by sin; and so death passed upon all men, for that all have sinned: 13 (For until the law sin was in the world: but sin is not imputed when there is no law. 14 Nevertheless death reigned from Adam to Moses, even over them that had not sinned after the similitude of Adam's transgression, who is the figure of him that was to come. 15 But not as the offence, so also is the free gift. For if through the offence of one many be dead, much more the **grace** of God, and the gift by grace, which is by one man, Jesus Christ, hath abounded unto many. 16 And not as it was by one that sinned, so is the gift: for the judgment was by one to condemnation, but the **free gift** is of many offences unto justification. 17 **For if by one man's offence death reigned by one; much more they which receive abundance of grace and of the gift of righteousness shall reign in life by one, Jesus Christ.**) 18 Therefore as by the offence of one judgment came upon all men to condemnation; even so by the **righteousness** of one the **free gift** came upon all men unto justification

of life. 19 **For as by one man's disobedience many were made sinners, so by the obedience of one shall many be made righteous.** 20 Moreover the law entered, that the offence might abound. But where sin abounded, grace did much more abound: 21 That as sin hath reigned unto death, even so might grace reign through righteousness unto **eternal life** by Jesus Christ our Lord.

And the doctrine of the atonement is not new to the New Testament. The word atonement is found 80 times in the Old Testament. An example:

Leviticus 17: 11 For **the life of the flesh is in the blood**: and I have given it to you upon the altar to make an **atonement** for your souls: for it is the **blood** that maketh an **atonement** for the soul. 12 Therefore I said unto the children of Israel, No soul of you shall eat blood, neither shall any stranger that sojourneth among you eat blood. 13 And whatsoever man there be of the children of Israel, or of the strangers that sojourn among you, which hunteth and catcheth any beast or fowl that may be eaten; he shall even pour out the blood thereof, and cover it with dust. 14 For it is the life of all flesh; the blood of it is for the life thereof: therefore I said unto the children of Israel, Ye shall eat the blood of no manner of flesh: for the life of all flesh is the blood thereof: whosoever eateth it shall be cut off.

Additional clarification:

Hebrews 9:11 But Christ being come an high priest of good things to come, by a greater and more perfect tabernacle, not made with hands, that is to say, not of this building; 12 Neither by the blood of goats and calves, but **by his own blood** he entered in **once** into the holy place, having obtained **eternal redemption** for us. 13 For if the blood of bulls and of goats, and the ashes of an heifer sprinkling the unclean, sanctifieth to the purifying of the flesh: 14 **How much more shall the blood of Christ, who through the eternal Spirit offered himself without spot to God, purge your conscience from dead works to serve the living God?**

8.1.8 Exposing deception #8

Is it true—as Meherally argues—"that Jesus **never**...said anything to indicate that forgiveness from God could only be granted 'after' or 'because of' the cross"'? No, this is not true. Jesus is God, and all of the verses of the Bible are the words of God. Note this verse:

Acts 5:30 The God of our fathers raised up **Jesus, whom ye slew and hanged on a tree**. 31 Him hath God exalted with his right hand to be a Prince and a Saviour, for to give repentance to Israel, and **forgiveness of sins**.

The "tree" in the above verse is referring to the cross.

Without the substitutionary death of Jesus Christ on the cross for our sins there could be no forgiveness of sins. It is needful to realize, however, that this forgiveness was also given to all the Old Testament believers in Christ at the moment they believed in the coming Messiah (Jesus) who would die for their sins.

Beware! Islamic deception follows:

HOT TIP:
"And there is no other God besides Me, A righteous God and a Saviour; There is none except Me. 'Turn to Me, and be saved, all the ends of the earth; For I am God, and there is no other." Isaiah 45:21-22. (please also read Hosea 13:4). When God said; "all the ends of the earth" He righteously meant it to be so. The era of "cross" should make no difference. BTW, if you truly accept the end part of the quoted Isaiah, you have accepted the first half of the 'Confession of Islamic Faith' called "Shahadah".

Quoting Isaiah 45:21-22 doesn't prove any points for Islam. Let's look at those verses in context.

Isaiah 45:11 Thus saith the **LORD**, the **Holy One of Israel**, and his Maker, Ask me of things to come concerning my sons, and concerning the work of my hands command ye me. 12 I have made the earth, and created man upon it: I, even my hands, have stretched out the heavens, and all their host have I commanded. 13 I have raised him up in righteousness, and I will direct all his ways: he shall build my city, and he shall let go my captives, not for price nor reward, saith the LORD of hosts. 14 Thus saith the LORD, The labour of Egypt, and merchandise of Ethiopia and of the Sabeans, men of stature, shall come over unto thee, and they shall be thine: they shall come after thee; in chains they shall come over, and **they shall fall down unto thee, they shall make supplication unto thee, saying, Surely God is in thee; and there is none else, there is no God.** 15 Verily thou art a God that hidest thyself, O God **of Israel**, the **Saviour**. 16 They shall be ashamed, and also confounded, all of them: they shall go to confusion together that are makers of idols. 17 **But Israel shall be saved in the LORD with an everlasting salvation: ye shall not be ashamed nor confounded world without end.** 18 For thus saith the LORD that created the heavens; God himself that formed the earth and made it; he hath established it, he created it not in vain, he formed it to be inhabited: **I am the LORD; and there is none else.** 19 I have not spoken in secret, in a dark place of the earth: I said not unto the seed of Jacob, Seek ye me in vain: I the LORD speak righteousness, I declare things that are right. 20 Assemble yourselves and come; draw near together, ye that are escaped of the nations: they have no knowledge that set up the wood of their graven image, and pray unto a god that cannot save. 21 Tell ye, and bring them near; yea, let them take counsel together: who hath declared this from ancient time? who hath told it from that time? have not I the LORD? and **there is no God else beside me; a just God and a Saviour; there is none beside me. 22 Look unto me, and be ye saved**, all the ends of the earth: for **I am God, and there is none else.** 23 I have sworn by myself, the word is gone out of my mouth in righteousness, and shall not return, That unto me every knee shall bow, every tongue shall swear. 24 Surely, shall one say, in

the LORD have I righteousness and strength: even to him shall men come; and all that are incensed against him shall be ashamed. 25 **In the LORD shall all the seed of Israel be justified, and shall glory.**

Note the important facts in the above verses that Muslim teachers don't want you to see:

⇨ It is not Allah that is speaking in these verses, but the LORD—JEHOVAH. Verse 11.

⇨ JEHOVAH is the Holy One of **Israel**, not the unholy one of Arabia. Verse 11.

⇨ JEHOVAH is the God of the **Israeli** nation, not the god of **Arab** nations. Verse 15. Though He will also be the God of any individual Arab who will trust Him as Savior.

⇨ **Israel** as a nation shall be saved in JEHOVAH with an **everlasting salvation**, and shall **not be ashamed nor confounded world without end**, not wiped off the face of the earth like Islam teaches. Verse 17.

⇨ In JEHOVAH "**all the seed of Israel** shall be **justified**, and shall **glory**." Verse 25. How different this is from what Israel-hating Islam teaches!

⇨ There is no God else beside JEHOVAH, so Allah is not God, but is an idol created in Muhammad's vain imagination. Verses 14, 18, 21, and 22.

⇨ JEHOVAH is the only Savior. Verse 15, and 21-22. You can't save yourself.

⇨ JEHOVAH is just. Verse 21. Therefore JEHOVAH does not make exceptions to His laws for anyone, and is thus very different from Allah who made exceptions many times for Muhammad.

The important question is, Who is JEHOVAH? We find the answer in Romans where the above verse is quoted.

> Romans 14:9 For to this end **Christ both died, and rose, and revived, that he might be Lord both of the dead and living.** 10 But why dost thou judge thy brother? or why dost thou set at nought thy brother? **for we shall all stand before the judgment seat of Christ.** 11 For it is written, **As I live, saith the Lord, every knee shall bow to me, and every tongue shall confess to God.** 12 So then every one of us shall give account of himself to God.

Jesus Christ is JEHOVAH, for JEHOVAH God was in Christ reconciling the world unto Himself.

> 2 Corinthians 5:18 And all things are of God, who hath reconciled us to himself by Jesus Christ, and hath given to us the ministry of reconciliation; 19 To wit, that **God was in Christ**, reconciling the world unto himself, not imputing their trespasses unto them; and hath committed unto us the word of reconciliation.

> Colossians 2:8 **Beware** lest any man spoil you through philosophy and vain deceit, after the tradition of men, after the rudiments of the world, and not after **Christ.** 9 **For in him dwelleth all the fulness of the Godhead bodily.**

Hosea 13:4 also doesn't help Islam, for it declares that the LORD (JEHOVAH) is Israel's God, and there is no savior beside Him. That excludes Allah or Muhammad from being a savior.

> Hosea 13:4 Yet I am the LORD thy God from the land of Egypt, and thou shalt know no god but me: for there is no saviour beside me.

HOTTER TIP than Meherally's hot tip:

God cannot be righteous if He is not just. Justice demands that sin be punished. The punishment for sin is death. "For the wages of sin is death" (Rom. 6:23a). Because God is just, He will not forgive a person whose sin has not first been punished. Jesus took the punishment for our sins so that we could be forgiven. Islam's Allah is an unjust god if he forgives people without first demanding punishment for their sins. And an unjust god cannot possibly be the true God. We shall see in a later chapter that Muhammad taught that all Muslims, including himself, will go to Hell to pay the price for their own sins. Is that where you want to go?

By the way, there is not even one verse in the Quran that says that Allah or Muhammad is the Savior. Islam teaches that people must be their own savior. Islam teaches that people must save themselves by refraining from sins and obeying the laws of Islam. The problem is that people do not refrain from sinning, but instead sin a lot. What about you, dear reader? Do you honestly think your good deeds outweigh your bad deeds? And even if you think they do, do you honestly think that God will allow a 25 or 30 percent bad person into Heaven? If a man murdered your loved one, would you consider it just for the judge to forgive him of the crime and let him go because he was religious and had done no other sin? Would you drink a glass of water if it had only one drop of sewer water in it? The true God is holy, and demands perfect holiness from everyone.

> James 2:8 If ye fulfil the royal law according to the scripture, Thou shalt love thy neighbour as thyself, ye do well: 9 But if ye have respect to persons, ye commit sin, and are convinced of the law as transgressors. 10 For whosoever shall keep the **whole** law, and yet offend in **one** point, **he is guilty of all.**

> Galatians 3:10 For as many as are of the works of the law are under the curse: for it is written, **Cursed** is every one that continueth not in **all** things which are written in the book of the law to **do** them.

8.2 Was not Jesus God from the beginning?

Question No.15 [from a Christian to Islamic teacher Meherally.]

From the prologue of John's Gospel, I have a very valid and legitimate three part question:- (a) Was not Jesus God from the beginning? Verse upholding (a); In the beginning was the Word, and the Word was with God, and the Word was God. (John 1:1) (b) Were not all things made through Jesus?? Verses upholding (b); He was in the beginning with God. All things came into being through him; and apart from him nothing came into being that has come into being. (John 1:2-3) (c) Was not Jesus made flesh and dwelt among us??? Verse upholding (c); And the Word became flesh, and dwelt among us, and we beheld his glory, glory as of the only begotten from the Father, full of grace and truth. (John 1:14)

| Beware! Islamic deception follows: |

Answer No.15
This three part question is so often repeated, collectively or individually, that I will try to answer them (God-willing), from various perspectives. For an uncomplicated comprehension, I am going to separate the three part question into three separate questions. In this number fifteen, I will deal with part (a) above.
1. The verse insinuates "Jesus was God from the beginning" because Christians have, for the last numerous generations, embraced the concept of SUBSTITUTING the word "Word" (Greek term 'Logos') with "Jesus". John did not write "Jesus". It is a SUBSTITUTION.
2. One can only SUBSTITUTE (of course with admissible logic), the original term *IF* the LITERAL translation of the used

term fails to reconcile with the rest of the text. Unfortunately, as you will soon discover, the situation here is the other way around.
3. Please read the last two lines from (a) with the SUBSTITUTION. It reads; "and Jesus was with God and Jesus was God." How can Jesus be "with" God and "was" God, as well? It defies the logic. The SUBSTITUTION creates an enigmatic dilemma to which the Christian scholars have yet to find an answer.
4. The norm of accepting the SUBSTITUTION has been so deep rooted that no believing Christian scholar has sincerely attempted to find out what in reality is the LITERAL translation. Let us do it together. The Greek term 'Logos' is derived from the root word 'Lego' meaning 'to speak'. The literal translation of 'Logos' is 'something spoken or thought'. The verification of the above translation is simple. Please pick up your English Dictionary and look for the word 'Decalogue'. Surprised! It reads; 'The Ten Commandments'. (deka=ten; logous=commands). Now please flip a few more pages of your dictionary and go to the word 'Logos'. Please look for the word origin. In my pocket 'Oxford Dictionary' it reads; "[Gk, = reason, discourse, (rarely) word]."
5. Having discovered the LITERAL translation of the word "Logos" used by apostle John, let us read (a): In the beginning was the 'spoken word, command', and the 'spoken word, command' was with God, and the 'spoken word, command' was Divine. (John 1:1)
6. The LITERAL translation is not only logical but it coincides perfectly with the prologue of the Book of Genesis. "In the beginning God created the heavens and the earth." "And the God said, Let there be light; and there was light." (Genesis 1:1 and 3) ^^^^^
7. You may now ask, why did I translate "Divine" instead of "God" in the last line?.

The answer is based upon the usage of Greek grammar. In the second line, the phrase used by John for "God" is 'ho theo', meaning 'the God'. In the last line it is simply 'theo', the definitive article 'the' is not used. Why? Because, it is a predicate of the subject 'ho theo'. The predicate is used to denote the nature, quality, attribute or property of the subject. Here the in this instance the nature of the God's spoken command was Divine.

8. In 'New translation of the Bible' (1922) by the famous Dr. James Moffatt, it reads; "the Logos was Divine." And, also in 'The Complete Bible - An American Translation' (Smith-Goodspeed) and 'The Authentic New Testament' by Hugh J. Schonfield. Please look for No. 16 and 17 for answers to (b) and (c) above.

First of all, I point out again that Meherally almost always quotes from some translation other than the King James Version of 1611. Why? Because the other translations were made from corrupted Greek texts which contain changes to the original text, and because the other translations were made by unbelievers like himself who do not like what the Bible says, and so have changed it to suit their own vain thinking.

Now concerning Meherally's talk about substitution, all he is trying to do is distract you from the obvious meaning of the text. He is simply lying to you. These verses disprove his religion, so he has to change their meaning somehow. Meherally claims to believe the Bible out of one side of his mouth, but out of the other side of his mouth he denies all it teaches. Such a man cannot be trusted to either translate or interpret the Bible. This is to say nothing of his obvious ignorance of the Greek language—he is just hoping that you are even more ignorant of Greek than he is so that you will not be able to realize his ignorance. Anyone can lie—that is easy to do. But we must not be

so naive as to believe the lies. Let us not be among "them that perish; because they received not **the love of the truth**, that they might be saved" (2 Thessalonians 2:10).

I recommend that you read John 1:1-14 carefully, and be honest with yourself as to its meaning. Here it is:

> John 1:1 In the beginning was the **Word**, and **the Word was with God**, and **the Word was God**. 2 The same was in the beginning with God. 3 All things were made by him; and without him was not any thing made that was made. 4 In him was life; and the life was the light of men. 5 And the light shineth in darkness; and the darkness comprehended it not. 6 There was a man sent from God, whose name was John. 7 The same came for a witness, to bear witness of the Light, that all men through him might believe. 8 He was not that Light, but was sent to bear witness of that Light. 9 That was the true Light, which lighteth every man that cometh into the world. 10 He was in the world, and the world was made by him, and the world knew him not. 11 He came unto his own, and his own received him not. 12 But as many as received him, to them gave he power to become the sons of God, even to them that believe on his name: 13 Which were born, not of blood, nor of the will of the flesh, nor of the will of man, but of God. 14 **And the Word was made flesh, and dwelt among us, (and we beheld his glory, the glory as of the only begotten of the Father,) full of grace and truth.**

Notice especially verse 14. God is called "the Father" in this verse. And the "the Word" is the "only begotten of the Father" who was "made flesh." In other words, the Word was in existence before He was made flesh. The Word is the "only begotten of the Father." This Word is Jesus.

Is it not exceedingly obvious now that Meherally is lying when he says that he believes the Bible to be Scripture? He does not believe the Bible, and he does not want you to believe it either.

The translators of the King James Version of 1611 were some of the very best Greek and Hebrew language scholars to ever be assembled. They did not mistranslate Theos. The Greek word for Divine is "Theias" (see 2 Pet. 1:3-4), not "Theos." However, even "Theias" is used only in reference to God, so Meherally's argument is meaningless. If Jesus is Divine then He is God.

Meherally asks, "How can Jesus be "with" God and "was" God, as well?" The answer is that God is omnipresent, omnipotent, and a Trinity. God is not like man. Man has only one person, but God has three separate Persons, and those three Persons are the one true God. The true God is too high for Meherally's logic, so he prefers instead to believe in Allah. Interestingly, the Quran's description of Allah fits the Bible's description of a very powerful being who was nevertheless impotent in the sense of being unable to father a child. This being will be discussed in chapter 12.

Beware! Islamic deception follows:

HOT TIP:
Paul wrote; "...if any man is preaching to you a Gospel contrary to which you received, let him be accursed (anathema)." Gal. 1:9.

DOUBLE HOT TIP: Meherally's quote of Gal. 1:9 can be made even stronger by showing the context. Here it is:

> Galatians 1:6 I marvel that ye are so soon removed from him that called you into **the grace of Christ** unto **another gospel**: 7 **Which is not another**; but there be some that trouble you, and would **pervert** the **gospel of Christ**. 8 **But though we, or an angel from heaven, preach any other gospel unto you than that which we have preached unto you, let him be accursed.** 9 As we said before, so say I now again, **If any man preach any other gospel unto you than that ye have received, let him be accursed**.

Note that we are warned in verse seven that there are people who would pervert the gospel of Christ, just as Meherally is doing. They will teach another gospel which is a false gospel. What is the true gospel? Here it is:

> 1 Corinthians 15:1 Moreover, brethren, I declare unto you **the gospel** which I preached unto you, which also ye have received, and wherein ye stand; 2 By which also ye are saved, if ye keep in memory what I preached unto you, unless ye have believed in vain. 3 For I delivered unto you first of all that which I also received, how that **Christ died for our sins according to the scriptures; 4 And that he was buried, and that he rose again the third day according to the scriptures.**

The true gospel is "how that Christ died for our sins according to the scriptures; and that he was buried, and that he rose again the third day according to the scriptures." If anyone preaches any other gospel, "let him be accursed."

What did Muhammad teach? The following verses from the Quran (shown in three translations) are generally interpreted by Muslims to mean that Jesus did not die for our sins, was not buried, and so did not rise from the dead, but rather was taken up to Heaven without dying.

004.157

YUSUFALI: That they said (in boast), "We killed Christ Jesus the son of Mary, the Messenger of Allah";- but they killed him not, nor crucified him, but so it was made to appear to them, and those who differ therein are full of doubts, with no (certain) knowledge, but only conjecture to follow, for of a surety they killed him not:-

PICKTHAL: And because of their saying: We slew the Messiah, Jesus son of Mary, Allah's messenger - they slew him not nor crucified him, but it appeared so unto them; and lo! those who disagree concerning it are in doubt thereof; they have no knowledge thereof save pursuit of a conjecture; they slew him not for certain.

SHAKIR: And their saying: Surely we have killed the Messiah, Isa son of Marium, the messenger of Allah; and they did not kill him nor did they crucify him, but it appeared to them so (like Isa) and most surely those who differ therein are only in a doubt about it; they have no knowledge respecting it, but only follow a conjecture, and they killed him not for sure.

004.158

YUSUFALI: Nay, Allah raised him up unto Himself; and Allah is Exalted in Power, Wise;-

PICKTHAL: But Allah took him up unto Himself. Allah was ever Mighty, Wise.

SHAKIR: Nay! Allah took him up to Himself; and Allah is Mighty, Wise.

Since Islam teaches the exact opposite of the gospel—Islam teaches that Christ did not die for our sins, and was not buried, and did not rise from the dead—the curse mentioned in Galatians 1:6-9 most certainly applies to Muhammad and every Islamic teacher. The **only way** for them to get out from under that curse is to repent of their false gospel, and believe the true gospel of Jesus Christ.

Note also that Galatians 1:8 says, "But though we, **or an angel from heaven,** preach any other gospel unto you than that which we have preached unto you, let him be accursed." Muhammad claimed that the angel Gabriel gave him the surahs of the Quran. It obviously was an angel that gave the Quran to Muhammad, but it wasn't Gabriel. Which angel it actually was will be discussed in chapter 12.

There is another related major problem that Muslims need to face. Muhammad claimed to believe the books of the former prophets, but his Quran totally denies the core doctrines taught in those books. This serious contradiction in the Quran proves it is not of God.

Figure 8.1: *Osama bin Laden did not hijack Islam, but rather Islam hijacked him, and coverted him into a lustful polygamist, hateful racist, and cruel, cold-blooded mass murderer of innocent people. He had a large collection of pornography is his home when he died. Did the life of this follower of Muhammad comfort you? Were his fruits righteous fruits or wicked fruits? Did his faith in Muhammad's theology cause him to be a good man or an evil man? Did he practice and promote love or hatred?*

Galatians 5:19 Now the works of the flesh are manifest, which are these; Adultery, fornication, uncleanness, lasciviousness, 20 Idolatry, witchcraft, hatred, variance, emulations, wrath, strife, seditions, heresies, 21 Envyings, murders, drunkenness, revellings, and such like: of the which I tell you before, as I have also told you in time past, that they which do such things shall not inherit the kingdom of God. 22 But the fruit of the Spirit is love, joy, peace, longsuffering, gentleness, goodness, faith, 23 Meekness, temperance: against such there is no law.

Figure 8.2: *Though she looks much older in this picture, this Somali girl was only 13 years old. Aisha, was raped by three men. When her family reported it to the Muslim authorities, they accused her of adultery, buried her in a hole chest deep, and 50 men stoned her as about 1,000 people watched. As they dug her out of the hole, they found her still alive. So, they buried her again, and stoned her till she died. But none of the rapists were arrested. So much for justice under sharia law. But some day those three rapists, and the Muslim authorities who so unjustly murdered this girl, will stand before Jesus at the Great White Throne Judgment, and justice will be done as Jesus has them cast into the Lake of Fire to be tormented day and night forever and ever.*

Chapter 9

Deceptive Muslim Answers To Christian's Questions 16–19

As will be shown in this chapter, the Bible clearly tells us that Jesus is God, the creator of all things, and that He became a sinless human by being born of a virgin so that He might save us from our sins. Muslim teachers use very cleaver deception to try to explain away these vital facts, as we will see.

9.1   Is Jesus the Creator?

Question No.16 [from a Christian to Islamic teacher Meherally.]

From the prologue of John's Gospel, I have a very valid and legitimate three part question:- (a) Was not Jesus God from the beginning? Verse upholding (a); In the beginning was the Word, and the Word was with God, and the Word was God. (John 1:1) (b) Were not all things made through Jesus?? Verses upholding (b); He was in the beginning with God. All things came into being through him; and apart from him nothing came into being that has come into being. (John 1:2-3) (c) Was not Jesus made flesh and dwelt among us??? Verse upholding (c); And the Word be-

came flesh, and dwelt among us, and we beheld his glory, glory as of the only begotten from the Father, full of grace and truth. (John 1:14)

Beware! Islamic deception follows:

Answer No.16
Below is a response to part (b) above. Part (a) has been replied under FAQ number 15. Part (c) will be replied under FAQ number 17. 1. The opening word of John 1:2 in the Greek text is 'houtos' (3778), which translates 'the same'. The usage of word "He" in the above quote, is based upon the traditional concept of SUBSTITUTING the Greek term "Logos" with "Jesus", as explained in FAQ 15. 2. In the King James Version, it reads; "The same was in the beginning with God", which supports the above clarification. 3. Based upon the LITERAL translation of the word "Logos" as explained in FAQ 15, the verse should read; "The same (i.e. the spoken divine word, command) was in the beginning with the God." This LITERAL translation coincides with the opening of the Old Testament. (Genesis 1:3,6,11,14,20 & 24). 4. In John 1:3 above, the Greek word used for "him" is 'autos' (846), which means;

her, it (-self); (self-) the same; (him-, my-, thy-,) self; etc. If one was to continue the LITERAL translation from the beginning, the verse should read; All things came into being through it; and apart from it nothing came into being that has come into being. (John 1:3) Here "it" stands for "the spoken divine word, command."

Meherally's use of Greek would really be funny were he not deceiving many people. He changes words to mean whatever he wants. Anything can be proven that way. The Quran could say, "Allah has no son." And we could just say that in the original Arabic all the words actually mean something else. Let's see, "Allah" could mean "Triune God," and "no" could mean "one." Thus the "LITERAL" meaning of "Allah has no son," would be the "Triune God has one Son." That is the same kind of silly logic that Meherally is using.

Beware! Islamic deception follows:

5. For some reason, one was to quote Colossians 1:16 which reads; "For in Him all things were created, both in the heaven and on earth, visible and invisible, whether thrones or dominions or rulers or authorities - all things have been created through Him and for Him." And, go on contending that in the above letter by Paul, "Him" refers to "Jesus", and his/her beliefs are valid, please let him/her read the following. 6. In 'The Oxford Companion to the Bible', edited by Bruce M. Metzger and Michael D. Coogan, published by the Oxford University Press, on page 127, it reads; "The Pauline authorship of Colossians has often been challenged over the last 160 years. The grounds for this questioning concern the language and style of the letter; more recently it has been argued that there are major differences between Colossians and the

theology of the main Pauline letters, particularly in relation to the person and cosmic work of Christ, the Church as the body of Christ, and early Christian tradition." 7. If all things, including men and women were created through Jesus, then the righteous Jesus would not have told the Pharisees that from the beginning "God" created man and woman. (Matt. 19:4). 8. However, if the person is unwilling to write-off the so called canonical letter by Paul on the basis of the above two observations, please ask him/her to read the quoted scripture below which unequivocally tells us that "God" created man, made the earth and stretched out the heavens with HIS OWN HANDS. HOT TIP:
"It is I who made the earth, and created man upon it. I stretched out the heavens with My hands, And I ordained all their host." (Isaiah 45:12). Please also read Psalms 147-148, where the Psalmist bids Zion to "Praise your (their) God", who has done multitude of things and created; the heavens, the heights, His angels, His hosts, Sun, Moon, Stars and the waters that are above the heavens, by His own Command.

The reader will be wise to note once again how Meherally changes words in verses to weaken or change the meaning of the verse. Here is the correct reading of Col. 1:16 in its context:

Colossians 1:12 Giving thanks unto **the Father**, which hath made us meet to be partakers of the inheritance of the saints in light: 13 Who hath delivered us from the power of darkness, and hath translated us into the kingdom of **his dear Son**: 14 **In whom we have redemption through his blood, even the forgiveness of sins**: 15 **Who is the image of the invisible God**, the firstborn of every creature: 16 **For by him were all things created, that are in heaven, and that are in earth, visible and invisible, whether they be thrones, or dominions, or principalities, or powers: all things were created by him, and for him**: 17 And he is **before** all things, and by him all things consist. 18 And he is the head of the body, the church: who is the beginning, **the firstborn from the dead**; that in **all things he** might have the **preeminence**. 19 For it pleased the Father that in him should all fulness dwell; 20 And, having made peace through **the blood of his cross**, by him to reconcile all things unto himself; by him, I say, whether they be things in earth, or things in heaven. 21 And you, that were sometime alienated and enemies in your mind by wicked works, yet now hath he reconciled 22 **In the body of his flesh through death**, to present you holy and unblameable and unreproveable in his sight: 23 If ye continue in the faith grounded and settled, and be not moved away from the hope of the gospel, which ye have heard, and which was preached to every creature which is under heaven; whereof I Paul am made a minister;

Some of the teachings in the above verses that disprove Islam have been placed in boldface.

Compare verse 16 to Meherally's rendering of it above. Meherally changed "**by** him were all things created" to "**in** him all things were created." Then in the last half of the verse he changed "**by** him" to "**through** him." Such changes are deceitful and dishonest. But even that is not sufficient for him, so he wants to throw out the whole book of Colossians! Actually, of course, he wants to throw out the whole Bible because it diproves Islam.

Meherally uses the testimony of unbelieving false Christians to try to discredit the Bible, while ignoring the evil fruits of the Quran which brand it as a Satan-inspired, man-made document. The Quran claims to quote the Bible, but not one copy of such a Bible as it supposedly quotes has ever been found! Every area of earth controlled by people that believe the Quran is devoid of freedom—free speech is forbidden, and people fear for their lives in expressing any criticism of Islam. The Quran is racist—it causes people to hate Jews and other non-Muslims. The Quran promotes terrorism and violence. Something is definitely phony about the Quran.

The Bible correctly prophesied what Ishmael's nature would be like:

> Genesis 16:11 And the angel of the LORD said unto her, Behold, thou art with child, and shalt bear a son, and shalt call his name **Ishmael**; because the LORD hath heard thy affliction.12 And **he will be a wild man**; his hand will be against every man, and every man's hand against him; and he shall dwell in the presence of all his brethren.

Those verses perfectly describe Ishmael's descendant, Muhammad, and Muhammad's Quran also—a wild man with a wild book. A terrorist with a terrorist manual. Islam is a religion of hatred and violence and insanity produced by demonic possession.

Do not forget what the Bible says will happen to people who add to or take away from the Bible:

> Revelation 22:18 For I testify unto every man that heareth the words of the prophecy of this book, **If any man shall add unto these things, God shall add unto him the plagues that are written in this book**: 19 And **if any man shall take away from the words of the book of this prophecy, God shall take away his part out of the book of life, and out of the holy city, and from the things which are written in this book.**

Muhammad **added** the Quran to the Bible; or, more accurately, **took away** everything in the Bible that he disagreed with (almost everything) and then **added**—to what little was left—his own vain beliefs. **Therefore, according to Rev. 22:18-19, unto Muhammad has been added the plagues written in the Bible, and God has taken away his part out of the book of life.** He is burning in the agonies of Hell today, and will be tormented in the flames of the Lake of Fire for eternity.

137

9.2 Was not Jesus made flesh to dwell among us?

Question No.17 [from a Christian to Islamic teacher Meherally.]

From the prologue of John's Gospel, I have a very valid and legitimate three part question:- (a) Was not Jesus God from the beginning? Verse upholding (a); In the beginning was the Word, and the Word was with God, and the Word was God. (John 1:1) (b) Were not all things made through Jesus?? Verses upholding (b); He was in the beginning with God. All things came into being through him; and apart from him nothing came into being that has come into being. (John 1:2-3) (c) Was not Jesus made flesh and dwelt among us??? Verse upholding (c); And the Word became flesh, and dwelt among us, and we beheld his glory, glory as of the only begotten from the Father, full of grace and truth. (John 1:14)

Beware! Islamic deception follows:

Answer No.17
Below is a response to part (c) above. Parts (a) and (b) have been replied under FAQ 15 and 16. 1. To comprehend what apostle John wrote in (c) above, one has to read what John wrote ten verses earlier, i.e. in John 1:4. According to the LITERAL translation, in that verse, John wrote; "In it was life; and the life was the light of men." 2. As demonstrated earlier the word "it" stands for "Logos" (the divine command that was in the beginning with the God). Consequently, "In it (in the God's command was life); and that life was the light (the guidance, enlightenment) for men." 3. I have rendered "light" as the guidance and enlightenment, because in 1:9 John wrote;

"There was the true light which, coming into the world, enlightens every man". 4. Unfortunately, "And the light shines in the darkness; and the darkness did not comprehend it (him)." (John 1:5). Note: In either case; the word "it" which stands for God's command, or "him" which stands for Jesus, makes sense. 5. Going back to (c) above; "And the Word became flesh, and dwelt among us, and we beheld his glory, glory as of the only begotten from the Father, full of grace and truth." (John 1:14). What the apostle LITERALLY meant was; "And the Logos (the God's command, which was from the beginning with God, wherein was the life) became flesh, and dwelt among us,..." 6. Briefly, the embodiment in flesh was of "Logos" - the God's command, and NOT of the God. The conception of Jesus within the womb of his mother, Virgin Mary, was in reality made possible by an act of God's command - the "Logos". Jesus was neither God nor the physical incarnation of God. 7. The entire text which reads; "and we be held his glory, the glory as of the only begotten of the Father" is written within parentheses in the Kings James Version. Hence, it is considered as the editor's enhanced notes or addendum. 8. As for the true meaning of the original term used by John in his Gospel, for the mistranslated phrase "the only begotten", please see the earlier answers.

Meherally continues to bring the curse of Revelation 22:18-19 upon himself by both taking from and adding to God's word. He takes away the word "him," and adds the word "it" to replace "him." Also, in spite of what Meherally says, "Him" does not LITERALLY mean "it"—not in the English and not in the Greek. Also, "Logos" does **not** mean "command;" "Logos" means "Word." Also, in the King James Bible—which is the only trustworthy English translation—putting words within parentheses does not make them into editor's notes or addendum—that is just more of Meherally's lying. The Bible is not a collection of silly poems like the Quran. The Bible literally means what it says in context. The Bible is not an attempt to hide God from us. Rather, the Bible is God's revelation of Himself to us.

Beware! Islamic deception follows:

HOT TIP:

To those who prefer to contend; (a) "and the Word (Jesus) was *with* God" (John 1:1). (b) "He (Jesus) was in the beginning *with* God" (John 1:2). (c) "And the Word (Jesus) *became* flesh" (John 1:14) they have no recourse but to admit that it was either at the *beginning* or after the act of *becoming* happened, "Jesus" who was "with" God or "became" flesh, had to be either an additional, other, different, distinct, or dissimilar entity than the God. Now, having no way to retreat, please read the following: "No one can serve two masters;..." Matthew 6:24 If you wish choose the ONE and the only Master, please read; "Now to the King eternal, immortal, invisible, the only God, be honour and glory forever and ever. Amen." 1 Timothy 1:17 Can any one deny; "Jesus" who dwelt among us, was "visible"!

HOTTER TIP:

Like most Muslim leaders, Meherally presents Christians as believing differently than they really believe, then he tries to disprove this make-believe belief. In this case, Meherally tries to make it appear that Christians believe that Jesus is God only. But that is not what the Bible teaches and is not what true Christians believe. The Bible teaches that Jesus is the invisible God, but also that Jesus is a visible man. That is why Jesus is called the "image of the invisible God."

Colossians 1:12 Giving thanks unto **the Father**, which hath made us meet to be partakers of the inheritance of the saints in light: 13 Who hath delivered us from the power of darkness, and hath translated us into the kingdom of **his dear Son**: 14 **In whom we have redemption through his blood, even the forgiveness of sins**: 15 **Who is the image of the invisible God**, the firstborn of every creature: 16 For **by him were all things created**, that are in heaven, and that are in earth, visible and invisible, whether they be thrones, or dominions, or principalities, or powers: all **things were created by him, and for him**: 17 **And he is before all things, and by him all things consist**.

Muslims should note all the deceit of their leaders, and should realize that they are being led astray. Does your leader want you to become a suicide bomber? If yes, that should show you that he cares nothing about your soul. Are you afraid right now that some other Muslims might see you reading this document and think that you are seriously considering what it says? If yes, then in your heart you know that Islam is a religion of threats and fear. Have you been taught to hate Jews? If yes, then you know that Islam is a racist religion full of hate for people simply because they were born into a certain ethnic group. How do you know that you are not a Jew? I read once of a man who was raised among Muslims. Out of fear of their neighbors, his parents led him to believe that they were Arab Muslims, when in fact they were Jewish. Most of his friends were Muslims, and from them he developed a fierce hatred of Jews. Imagine his shock the day he learned that he was one of those "monkeys and pigs" he had learned to so despise. You might be a jew also.

1 John 2:11 But **he that hateth his brother is in darkness**, and walketh in darkness, and knoweth not whither he goeth, because that darkness hath blinded his eyes.

1 John 3:15 **Whosoever hateth his brother is a murderer**: and ye know that **no murderer hath eternal life** abiding in him.

1 John 4:20 **If a man say, I love God, and hateth his brother, he is a liar**: for he that

loveth not his brother whom he hath seen, how can he love God whom he hath not seen?

Clearly, according to the Bible, if you say you love God, but you hate Jews, then you are a liar and murderer, walking in darkness, and do not have eternal life.

We love Muslims enough to tell them the truth. We do not want Muslims to go to Hell. We want Muslims to go to Heaven. The only way to be saved from going to Hell so as to be allowed into Heaven is to separate from Islam, and believe in the Lord Jesus Christ. It would be hatred for us not to tell Muslims the truth about these things, and thereby let them proceed ignorantly into a Devil's Hell.

> John 3:16 For **God so loved the world**, that he gave **his only begotten Son**, that **whosoever believeth in him should not perish, but have everlasting life**. 17 For **God** sent not **his Son** into the world to condemn the world; but that the world through him might be saved. 18 **He that believeth on him is not condemned: but he that believeth not is condemned already**, because he hath not believed in the name of **the only begotten Son of God**. 19 And this is the condemnation, that light is come into the world, and men loved darkness rather than light, because their deeds were evil. 20 For **every one that doeth evil hateth the light, neither cometh to the light, lest his deeds should be reproved**. 21 **But he that doeth truth cometh to the light, that his deeds may be made manifest, that they are wrought in God**.

> John 3:35 **The Father** loveth **the Son**, and hath given all things into his hand. 36 He that believeth on **the Son** hath everlasting life: and he that **believeth not the Son** shall not see life; but **the wrath of God abideth on him**.

Christians take note: Bruce Metzger (often quoted by Meherally) was a major adviser for many of the modern corrupt translations of the Bible. He did not believe that the Bible has been preserved through time by God. In fact, he really didn't believe the Bible at all. Muslim teachers love his work, because it makes it much easier for them to deceive people about the deity of Christ so as to recruit them into Islam.

9.3 Did God the Father say that Jesus is God?

> **Question No.18 [from a Christian to Islamic teacher Meherally.]** While declaring Christ's superiority to the Angels, in the Epistle to the Hebrews, God said to Jesus: 1. Thou art My Son, Today I have begotten Thee. 1:5 2. Let all the Angels worship you. 1:6 3. Sit on My right hand, until I make thine enemies thy footstool. 1:13 How can you deny these "Words of God"?

Beware! Islamic deception follows:

Answer No.18
1. Before I answer your question, please tell me who was the author of this letter (Epistle) to the Hebrews from which you have submitted the above "Words of God"? Before one places his/her confidence in the quoted texts and builds up the faith, it is equitable and fair to first identify the authorship of the letter. 2. Have you noticed that the name of the author, which is invariably mentioned in the title (heading) of every Epistle, is conspicuously missing in the Hebrews. To know the reason why, please read the followings: 3. The King James Version is supposed to be the most conservative biblical version. The editors of K.J.V. (New Revised and Updated 6th, the Hebrew/Greek Key Study, Red Letter Edition), in their introduction to the Epistle to the Hebrews, write: "The author of the Book of Hebrews is unknown. Martin Luther suggested that Apollos was the author...Tertullian said that Hebrews was a

letter of Barnabas...Adolf Harnack and J. Rendel Harris speculated that it was written by Priscilla (or Prisca). William Ramsey suggested that it was done by Philip. However, the traditional position is that the Apostle Paul wrote Hebrews...Eusebius believed that Paul wrote it, but Origen was not positive of Pauline authorship." 4. The traditional position that "Apostle Paul wrote Hebrews" is seriously undermined by the fact that the Epistle to Hebrews does not begin with his personal name. For your information, each and every other Epistle of Paul begins with his personal name. The Hebrews begin with God's name. Further, Paul had specified that his letters will bear his signature. 5. The Epistle to the Hebrews is not listed in the 6th century list of the manuscripts called Codex Claromon. This leads to the suspicion that it could have been written at a later date. 6. The critics who have studied the text of Hebrews suggest, it is not likely the work of Paul. It was written much later to prove the superiority of God's Son (Jesus) over God's Prophets (Abraham and others). In other words, the document was created by a pseudo author to prove the superiority of Christianity over Judaism. 7. All the three quoted passages from the Hebrews are in fact the direct quotes from Psalms. (Psalms 2:7; 97:7; 110:1). To say that the Psalmist had written these Songs "about Jesus" and not "about characters from their history" needs hard evidence, which is not to be found in the Psalms. Lack of such evidences have lead the bible critics to question: Were the prophecies of the Old Testament fulfilled by the history, or, the history was written to fulfil the prophecies? (May I add, specially when the authorship is questioned, not by the outsiders, but the insiders! KJV).

Muslims claim to believe the Bible. Why then does Meherally constantly and hypocrit-ically question the authorship of the Bible? Let me state very clearly that I do **not** believe the Quran. Why? Because it is very obvious that the whole Quran is of questionable authorship. It is said that Muhammad would have a fit and start foaming at the face, and during this fit would begin reciting words that were written down by other people. How do we know that they actually wrote down what Muhammad said? How do we know they even heard him correctly? Was he not foaming at the face? Is it not safe to assume that that foam was coming out of his mouth? Muhammad could neither read nor write, so he couldn't even check to make sure that what was written was what he had said. After Muhammad died, there came into existence many different versions of the various surah that now make up the Quran. Which ones were genuine? The contradictions of these various versions were making Islam look silly. So, some Muslim leaders that happened to be in power at the time picked out the surahs they wanted to be considered genuine, and burned the rest. How do we know that they did not pick wrong? Perhaps they chose the counterfeits and burned the originals. One thing for certain, the supposed Bible quotations found in the Quran are different from all known ancient Bible manuscripts—and there are thousands of ancient Bible manuscripts that support the genuineness of the Textus Receptus Greek New Testament from which the King James Bible is translated. The Jews and Christians don't agree. Yet they both use the same Hebrew Old Testament to this day. How can that be if both Jews and Christians corrupted the Bible. How could two groups who do not cooperate with each other corrupt the Bible in exactly the same way? There is not one single copy of the Bible that agrees with the phony Bible quotations found in the Quran. So the whole Quran is obviously a fraud written to deceive the ignorant.

Now, what about the book of Hebrews? Obviously it is such a powerful refutation of Islam that Meherally realizes that he cannot answer it. His only recourse is to try to discredit the book. To do this he lists the doubting and blasphemy of other unbelievers like himself, mere sinful men who do not care what the truth is because they hate what the Bible teaches. Why do they hate what the Bible teaches? Because the Bible exposes their evil deeds and their wickedness before a righteous and holy God.

> John 3:19 And this is the condemnation, that light is come into the world, and **men loved darkness rather than light, because their deeds were evil**. 20 For every one that doeth evil hateth the light, neither cometh to the light, lest his deeds should be reproved. 21 But he that doeth truth cometh to the light, that his deeds may be made manifest, that they are wrought in God.

So you can realize why Meherally so hates and fears this book of Hebrews, note how Hebrews begins:

> KJV Hebrews 1:1 **God**, who at sundry times and in divers manners spake in time past unto the fathers by the prophets, 2 Hath in these last days spoken unto us by **his Son**, whom he hath appointed heir of all things, by whom also he made the worlds; 3 Who being the brightness of his glory, and the express image of his person, and upholding all things by the word of his power, when he had **by himself purged our sins**, sat down on the right hand of the Majesty on high; 4 Being made so much better than the angels, as he hath by inheritance obtained a more excellent name than they. 5 For unto which of the angels said he at any time, **Thou art my Son, this day have I begotten thee**? And again, **I will be to him a Father, and he shall be to me a Son**? 6 And again, when he bringeth in the firstbegotten into the world, he saith, And **let all the angels of God worship him**. 7 And of the angels he saith, Who maketh his angels spirits, and his ministers a flame of fire. 8 **But unto the Son he saith, Thy throne, O God**, is for ever

and ever: a sceptre of righteousness is the sceptre of thy kingdom. 9 Thou hast loved righteousness, and hated iniquity; therefore God, even thy God, hath anointed thee with the oil of gladness above thy fellows. 10 **And, Thou, Lord**, in the beginning hast laid the foundation of the earth; and the heavens are the works of thine hands: 11 They shall perish; but thou remainest; and they all shall wax old as doth a garment; 12 And as a vesture shalt thou fold them up, and they shall be changed: but thou art the same, and thy years shall not fail. 13 But to which of the angels said he at any time, Sit on my right hand, until I make thine enemies thy footstool? 14 Are they not all ministering spirits, sent forth to minister for them who shall be heirs of salvation?

Note in verse 8 that **God the Father calls Jesus "God," and in verse 10 God the Father calls Jesus "Lord."**

Now, who is the author of Hebrews? God.

> 2 Peter 1:21 For the prophecy came not in old time by the will of man: but **holy men of God spake as they were moved by the Holy Ghost**.

> 2 Timothy 3:16 **All scripture is given by inspiration of God**, and is profitable for doctrine, for reproof, for correction, for instruction in righteousness: 17 That the man of God may be perfect, throughly furnished unto all good works.

As Meherally admits, the traditional position held by all Bible-believing Christians is that Paul penned the words of the book of Hebrews. But God is the author—the words in the book of Hebrews are inspired of the one and only true God—they are God's words.

> **Beware! Islamic deception follows:**
>
> HOT TIP:
> Al-Hamdulillah (Praise be to "the God"), you yourself have indirectly admitted, by submitting the above three quotations that there is only ONE who is: 1. The Eter-

142

nal 2. The Worthy of Prayers 3. The Supreme. Your quotes and my submissions: 1. Thou art My Son, Today I have begotten Thee. ^^^^^ Yesterday, the Son did not exist. "The God" alone is "The Eternal". ^^^^^^^^^ 2. Let all the Angels worship you. If you believe, since Angels worshipped Jesus, 'Jesus is Worthy of Prayers' then in the Garden of Gethsemane, Jesus "fell on his face and prayed, saying, 'My Father, if it is possible, let this cup pass from me." (Matthew 26:39). Hence, the Heavenly Father - "The God" is "The Worthy of Prayers" from Jesus, Angels and every one. 3. Sit on My right hand,.... Does not the above sentence clearly demonstrate (manifest) that "The God" who articulated or commanded the above, was sitting on the "Throne" and Jesus was standing and waiting to be told to sit down, next to him? "The God" is "THE SUPREME". Note: All the prophets, including Jesus used to "fall on their ^^^^^ faces" like we Muslims do, while praying. See; Abraham, Genesis 17:3; Job, Job 1:20; Moses and Aaron, Numbers 16:22; Jesus, Mt.26:39.

HOTTER TIP:
Note that Meherally admits that the "Heavenly Father" is "The God." So, Meherally knows in his heart that Allah—who cannot father a son—is not the true God! Allah is impotent, but the true God is omnipotent. Allah is only one person like a mere human, but the true God is three Persons—the Father, the Son, and the Holy Spirit. Take away any of these three Persons and you no longer have the one true God. For the Son to be in submission to, and pray to, the Father subtracts nothing from the Son's Godhead. It is natural for the Son to be in perfect submission to the Father for they are one and the same God. They agree in all things, and desire the same things. Jesus said:

KJV John 14:1 Let not your heart be troubled: **ye believe in God, believe also in me.** 2 In **my Father's** house are many mansions: if it

were not so, I would have told you. I go to prepare a place for you. 3 And if I go and prepare a place for you, I will come again, and receive you unto myself; that where I am, there ye may be also. 4 And whither I go ye know, and the way ye know. 5 Thomas saith unto him, **Lord**, we know not whither thou goest; and how can we know the way? 6 Jesus saith unto him, **I am the way, the truth, and the life: no man cometh unto the Father, but by me.** 7 If ye had known me, ye should have known **my Father** also: and from henceforth ye know him, and have seen him. 8 Philip saith unto him, Lord, shew us **the Father**, and it sufficeth us. 9 **Jesus** saith unto him, Have I been so long time with you, and yet hast thou not known me, Philip? **he that hath seen me hath seen the Father**; and how sayest thou then, Shew us **the Father**? 10 Believest thou not that I am in **the Father**, and **the Father** in me? the words that I speak unto you I speak not of myself: but **the Father** that dwelleth in me, he doeth the works. 11 **Believe me that I am in the Father, and the Father in me: or else believe me for the very works' sake.**

Meherally said, "Yesterday, the Son did not exist. 'The God' alone is 'The Eternal.'" This idea was refuted in depth in section 7.1.1 on page 89, so it will not be repeated here.

Meherally also said, "All the prophets, including Jesus used to 'fall on their faces' like we Muslims do, while praying." It is true that the prophets often fell on their faces while praying, but that is not the only way they prayed.

1 Kings 8:22 And Solomon **stood** before the altar of the **LORD** in the presence of all the congregation of Israel, and spread forth his hands toward heaven: 23 And he said, **LORD God of Israel**, there is no God like thee, in heaven above, or on earth beneath, who keepest covenant and mercy with thy servants that walk before thee with all their heart.

And it is **not** true that they prayed like the Muslims do—their prayers were **not** like salat (see page 17). They did **not** pray toward Mecca. Their prayers were **not** vain repetitions using rosaries, but were spoken from the heart, as talking to God. Jesus admonished:

> Matthew 6:7 But when ye pray, **use not vain repetitions, as the heathen do**: for they think that they shall be heard for their much speaking.

Perhaps the most important difference between the prayers of the prophets before the birth of Islam and the prayers of Muslims is that the prophets did not pray to Allah, but rather to JEHOVAH (translated as LORD in all capital letters in the King James Bible) whereas Muslims pray to Allah. See 1 Kings 8:22 for an example of this. Another example:

> Numbers 11:1 And when the people complained, it displeased the LORD: and the LORD heard it; and his anger was kindled; and the fire of the LORD burnt among them, and consumed them that were in the uttermost parts of the camp. 2 And the people cried unto Moses; and when **Moses prayed unto the LORD**, the fire was quenched.

Muslims are required to pray toward Mecca five times a day. This is called salat, and is supposed to wash away sins. (What if a Muslim sins during the night, then dies on the way to morning salat?) Rakahs (positions of the body during Muslim prayers) are considered very important. In contrast, Christians can pray while walking, driving a vehicle, laying in bed, or sitting at the table. And a born-again believer in Christ doesn't pray to save himself, but because he is thankful that he is already saved forever, and wants to express love and thankfulness to God.

9.4 Is Jesus the Almighty God of Isaiah 9:6?

Question No.19 [from a Muslim to Islamic teacher Akbarally Meherally.]

Below is a question from Brother Muhammad Ali Siddiqui.

Br. Assalamu alaykum Here's a question. According to following verse of Isaiah, Jesus was born and he was "everlasting father". How do u explain this? Wassalam "Unto us a Child is born, unto us a son is given, and the government shall be upon His shoulders. And His name shall be called Wonderful Counselor, Almighty God, the Everlasting Father, the Prince of Peace." Is. 9:6

Beware! Islamic deception follows:

Answer No.19
Jesus was not born according to the above verse of Isaiah. This and several others verses from the Book of Isaiah have been *alluded* to Jesus Christ by the Christian clergy and theologians. Majority of these allusions do not have the authenticated supports. In John's gospel there is a narration about the multitude challenging Jesus by saying; "We have heard out of the Law that the Christ is to remain forever; and how can you say, 'The Son of Man must be lifted up'? Who is this Son of Man?" John 12:34. The theologians imply that the multitude was alluding to the above quoted verse (Isaiah 9:6), while speaking of having heard from the Law. Jesus Christ used to call himself, "Son of Man" (See Matthew 16:13). Disciple Stephen before he was stoned to death called Jesus, the "Son of Man" (Acts 7:55-56). However, Jesus is not the only person in the Bible to be so called. God addressed Ezekiel as the "Son of Man" (Ezekiel 2:1).

Let's start by reading all of Isaiah 9:6-7 so we can see the context which Meherally does not want you to see:

> Isaiah 9: 6 For **unto us a child is born**, unto us a **son** is given: and the government shall be upon his shoulder: and his **name** shall be called **Wonderful, Counsellor, The mighty**

God, The everlasting Father, The Prince of Peace. 7 Of the increase of his government and peace there shall be no end, upon **the throne of David**, and upon his kingdom, to order it, and to establish it with judgment and with justice from henceforth even for ever. The zeal of the LORD of hosts will perform this.

Isaiah 9:6 is yet another verse that shows that the Triune God is not a doctrine new to the New Testament, but is found in the Old Testament also. Meherally says that this verse does not refer to Jesus. But, the fact is, Jesus is the only person in history who fits the description found in Isaiah 9:6-7. These verses point blank contradict Islamic teachings. All Meherally can do here is say that verse 6 doesn't mean what it says, or claim it is mistranslated, and ignore verse 7. As will be seen below, his proof is once again only quotations from a group of insignificant unbelievers like himself—proponents of a false anti-Christ religion.

| Beware! Islamic deception follows: |

Notwithstanding the authentication of the above allusion, here is an answer to your original question; how do you explain Jesus was "the everlasting father"? In the Bible, the term "everlasting" or "forever" is often used as a figurative term and does not necessarily mean in its literal sense, e.g., It says; "and David My servant shall be their prince forever." Ezekiel 37:25. The same goes for the use of the term "Father". It does not necessarily mean; "the Heavenly Father" (God), or the biological. Joseph is called a father to Pharaoh. Genesis 45:8, Abraham is called the father of a multitude of nations. Gen. 17:5, and Job is called the father of the needy. Job 29:16. Again by theologians alluding to Psalms 110; Jesus is a called Priest or a Father of the priesthood, forever. Before some one reads the above quoted Isaiah 9:6 and wants to question;

How do you explain the phrase; "Almighty God", let me clear that issue in advance. "Almighty God" is a deliberate mistranslation of the Hebrew phrase "El-Gibbor" used by Isaiah. The Hebrew phrase for "God Almighty" is "El-Shadday". In the famous Hebrew and Chaldee Dictionary by James Strong the word "gibbowr" or short "gibbor" (1368), is translated as; warrior, tyrant:-champion, chief, X excel, giant, man, mighty (man, one), strong (man), valiant man. The word "shadday" (7706), is translated as, the Almighty:- Almighty. If one was to read the verses preceeding the quoted Isaiah 9:6, the on going subject there is; "at the battle of Midian", and "the booted warrior in the battle tumult". HOT TIP: ^^^^^^^ It is very interesting to read and note; "And whoever shall speak a word against the Son of Man, it shall be forgiven him; but whoever shall speak against the Holy Spirit, it shall not be forgiven him, either in this age or in the age to come." Matthew 12:32. Now please read and also note this; "But the Comforter (Greek, Paraclete), the Holy Spirit, whom the Father will send in my name, *He* will teach you all things, and bring to your remembrance all that I said to you. (John 14:26). If one was to honestly look at the historical records of the Great Religious Teachers, and try to discover *He* "a male salvific figure"; that came after Jesus, taught "all things", spoke of Jesus and his teachings, he would but have to point his finger to the prophet of Islam. The Christian traditions have indeed "confused" this "male salvific figure" with "Spirit", in spite of the fact that the word "Spirit" (Greek, 'pneu'ma'), is of a neutral gender and is *always* referred to by the pronoun "it". Below is a direct quote from the world famous 'The Anchor Bible' published by Doubleday & Company, Inc, Garden City, N.Y. 1970. "Christian tradition has identified this figure (Paraclete) as the Holy Spirit, but scholars like Spitta, De-

145

lafosse, Windisch, Sasse, Bultmann, and Betz have doubted whether this identification is true to the original picture and have suggested that the Paraclete was once an independent salvific figure, later confused with the Holy Spirit." (page 1135). Al-Hamdulillah, what a mighty statement of truth.

Meherally is simply lying. The Hebrew word "gibbor" is an adjective which means "mighty." "El" means God. Thus, El-Gibbor means Mighty God. The translation of this verse in the King James Version of 1611 is correct. God's word is able to correct Meherally, but Meherally has no power whatsoever to correct God's word. There is a verse for those who desire to add words (whether they be from the Quran or any other words) to God's words:

KJV Proverbs 30:6 Add thou not unto his words, lest he reprove thee, and thou be found a liar.

Concerning the identity of the Comforter, this was covered in depth in chapter 3 on page 21, so will not be repeated here, except to say that the obvious fact is that the history of Muhammad and his followers right down to today shows that he is a discomforter, not the Comforter. Have he and his followers brought any comfort to you?

Figure 9.1: *Christians in Maluku, Indonesia who were "comforted" by followers of Muhammad who traveled over 1,000 miles by ship from Java to wage jihad against them with a surprise raid upon their village in 2001. Many of their women were raped, and with the children taken as slaves to another island. And the Muslims of Indonesia are generally considered to be the most moderate of all Muslims. Do all professed Muslims agree with such violence? Of course not, but those that study the Quran and believe what it says do, and they are the devout Muslims. And the Muslims that disagree with such violence greatly fear those devout Muslims who practice jihad violence, and dare not publicly disagree with them, and—with few exceptions—in a war will side with them, even though they know it is wrong. Why? Because they fear for their lives.*

Chapter 10

Deceptive Muslim Answers To Christians' Questions 20–24

10.1   Is Jesus God with us?

> **Question No.20 [from a Christian to Islamic teacher Meherally.]**
>
> **Apostle Matthew while recording the prophecy by Isaiah writes: "Behold, the virgin shall be with child, and shall bear a Son, and they shall call His name Immanuel; which translated means, "God with us." Matthew 1:23. Do you disagree, Jesus - born to virgin Mary, was the God with us?**

> **Beware! Islamic deception follows:**

Answer No.20

1. The text of the original prophecy in the Book of Isaiah reads; "...a virgin will be with child and bear a son, and *she* will call His name Immanuel." Isaiah 7:14 (NASB). In other words, the virgin mother was to call her son "Immanuel", which the virgin Mary did not. The prophecy thus does not apply to Jesus. Note: The K.J.V. has REPLACED the word "she" of the above prophecy with "they". Those who wish to argue KJV is more reliable; please read (2) below. 2. Before the birth of Jesus, an angel of the God told Mary;

> "You shall call His name Jesus," (Matthew 1:21). The question is; If the son of Mary was to be called "Immanuel", why did the angel of God tell Mary to call him Jesus, INSTEAD? Did the angel of God, ERR? OR, to demonstrate that the child to be born to this virgin Mary was NOT "Immanuel" but was "JESUS"?

Let's deal first with Meherally's point numbered one. Meherally claims: "The K.J.V. has REPLACED the word 'she' of the above prophecy with 'they.'" Note that Meherally is powerless against the King James Version of 1611 for it is sharper than any twoedged sword. The only way he can find anything to support his arguments is to resort to one of the modern perverted translations—in this case the NASB. But actually in this case even that does not help him as his whole argument is weak as water. In the King James Bible—which is the only trustworthy translation of the Bible in the English language—neither the pronoun "she" nor the pronoun "they" are found in Isaiah 7:14, so "she" **wasn't** changed to "they" in that verse. In Matthew 1:23 the pronoun "they" would include "she." **In light of Matthew 1:23 it is obvious that both "she" and "they" called His name Immanuel.**

Isaiah 7:14 Therefore the Lord himself shall give you a sign; Behold, a virgin shall conceive, and bear a son, and shall call his name Immanuel.

Matthew 1:23 Behold, a virgin shall be with child, and shall bring forth a son, and they shall call his name Emmanuel, which being interpreted is, God with us.

In his point numbered 2, Meherally says that the virgin Mary did not call Jesus by the name Immanuel. Where is his proof of that? He gives none! Then Meherally says that since Mary's son was named Jesus He could not also be named Immanuel. That is really silly logic. That is like saying that since Meherally is named Akbarally his name could not possibly be Meherally! Meherally asks, "If the son of Mary was to be called 'Immanuel', why did the angel of God tell Mary to call him Jesus, INSTEAD?" The obvious answer is that the virgin-born Son of God wasn't named Jesus **instead** of Immanuel, but was named Jesus **in addition to** Immanuel. Why two names? Immanuel means "God with us," and Jesus means "JEHOVAH saves." Jesus is Jehovah God with us—the only Savior.

Beware! Islamic deception follows:

HOT TIP:
When Judas approached Jesus to kiss him, Jesus said to him; "Judas, are you betraying the Son of Man with a kiss?" Luke 22:48. This is the practical dilemma:- In the above question, you call Jesus; "the God with us." Earlier, you had called Jesus; "the Begotten Son of God." Paul, in 2 Corin. 4:4, calls Jesus; "the Image of God." Jesus calls himself; "the Son of Man." What and whom to believe? There are many who claim Jesus was the Son of God as well as the Son of Man. They who claim "dual" Sonhood for Jesus better admit that only ONE (what Jesus affirmed), was a REALITY and the

---

other a metaphorical term. If they don't, then all I can say is; "O God, forgive them for they do not know what they are saying."

Meherally's reasoning gets sillier and sillier as we approach the end of his document. Meherally, himself, is called **dad** by his children, **husband** by his wife, **employee** by his boss, **teacher** by his students, etc. What and whom do we believe? Why obviously he could possibly be all of those things, and we should at least check the facts before calling those people liars. Meherally is **son of his mother**. Does that stop him for also being **son of his father**? Of course not! So Christ is God with us, the only begotten Son of God, Son of Man, and the image of the invisible God. Jesus is all of that and more, and we can believe in the validity of all those titles.

10.2 Does not Jesus defeating death make Him the Authority?

Question No.21 [from a Christian to Islamic teacher Meherally.]

According to Paul, upon the second coming; "Jesus Christ must reign until he has put all his enemies under his feet. The last enemy that will be abolished is death." (1 Corin. 15:25-26). Does this not prove Jesus Christ will be the Supreme Authority, upon his second coming?

Beware! Islamic deception follows:

Answer No.21
If one was to continue reading further, one would discover; "And when all things are subjected to him, then the Son himself also will be subjected to the one who subjected all things to him, that God may be all in all." (1 Corin. 15:28). This proves that God

alone is the Ultimate Supreme Authority and Jesus Christ, one of His subjects. Furthermore, it will be God that will subject all other things, including the death, to Jesus Christ. HOT TIP: ^^^^^^^^ God said to prophet Isaiah; "I am the first and I am the last, And there is no God besides Me." Isaiah 44:6

The God who is the first and the last in Isaiah 44:6 is the same God who is the first and the last in the book of Revelation:

Revelation 1: 4 John to the seven churches which are in Asia: Grace be unto you, and peace, from him which is, and which was, and which is to come; and from the seven Spirits which are before his throne; 5 And from **Jesus Christ**, who is the faithful witness, and the first begotten of the dead, and the prince of the kings of the earth. Unto him that loved us, **and washed us from our sins in his own blood**, 6 And hath made us kings and priests unto God and **his Father**; to him be glory and dominion for ever and ever. Amen. 7 Behold, he cometh with clouds; and every eye shall see him, and they also which **pierced him**: and all kindreds of the earth shall wail because of him. Even so, Amen. 8 **I am Alpha and Omega, the beginning and the ending, saith the Lord, which is, and which was, and which is to come, the Almighty.** 9 I John, who also am your brother, and companion in tribulation, and in the kingdom and patience of Jesus Christ, was in the isle that is called Patmos, for the word of God, and for the testimony of Jesus Christ. 10 I was in the Spirit on the Lord's day, and heard behind me a great voice, as of a trumpet, 11 Saying, **I am Alpha and Omega, the first and the last**: and, What thou seest, write in a book, and send it unto the seven churches which are in Asia; unto Ephesus, and unto Smyrna, and unto Pergamos, and unto Thyatira, and unto Sardis, and unto Philadelphia, and unto Laodicea. 12 And I turned to see the voice that spake with me. And being turned, I saw seven golden candlesticks; 13 And in the midst of the seven candlesticks one like unto **the Son of man**, clothed with a garment down to the

foot, and girt about the paps with a golden girdle. 14 His head and his hairs were white like wool, as white as snow; and his eyes were as a flame of fire; 15 And his feet like unto fine brass, as if they burned in a furnace; and his voice as the sound of many waters. 16 And he had in his right hand seven stars: and out of his mouth went a sharp twoedged sword: and his countenance was as the sun shineth in his strength. 17 And when I saw him, I fell at his feet as dead. And he laid his right hand upon me, saying unto me, **Fear not; I am the first and the last: 18 I am he that liveth, and was dead; and, behold, I am alive for evermore**, Amen; and have the keys of hell and of death.

HOTTER TIP: Isaiah 44:6: "Thus saith the LORD the King of Israel, and his redeemer the **LORD** of hosts; I am the first, and I am the last; and beside me there is no God." When LORD is in all capitals as in this verse it means "JEHOVAH." JEHOVAH (who is also called Jesus and Immanuel) is the one and only true God. Allah is an impostor.

10.3 Do Muslims really believe in Jesus?

Question No.22 [from a Christian to Islamic teacher Meherally.]

"Jesus said to her (Martha), 'I am the resurrection, and the life; he who believes in me shall live even if he dies, and everyone who lives and believes in me shall never die. Do you believe in this?" (John 11:25/26). I repeat the question to you, do you believe in this?**

Beware! Islamic deception follows:

Answer No.22
Do you know there are two kinds of Resurrections according to the recorded words of Christ Jesus? 'The Resurrection of Life' and 'The Resurrection of Judgment'. "...all who are in the tombs shall hear His

voice, and shall come forth; those who did the good deeds, to a resurrection of life, those who committed the evil deeds to a resurrection of judgment." (John 5:28/29). What exactly is one supposed to do to have 'The Resurrection of Life' according to the words of Christ Jesus? "Truly, truly, I say to you, he who hears my word, and believes Him who sent me, has eternal life, and does not come into judgment, but has passed out of death into life." (John 5:24) I hear the above words of Christ Jesus. I also believe as well as glorify Him, who had sent His Messenger Christ Jesus, to convey the above words? HOT TIP: ^^^^^^^^ "Truly, truly, I say to you, if anyone keeps my word he shall never see death." (John 8:51). "And why do you call me, 'Lord, Lord,' and do not do what I say? (Luke 6:46)

Note that Meherally does not answer the man's question. Instead, he quotes a different verse which he says he believes. So, obviously, Meherally does not believe the verses in question:

> John 11:25 **Jesus** said unto her, **I** am **the resurrection, and the life**: he that believeth in **me**, though he were dead, yet shall he live: 26 And whosoever liveth and **believeth** in **me** shall **never die**. Believest thou this?

The problem that Meherally faces is that if he is going to use verses in the Bible as proof of his beliefs, then he is going to have to accept all of the verses. He cannot pick and choose. Meherally cannot truthfully say he believes the words of Christ if he refuses to believe that Jesus is the resurrection and the life.

Meherally quotes John 5:24 in an effort to prove that we should believe in "God," and not in "Jesus." To Meherally Allah is that God. But Meherally does not give the context. Always read the context. Here it is:

> John 5:22 For **the Father** judgeth no man, but hath committed all judgment unto **the Son**: 23

That all men should honour **the Son**, even as they honour **the Father**. **He that honoureth not the Son honoureth not the Father which hath sent him**. 24 Verily, verily, I say unto you, **He that heareth my word, and believeth on him that sent me, hath everlasting life, and shall not come into condemnation; but is passed from death unto life**. 25 Verily, verily, I say unto you, The hour is coming, and now is, when **the dead shall hear the voice of the Son of God: and they that hear shall live**. 26 For as **the Father** hath life in himself; so hath he given to **the Son** to have life in himself; 27 And hath given him authority to execute judgment also, because he is the Son of man. 28 Marvel not at this: for the hour is coming, in the which all that are in the graves shall hear his voice, 29 And shall come forth; they that have done good, unto the resurrection of life; and they that have done evil, unto the resurrection of damnation. 30 I can of mine own self do nothing: **as I hear, I judge: and my judgment is just**; because I seek not mine own will, but the will of **the Father** which hath sent me. 31 If I bear witness of myself, my witness is not true. 32 There is another that beareth witness of me; and I know that the witness which he witnesseth of me is true. 33 Ye sent unto John, and he bare witness unto the truth. 34 But I receive not testimony from man: but these things I say, that ye might be saved. 35 He was a burning and a shining light: and ye were willing for a season to rejoice in his light. 36 But I have greater witness than that of John: for the works which **the Father** hath given me to finish, the same works that I do, bear witness of me, that **the Father** hath sent me. 37 **And the Father himself, which hath sent me, hath borne witness of me**. Ye have neither heard his voice at any time, nor seen his shape. 38 And ye have not his word abiding in you: for whom he hath sent, him ye believe not. 39 **Search the scriptures; for in them ye think ye have eternal life: and they are they which testify of me. 40 And ye will not come to me, that ye might have life**. 41 I receive not honour from men. 42 But I know you, that ye have not the love of God in you. 43 I am come in **my Father's** name, and ye receive me not: if another shall come in his own name, him ye will receive. **44 How can ye believe, which receive honour one of another, and seek not the honour that cometh from God only?** 45 Do not think that I will accuse you to **the Father**: there is one that accuseth you, even Moses, in whom ye trust. 46 **For had ye believed Moses, ye would have believed me: for he wrote of me. 47 But if ye believe not his writings, how shall ye believe my words?**

Meherally claims to believe in the One that sent Jesus. But notice in verse 23 who sent Jesus: "the **Father**." Not the impotent eunuch, Allah, who cannot have a son and therefore cannot be a father, but God **the Father**. Notice in verse 22 that the Father has committed all judgment unto the Son, that men would honor the Son, even as they honor the Father. Notice in verse 23 that if a person does not honor the Son, he does not honor God the Father either.

10.4 Do Jesus' miracles prove Him to be God?

Question No.23 [from a Christian to Islamic teacher Meherally.]

Jesus Christ; Walked upon a Sea (Mt.14:25), and he raised Lazarus from the Dead (Jn.11:44). Who else can do such extraordinary deeds but God?

Beware! Islamic deception follows:

Answer No.23
If the performance of extraordinary miracles was the litmus test for being a God, then, we may as well have many other Gods from the Bible. The following prophets performed deeds that could even surpass to what Jesus Christ did during his entire ministry. 1. Prophet Joshua commanded the Sun and the Moon to stop for one whole day. Moved a shadow of the sun-dial ten degrees backward. (Joshua 10:13 and 2 Kings 20:10). 2. Prophet Elisha brought back to life a dead son of a Shunammite woman. Resurrected himself. After being dead and buried, he stood up on his feet. Healed a Syrian named Naaman of leprosy. (2 Kings 4:35; 13:21 and 5:14). 3. Prophet Ezekiel made dry bones come together, grow flesh, cover with skin and come to life. (Ezekiel 37:3-10). 4. Prophet Elijah brought back to life a son of a widow. Made a bowl of flour and a jar of oil inexhaustible for many days. (1 Kings 17:22 and 14).

Meherally is partly correct about this. Miracles accompanied the giving of God's word through all of the prophets. The miracles were to establish the fact that the words they spoke and wrote were inspired of God. The miracles did not mean that the prophets were God, but rather that they spoke God's words as moved by the Holy Ghost.

However, since Jesus preformed many miracles, even raising the dead, then it is certain that the words He spoke were indeed of God and therefore infallibly true. Why then does Meherally not believe God's words?

Another closely related question is, Why do Muslims believe the Quran is from God, seeing that, according to the Quran, Muhammad performed no miracles? Here is what the Quran says (shown in three translations):

029.048

YUSUFALI: And thou wast not (able) to recite a Book before this (Book came), nor art thou (able) to transcribe it with thy right hand: In that case, indeed, would the talkers of vanities have doubted.

PICKTHAL: And thou (O Muhammad) wast not a reader of any scripture before it, nor didst thou write it with thy right hand, for then might those have doubted, who follow falsehood.

SHAKIR: And you did not recite before it any book, nor did you transcribe one with your right hand, for then could those who say untrue things have doubted.

029.049

YUSUFALI: Nay, here are Signs self-evident in the hearts of those endowed with knowledge: and none but the unjust reject Our Signs.

PICKTHAL: But it is clear revelations in the hearts of those who have been given knowledge, and none deny Our revelations save wrong-doers.

SHAKIR: Nay! these are clear communications in the breasts of those who are granted knowledge; and none deny Our communications except the unjust.

029.050

YUSUFALI: Ye they say: **"Why are not Signs sent down to him from his Lord?"** Say: "The signs are indeed with Allah: and I am indeed a clear Warner."

PICKTHAL: And they say: **Why are not portents sent down upon him from his Lord?** Say: Portents are with Allah **only**, and **I am but a plain warner**.

SHAKIR: And they say: **Why are not signs sent down upon him from his Lord?** Say: The signs are **only** with Allah, and I am **only** a plain warner.

029.051

YUSUFALI: And **is it not enough for them that we have sent down to thee the Book** which is rehearsed to them? Verily, in it is Mercy and a Reminder to those who believe.

PICKTHAL: **Is it not enough for them that We have sent down unto thee the Scripture** which is read unto them? Lo! herein verily is mercy, and a reminder for folk who believe.

SHAKIR: **Is it not enough for them that We have revealed to you the Book** which is recited to them? Most surely there is mercy in this and a reminder for a people who believe.[1]

Note in verse 50 that people were asking **"Why are not Signs sent down to him from his Lord?"** Clearly, people had noticed that Muhammad was performing no miracles, and this was causing them to doubt that the surahs of the Quran were genuinely inspired of God. Muhammad's response to these doubts was, "I am **only** a plain warner," thus implying that Allah had not given him power to perform miracles. Then to make it crystal clear that Muhammad preformed no miracles, in verse 51 Allah says, "And **is it not enough for them that we have sent down to thee the Book** which is rehearsed to them?" And to answer Allah's question, no, it is not enough—no miracles by Muhammad means the Quran is not true scriptures from God.

I'm aware that there is a hadith that claims that Muhammad split the moon, and a few more hadiths that claim he did other miracles. But if they are true, then the Quran is wrong. These contradictions are more proofs that Islam is a false religion.[2]

| Beware! Islamic deception follows: |

HOT TIP:
Two important questions: 1. Who in reality performed the miracles? The answer is; "...Jesus the Nazarene, a man attested to you by God with miracles and wonders and signs which God performed through him in your midst..." (Acts 2:22). 2. Why were these miracles performed? The answer is; Before raising Lazarus, Jesus said to God; "And I knew that Thou hearest me always; but because of the people standing around I said it, that they may believe that Thou didst send Me." (John 11:42). Do you believe Jesus was sent by "Thou" - the God?

---

[1] http://www.usc.edu/schools/college/crcc/engagement/resources/texts/muslim/quran/029.qmt.html

[2] To study this in more depth, read: http://www.answering-islam.org/Responses/Azmy/mhd_miracles.htm

> If he was sent by the God, then obviously he was not the God that sent him.

Meherally asked, "Who in reality performed the miracles?" Meherally answered his own question correctly: God performed the miracles. But he neglected to say—**"through Jesus."**

Meherally asked, "Why were the miracles performed?" Meherally answered his second question correctly also: **that we might know that Jesus was sent of God.**

Meherally says, "If he was sent by the God, then obviously he was not the God that sent him." Here Meherally draws a wrong conclusion. The reason he draws this wrong conclusion is because he refuses to accept the many Bible verses that show that God is a Trinity. Meherally insists that God is only one person like a mere human or angel. Meherally refuses to accept the fact that God is infinitely higher than humans, being three Persons.

Meherally asked, "Do you believe Jesus was sent by 'Thou' - the God?" We answer, of course we believe that Jesus was sent by God. That is the reason we believe every word that Jesus spoke. Does Meherally believe every word that Jesus spoke? If he does, then he must believe these words which Jesus spoke:

> John 3:16 For **God** so loved the world, that he gave **his only begotten Son**, that whosoever **believeth** in him should **not perish**, but have **everlasting life**. 17 For God sent not his **Son** into the world to condemn the world; but that the world through him might be saved. 18 **He that believeth on him is not condemned: but he that believeth not is condemned already**, because he hath not believed in the name of the **only begotten Son of God**.

Note that Jesus said that to be saved we must believe in the "only begotten Son" of God. According to verse 18, the person that does not believe in the **only begotten Son of God** is **already** condemned to Hell. The unbe-

liever's only hope is to repent and believe on the only begotten Son of God.

Also, it is needful for the reader to see that the context of the verses Meherally quotes for proof texts disprove some of the most basic teachings of Islam. For example, note the verses immediately following Acts 2:22 which was just quoted above by Meherally:

> Acts 2:22 Ye men of Israel, hear these words; **Jesus** of Nazareth, a man approved of God among you by miracles and wonders and signs, which God did by him in the midst of you, as ye yourselves also know: 23 Him, being delivered by the determinate counsel and foreknowledge of God, ye have taken, and by wicked hands have **crucified and slain**: 24 **Whom God hath raised up**, having loosed the pains of death: because it was not possible that he should be holden of it. 25 For David speaketh concerning him, I foresaw the Lord always before my face, for he is on my right hand, that I should not be moved: 26 Therefore did my heart rejoice, and my tongue was glad; moreover also my flesh shall rest in hope: 27 Because thou wilt not leave my soul in hell, neither wilt thou suffer thine **Holy One** to see corruption. 28 Thou hast made known to me the ways of life; thou shalt make me full of joy with thy countenance. 29 Men and brethren, let me freely speak unto you of the patriarch David, that he is both dead and buried, and his sepulchre is with us unto this day. 30 Therefore being a prophet, and knowing that God had sworn with an oath to him, that of the fruit of his loins, according to the flesh, he would raise up Christ to sit on his throne; 31 He seeing this before spake of the **resurrection of Christ**, that his soul was not left in hell, neither his flesh did see corruption. 32 **This Jesus hath God raised up**, whereof we all are witnesses. 33 Therefore **being by the right hand of God exalted**, and having received of **the Father** the promise of the Holy Ghost, he hath shed forth this, which ye now see and hear. 34 For David is not ascended into the heavens: but he saith himself, **The LORD** said unto my **Lord**, Sit thou on my right hand, 35 Until I make thy foes thy footstool. 36 Therefore let all the house of Israel know assuredly, that **God** hath made that same **Je-**

sus, whom ye have **crucified**, both **Lord** and **Christ**.

These verses clearly teach that Jesus was crucified, and buried, and resurrected. Therefore, Islam clearly lies about what the Bible teaches concerning Jesus who is both **Lord** and **Christ**.

10.5 Is Jesus equal with God?

Question No.24 [from a Christian to Islamic teacher Meherally.]

The following verses tell us that Jesus Christ had "equality with God", but he emptied himself and acted as "a bond servant" while upon this earth, which is a thing to be grasped; "...although he (Jesus Christ) existed in the form of God, did not regard equality with God a thing to be grasped, but emptied himself, taking the form of a bond servant, and being made in the likeness of men." Philippians 2:6-7 (NASB). Jesus Christ who was in "the form of God" may have acted as "a bond servant" to avoid heresy, do you grasp that?

| Beware! Islamic deception follows: |

Answer No.24
1. The Greek word used for "form" is 'morphe' (3444) which means; shape, fig, image, appearance. Hence, the phrase simply means, "in the image of God", as it reads in 2 Corinthians 4:4, "...Christ, who is the image of God." 2. One may be tempted to say; "the image of God" is no different from God. I suggest, please read Genesis 1:26 where it says; *man* was made in the image and likeness of God. Man though an image of God is not God, nor the God is man. 3. In the New English Bible the word 'morphe' is translated as

"nature". The text conveys; Jesus had the Divine nature. 4. The very notion of regarding "equality with God" is contrary to the basic fundamental concept of "monotheism". Jesus had to be regarded either as "The God" or "Not God". A few verses after the verses under scrutiny, it reads; "God highly exalted Jesus" after his death. This conclusively proves Jesus was not equal or even "highly exalted" before that date. 5. Here is an interesting statement reproduced from the K.J.V.'s commentary on the verses under scrutiny; "What is to be understood here is that Christ merely relinquished His glory which He had due to the fact that He was deity. Prior to His death, He asked the Father to glorify Him in a position next to God with the glory which He had even before the world was created (John 17:5)." The phrase "a position next to God" clearly tells us Jesus did not have the "equality with God" during his ministry or before or after. 6. You write; Jesus "acted as a bond servant" to avoid heresy. Was the righteous Jesus then also "acting" or intentionally misleading his disciples, when he said; "the Father is greater than I"? (Jn.14:28). The fact that Jesus did act as "a bond servant", because he was "a bond servant". Read Acts 3:13, 3:26, 4:27 NASB.
HOT TIP:
"and you belong to Christ; and Christ belongs to God." 1 Corin. 3:23 If you consider yourself a bond servant of Jesus, so was Jesus a bond servant to God.
Note: The above FAQ is based upon a recently asked question to me by a Christian, on a Christian Discussion Net Group.

The Christian asking question number 24 was obviously a very weak and uninformed Christian. This is seen at once from the fact that he quoted from the New American Standard Bible (NASB) instead of the King James Bible. His weakness and ignorance is seen again in his or her saying, "Jesus Christ who was in 'the form of God' may have acted as 'a bond servant' to avoid heresy." Just exactly what he was trying to prove by this statement is not clear—the statement makes no sense.

The correct reading of that passage of Scripture is as follows:

> Philippians 2:5 Let this mind be in you, which was also in **Christ Jesus**: 6 Who, being in the form of God, thought it not robbery to be **equal with God**: 7 But made himself of no reputation, and took upon him the form of a servant, and was made in the likeness of men: 8 And being found in fashion as **a man**, he humbled himself, and became **obedient unto death, even the death of the cross**. 9 Wherefore God also hath highly exalted him, and given him a name which is above every name: 10 That **at the name of Jesus every knee should bow**, of things in heaven, and things in earth, and things under the earth; 11 And that every tongue should confess that **Jesus Christ is Lord**, to the glory of God **the Father**.

Muhammad's knees will also bow to Jesus. Meherally says, "The very notion of regarding 'equality with God' is contrary to the basic fundamental concept of 'monotheism.'" This is the hangup that Islamic teaching causes people to have. The Islamic god, Allah, is an impotent god with only one person or none at all. He is like a human in having only one person, but he is less than human in that he is impotent—like a castrated man he cannot father children. The one and only true God is omnipotent—He does have a Son—, and is three Persons. For the Son—the second Person of the Godhead—to be in submission to the Father—the first Person of the Godhead—does not mean that Jesus is not God. When a son honors his father does that mean that the father is smarter, or stronger, or wiser than the son? No. It means that the father is in a position of greater authority. The Father is the one God, and Jesus is the one God, and the Holy Spirit is the one God. These three Persons are the one God. Jesus is equal to God because Jesus is God and God is one. But the Person of the Father is in a position of authority over the Person of the Son. Do you, dear reader, have trouble understanding this? God does not require us to understand that which is too high for us to be capable of understanding. God, therefore does not require us to understand Him, but He does require that we believe what He says about Himself!

> Colossians 2:8 **Beware** lest any man spoil you through philosophy and **vain deceit**, after the tradition of men, after the rudiments of the world, and not after **Christ**. 9 **For in him dwelleth all the fulness of the Godhead bodily**.

In the human body of Christ dwells all the fulness of **the Godhead**. Jesus is the "image" of God because the body of Jesus is all we will ever see of the invisible God. That is what Jesus meant when He said, "he that hath seen **me** hath seen **the Father**" (John 14:9).

MUHAMMAD IS INSIGNIFICANT COMPARED TO JESUS

Muhammad	Jesus
Did not exist before his conception.	Existed in eternity past.
Son of a sinful human father.	Only begotten Son of God the Father.
Son of a non-virgin mother.	Son of a virgin mother.
Circumcised at age of 13 years.	Circumcised the 8th day after birth as commanded by God's law.
Performed no miracles.	Performed many miracles.
Lied often and broke promises.	Never lied or broke a promise.
Sinful.	Sinless.
Illiterate.	Literate.
Ordered his critics to be murdered.	Died on the cross for His critics so they could have eternal life.
Forced people to follow.	Persuaded people to follow.
Terrorizes.	Gives peace.
Robbed innocent people.	Gives and makes rich.
Enslaves.	Frees.
Committed adultery and rape.	Morally pure.
Corrupt man.	Sinless Man and Holy God.

Chapter 11

Why is the doctrine of the Trinity so important?

The doctrine of the Trinity is vitally important because the salvation of your soul depends upon God being a Trinity. If God is not the Trinity—one God with three Persons—then God cannot be loving, merciful, and gracious, **and also** holy, righteous, and just. It is precisely at this point that Islamic theology breaks down completely in contradictions and silliness.

Because the true God is loving, merciful, and gracious, He wants to forgive us our sins so as to allow us into Heaven. But because God is holy, righteous and just, He hates sin and He hates sinners and demands that they be punished. A mono-person god such as Allah cannot reconcile these two conflicting aspects of God's attributes. **Allah** must **either** forgive without requiring justice, **or else** require justice without forgiving. Allah—because he, she, or it—is not three Persons—can be **either** just or forgiving, **but not both**.

Perhaps realizing this serious theological problem with mono-person Allah, many Muslim commentators believe that Muhammad taught that **everyone, including Muhammad and all good Muslims,** will have to suffer in Hell for their sins for an unspecified length of time until Allah sees fit to let them out. They base this belief on Surah 19:70–72 of the Quran.

> 019.070
>
> YUSUFALI:
>
> And certainly We know best those who are most worthy of being burned therein.
>
> PICKTHAL: And surely We are Best Aware of those most worthy to be burned therein.
>
> SHAKIR: Again We do certainly know best those who deserve most to be burned therein.
>
> 019.071
>
> YUSUFALI: Not one of you but will pass over it: this is, with thy Lord, a Decree which must be accomplished.
>
> PICKTHAL: There is not one of you but shall approach it. That is a fixed ordinance of thy Lord.
>
> SHAKIR: And there is not one of you but shall come to it; this is an unavoidable decree of your Lord.
>
> 019.072
>
> YUSUFALI: But We shall save those who guarded against evil, and We shall leave the wrong-doers therein, (humbled) to their knees.
>
> PICKTHAL: Then We shall rescue those who kept from evil, and leave the evil-doers crouching there.

SHAKIR: And We will deliver those who guarded (against evil), and We will leave the unjust therein on their knees.

Yusuf Ali makes the following comment concerning the above passage from the Quran:

Three interpretations are possible, (1) The **general** interpretation is that **everyone** must pass through or by or over the Fire. Those who have Taqwa (see n. 26 to ii.2) will be saved by Allah's Mercy, while unrepentant sinners will suffer the torments in ignominy, (2) If we refer the pronoun "you" to those "in obstinate rebellion" in verse 69 above, both leaders and followers in sin, this verse only applies to the wicked, (3) Some refer this verse to the Bridge over **Hell**, the Bridge Sirat, over which all must pass to their final Destiny. **This Bridge is not mentioned in the Qur'an.** (Ali, The Holy Qur'an: Translation and Commentary, footnote 2518.)

Muslim teacher al-Jalalayn interpretes surah 19:71 of the Quran as follows:

There is not one of you but shall come to it, **that is, [but] shall enter Hell.** That is an inevitability [already] decreed by your Lord, [something which] He made inevitable and [which] He decreed; **He will not waive it.**[1]

This is why Muslims are still to this day praying that Allah might have mercy on Muhammad. Has Muhammad suffered in Hell long enough to pay the price for his own sins? Muslims aren't sure, so they keep praying for him.[2]

Some Muslims say that the fire in Hell will be cool for Muslims. But there are no surahs in the Quran which says that, and if it be so then Hell is not actually punishment for sins,

and Allah is still unjust when he forgives a sinner.[3]

The true God, JEHOVAH, because He is three Persons, can be both just and forgiving. And people who believe in the Lord Jesus Christ **will never** go to Hell. Let us now study these facts in detail.

11.1 JEHOVAH is holy and hates wicked people

Leviticus 11:45 For I am the **LORD** that bringeth you up out of the land of Egypt, to be your God: ye shall therefore be holy, for **I am holy.**

Psalms 5:4 For thou art not a God that hath pleasure in wickedness: neither shall evil dwell with thee. 5 The foolish shall not stand in thy sight: **thou hatest all workers of iniquity.**

Psalms 45:6 Thy throne, **O God**, is for ever and ever: the sceptre of thy kingdom is a right sceptre. 7 Thou lovest righteousness, and **hatest wickedness**: therefore God, thy God, hath anointed thee with the oil of gladness above thy fellows.

Psalms 11:5 The **LORD** trieth the righteous: **but the wicked and him that loveth violence his soul hateth.** 6 Upon the wicked he shall rain snares, fire and brimstone, and an horrible tempest: this shall be the portion of their cup.

11.2 JEHOVAH is just and severely punishes sin

Ezekiel 18:4 Behold, all souls are mine; as the soul of the father, so also the soul of the son is mine: **the soul that sinneth, it shall die.**

---

[1]http://altafsir.com/Tafasir.asp?tMadhNo=0&tTafsirNo=74&tSoraNo=19&tAyahNo=71&tDisplay=yes&UserProfile=0

[2]For a long article discussing the implications of Muslims being required to pray for Muhammad, read: http://www.answering-islam.org/authors/shamoun/praying_for_mo.html

[3]For a long article documenting what the Quran and other Islamic writing say about Muslims going to Hell, and the serious contradictions this exposes in the Quran, read: http://www.answering-islam.org/Shamoun/muslims_in_hell.htm#3

Ezekiel 18:20 **The soul that sinneth, it shall die**. The son shall not bear the iniquity of the father, neither shall the father bear the iniquity of the son: the righteousness of the righteous shall be upon him, and the wickedness of the wicked shall be upon him.

Romans 6:23 For **the wages of sin is death**; but the gift of God is eternal life through Jesus Christ our Lord.

Isaiah 45:21 Tell ye, and bring them near; yea, let them take counsel together: who hath declared this from ancient time? who hath told it from that time? have not I the **LORD**? and there is no God else beside me; **a just God and a Saviour**; there is none beside me.

And because God is just, He must carry out the punishment for sin. Justice by definition is the punishment of sinners and only sinners. If God does not punish sinners, then He is not just. And if God is not just, then God is not God. So without exception God does punish sin.

Revelation 20:11 And I saw a great white throne, and him that sat on it, from whose face the earth and the heaven fled away; and there was found no place for them. 12 And I saw the dead, small and great, stand before God; and the books were opened: and another book was opened, which is the book of life: and **the dead were judged out of those things which were written in the books, according to their works**. 13 And the sea gave up the dead which were in it; and death and hell delivered up the dead which were in them: and **they were judged every man according to their works**. 14 And death and hell were cast into the lake of fire. This is the second death. 15 **And whosoever was not found written in the book of life was cast into the lake of fire.**

Revelation 21: 8 ...the **fearful**, and unbelieving, and the abominable, and **murderers**, and whoremongers, and sorcerers, and idolaters, **and all liars, shall have their part in the lake which burneth with fire and brimstone: which is the second death.**

Galatians 6:7 Be not deceived; God is not mocked: for **whatsoever a man soweth, that shall he also reap**. 8 For he that soweth to his flesh shall of the flesh reap corruption; but he that soweth to the Spirit shall of the Spirit reap life everlasting.

2 Peter 2:4 ...**God spared not the angels** that sinned, but cast them down to hell, and delivered them into chains of darkness, to be reserved unto judgment; 5 **And spared not the old world**, but saved Noah the eighth person, a preacher of righteousness, bringing in the flood upon the world of the ungodly; 6 **And turning the cities of Sodom and Gomorrha into ashes** condemned them with an overthrow, making them an ensample unto those that after should live ungodly;

Romans 11:21 ...if **God spared not the natural branches**, take heed lest he also spare not thee.

Romans 8:32 He that **spared not his own Son**, but delivered him up for us all, how shall he not with him also freely give us all things?

Note the last verse. When all our sins were placed upon Jesus, God did not even spare His own Son. That is how just God is. So do not think that God will spare you if you reject His Son. Outside of the Lord Jesus Christ there is no forgiveness of sins. God is absolutely just. Do not test His justice, for if you do you will come to regret that foolish decision for eternity.

11.3 God's mercy and love are reconciled with His justice in Christ

So how does the true God show forgiveness, mercy, and grace to us sinners? It is only possible because the one God is three Persons.

God is a Spirit, and cannot die. So the second person of the Godhead—the Son—came to earth and became a human through the process of the virgin birth, so that **as a**

human with a fleshly body He could die on the cross as our **substitute** for our sins. In other words, in a human body such as we have, Jesus suffered capital punishment for our sins, so that we would not have to be punished for eternity in the Lake of Fire.

> Romans 5:6 For when we were yet without strength, in due time **Christ died for the ungodly**. 7 For scarcely for a righteous man will one die: yet peradventure for a good man some would even dare to die. 8 But **God commendeth his love toward us, in that, while we were yet sinners, Christ died for us**. 9 Much more then, being now justified by his blood, we shall be saved from wrath through him. 10 For if, when we were enemies, **we were reconciled to God by the death of his Son**, much more, being reconciled, we shall be saved by his life. 11 And not only so, but we also joy in God through our Lord Jesus Christ, by whom we have now received the **atonement**. 12 Wherefore, as by one man sin entered into the world, and death by sin; and so death passed upon all men, for that all have sinned: 13 (For until the law sin was in the world: but sin is not imputed when there is no law. 14 Nevertheless death reigned from Adam to Moses, even over them that had not sinned after the similitude of Adam's transgression, who is the figure of him that was to come. 15 But not as the offence, so also is the **free gift**. For if through the offence of one many be dead, much more the grace of God, and the gift by grace, which is by one man, Jesus Christ, hath abounded unto many. 16 And not as it was by one that sinned, so is the gift: for the judgment was by one to condemnation, but the **free gift** is of many offences unto justification. 17 **For if by one man's offence death reigned by one; much more they which receive abundance of grace and of the gift of righteousness shall reign in life by one, Jesus Christ**.) 18 Therefore as by the offence of one judgment came upon all men to condemnation; even so by the righteousness of one the **free gift** came upon all men unto justification of life. 19 For as by one man's disobedience many were made sinners, so **by the obedience of one shall many be made**

> righteous. 20 Moreover the law entered, that the offence might abound. **But where sin abounded, grace did much more abound**: 21 That as sin hath reigned unto death, even so might grace reign through righteousness unto **eternal life** by **Jesus Christ our Lord**.

Note that Jesus Christ died for us ungodly sinners while we were yet His enemies—that is unconditional love. Jesus—the only begotten Son of God—died for our sins to satisfy God's attribute of justice. In Christ hanging on that cross for our sins, we see the holiness, righteousness, and justice of God reconciled with God's love, mercy, and grace.

But even that would not be sufficient without the work of regeneration performed by the third Person in the Godhead—the Holy Spirit.

11.4 The vital work of the Holy Spirit

Even though Jesus died on the cross for the sins of every man, God would still not be just to allow into Heaven an unregenerate sinner whose nature still lusted to do wickedness, for such a person would surely do wickedness again in Heaven, thereby ruining Heaven for everyone else. There will be no sin in the new Heaven—no murder, no rape, no stealing, no lying, no greed, no envy, no disrespect, no hatred, no sin of any kind. So even though Jesus died on the cross for our sins so that every person on earth can be saved, God still will not forgive or save anyone who is not sorry for his sins, and who is unwilling to allow the Holy Spirit to perform the miracle of the new birth upon him so as to give him a new nature.

> John 3:3 Jesus answered and said unto him, Verily, verily, I say unto thee, **Except a man be born again, he cannot see the kingdom of God**. 4 Nicodemus saith unto him, How can a man be born when he is old? can he enter the second time into his mother's womb, and

be born? 5 Jesus answered, Verily, verily, I say unto thee, **Except a man be born of water and of the Spirit, he cannot enter into the kingdom of God.** 6 That which is born of the flesh is flesh; and that which is born of the Spirit is spirit. 7 Marvel not that I said unto thee, **Ye must be born again.** 8 The wind bloweth where it listeth, and thou hearest the sound thereof, but canst not tell whence it cometh, and whither it goeth: so is every one that is born of the Spirit.

The water referred to in John 3:5 is not baptism as some have imagined, but rather is referring to the water in the womb—to be born of water is to be born physically. This is made clear in verse six. The physical birth is not sufficient; a spiritual birth is also necessary to impart to us a new nature. This new birth is the work of the Holy Spirt, and results in a drastic change in a person's life.

2 Corinthians 5:17 **Therefore if any man be in Christ, he is a new creature: old things are passed away; behold, all things are become new.** 18 And all things are of God, who hath reconciled us to himself by Jesus Christ, and hath given to us the ministry of reconciliation; 19 To wit, that **God was in Christ, reconciling the world unto himself**, not imputing their trespasses unto them; and hath committed unto us the word of reconciliation. 20 Now then we are ambassadors for Christ, as though God did beseech you by us: we pray you in Christ's stead, be ye reconciled to God. 21 **For he hath made him to be sin for us, who knew no sin; that we might be made the righteousness of God in him.**

Verse 21 above does not mean the Jesus became a sinner for us, for Jesus never sinned. Rather, Jesus became the sacrifice for our sins. All our sins were placed upon him, and he died in our place so that we can be saved from those sins.

11.5 God the Father must draw us to Himself

Furthermore, because the unbeliever is "dead in trespasses and sins" (Eph. 2:1), he cannot come to God on his own power. The first Person of the Godhead—the Father—must draw him:

John 6:43 **Jesus** therefore answered and said unto them, Murmur not among yourselves. 44 **No man can come to me, except the Father which hath sent me draw him**: and I will raise him up at the last day. 45 It is written in the prophets, And they shall be all taught of God. Every man therefore that hath heard, and hath learned of the Father, cometh unto me. 46 Not that any man hath seen the Father, save he which is of God, he hath seen the Father. 47 Verily, verily, I say unto you, **He that believeth on me hath everlasting life**.

11.6 Conclusion

So we see that the mono-person (or none-person) Allah, being impotent, can be either merciful or just, but not both, and so is unable to forgive our sins and save our souls. But the one and only triune LORD God is omnipotent, and being triune can be **both** merciful **and** just and so is fully able to forgive our sins and save our souls. Trust in Jesus now, and he will forgive you of your sins, and give you everlasting life and eternal salvation now. At the moment you place your faith in Him, Jesus will save you from your sins, and will keep you saved forever.

John 5:24 Verily, verily, I say unto you, He that heareth my word, and **believeth** on him that sent me, **hath everlasting life, and shall not come into condemnation; but is passed from death unto life.**

Romans 8:1 **There is therefore now no condemnation to them which are in Christ Jesus,** who walk not after the flesh, but after the Spirit.

John 10:24 Then came the Jews round about him, and said unto him, How long dost thou make us to doubt? If thou be the Christ, tell us plainly. 25 **Jesus** answered them, I told you, and ye believed not: the works that I do in my Father's name, they bear witness of me. 26 But ye believe not, because ye are not of my sheep, as I said unto you. 27 My sheep hear my voice, and I know them, and they follow me: 28 **And I give unto them eternal life; and they shall never perish, neither shall any man pluck them out of my hand.** 29 My Father, which gave them me, is greater than all; and no man is able to pluck them out of my Father's hand. 30 **I and my Father are one.**

ALLAH AND **JEHOVAH** ARE NOT THE SAME GOD

Allah	JEHOVAH
Only one person like a human or angel.	Three persons.
Impotent—cannot have children.	Omnipotent—has a beloved Son.
Is hatred.	Is love.
Exalts lying.	Exalts truth.
Immoral—justifies murder, slavery, robbery, and rape.	Holy—condemns murder, slavery, robbery, and rape.
Tells people who call upon him to save themselves.	Saves people who call upon His dear Son.
Exalts self-mutilation.	Condemns self-mutilation.
Exalts death.	Exalts life.
Makes people bitter and unhappy.	Makes people satisfied and happy.
Fickle—changed mind to meet Muhammad's lusts.	Immutable—changes for no one.
Racist—hates Jews.	Loves all ethnic groups.

Chapter *12*

Why Allah doesn't have a son

Muslim teachers place great stress upon the idea that God does not have a Son. They think that this is one of the major strengths of Islam. In fact, the Islamic idea that God has no Son is the greatest weakness of Islam, and proves that Islam is a sham. Consider the following:

Gen. 1:1 In the beginning God created the heaven and the earth.

During the sixth day of creation God created humans.

Genesis 1:26 And God said, Let us make man in our image, after our likeness: and let them have dominion over the fish of the sea, and over the fowl of the air, and over the cattle, and over all the earth, and over every creeping thing that creepeth upon the earth. 27 So God created man in his own image, in the image of God created he him; male and female created he them.

Sometime during the six days of creation God also created angels. One of the angels God created was Lucifer, who was created perfect, but fell into sin.

Ezekiel 28:12 Son of man, take up a lamentation upon the king of Tyrus, and say unto him, Thus saith the Lord GOD; Thou sealest up the sum, full of wisdom, and perfect in beauty. 13 **Thou hast been in Eden the garden of God;**

every precious stone was thy covering, the sardius, topaz, and the diamond, the beryl, the onyx, and the jasper, the sapphire, the emerald, and the carbuncle, and gold: the workmanship of thy tabrets and of thy pipes was prepared in thee in the day that **thou wast created**. 14 Thou art the anointed cherub that covereth; and I have set thee so: thou wast upon the holy mountain of God; thou hast walked up and down in the midst of the stones of fire. 15 Thou wast **perfect** in thy ways **from the day that thou wast created, till iniquity was found in thee.** 16 By the multitude of thy merchandise they have filled the midst of thee with violence, and thou hast sinned: therefore I will cast thee as profane out of the mountain of God: and I will destroy thee, **O covering cherub**, from the midst of the stones of fire. 17 **Thine heart was lifted up** because of thy beauty, thou hast **corrupted** thy wisdom by reason of thy brightness: I will cast thee to the ground, I will lay thee before kings, that they may behold thee.

Lucifer's sin was pride—he wanted to be like God.

Isaiah 14:12 How art thou **fallen from heaven, O Lucifer**, son of the morning! how art thou cut down to the ground, which didst weaken the nations! 13 For thou hast said in thine heart, I will ascend into heaven, I will exalt my throne above the stars of God: I will sit also upon the mount of the congregation, in the sides of the north: 14 I will ascend above the heights of the clouds; **I will be like the most High**. 15 Yet thou shalt be brought down to hell, to the sides of the pit.

Lucifer persuaded one third of the angels to follow him in an attempt to dethrone God. Of course he failed and both he and the other angels that followed him were cast out of Heaven to become Satan and his demons.

Revelation 12:1 And there appeared a great wonder in heaven; **a woman** clothed with the sun, and the moon under her feet, and upon her head a crown of twelve stars: 2 And she **being with child** cried, travailing in birth, and pained to be delivered. 3 And there appeared another wonder in heaven; and behold **a great red dragon**, having seven heads and ten horns, and seven crowns upon his heads. 4 **And his tail drew the third part of the stars of heaven, and did cast them to the earth: and the dragon stood before the woman which was ready to be delivered, for to devour her child as soon as it was born. 5 And she brought forth a man child, who was to rule all nations with a rod of iron: and her child was caught up unto God, and to his throne.** 6 And the woman fled into the wilderness, where she hath a place prepared of God, that they should feed her there a thousand two hundred and threescore days. 7 And there was **war in heaven: Michael and his angels fought against the dragon; and the dragon fought and his angels,** 8 And prevailed not; neither was their place found any more in heaven. 9 **And the great dragon was cast out, that old serpent, called the Devil, and Satan, which deceiveth the whole world: he was cast out into the earth, and his angels were cast out with him.** 10 And I heard a loud voice saying in heaven, Now is come salvation, and strength, and the kingdom of our God, and the power of his **Christ**: for **the accuser** of our brethren is cast down, which accused them before our God day and night. 11 And **they overcame him by the blood of the Lamb**, and by the word of their testimony; and they loved not their lives unto the death. 12 Therefore rejoice, ye

heavens, and ye that dwell in them. Woe to the inhabiters of the earth and of the sea! for **the devil** is come down unto you, having great wrath, because he knoweth that he hath but a short time. 13 And when **the dragon** saw that he was cast unto the earth, **he persecuted the woman which brought forth the man child.** 14 And to the woman were given two wings of a great eagle, that she might fly into the wilderness, into her place, where she is nourished for a time, and times, and half a time, from the face of the serpent. 15 And the serpent cast out of his mouth water as a flood after the woman, that he might cause her to be carried away of the flood. 16 And the earth helped the woman, and the earth opened her mouth, and swallowed up the flood which the dragon cast out of his mouth. 17 And **the dragon** was wroth with **the woman**, and went to make war with the remnant of **her seed**, which keep the commandments of God, and have the testimony of **Jesus Christ**.

The woman mentioned in the above verses is the nation of Israel. The man child which she brought forth is the Lord Jesus Christ. The red dragon is the devil. The third part of the stars of Heaven which the devil cast to the earth with his tail are the angels which had followed him in his rebellion against God. Satan hates Israel because she produced the seed of the woman who is predestined to bruise Satan's head.

Genesis 3:14 And the LORD God said unto **the serpent**, Because thou hast done this, thou art **cursed** above all cattle, and above every beast of the field; upon thy belly shalt thou go, and dust shalt thou eat all the days of thy life: 15 And I will put **enmity** between **thee** and **the woman**, and between **thy seed** and **her seed**; it shall **bruise thy head**, and thou shalt **bruise his heel**.

Satan thought he had defeated God when Jesus was crucified—but he had only bruised Christ's heel. When Christ rose from the dead Satan knew "that he hath but a short time" before his head will be bruised by Christ. But Satan is insane, and so is intent on motivating his followers to murder as many of Christ's relatives in the flesh as he can while he can—just to spite Christ.

And so today there is the true God on the one hand, and on the other hand a great impostor, claiming to be God, but in fact being only a fallen angel. Now an important thing to realize about angels is that they are sexless beings.

> Mark 12:18 Then come unto him the Sadducees, which say there is no resurrection; and they asked him, saying, 19 Master, Moses wrote unto us, If a man's brother die, and leave his wife behind him, and leave no children, that his brother should take his wife, and raise up seed unto his brother. 20 Now there were seven brethren: and the first took a wife, and dying left no seed. 21 And the second took her, and died, neither left he any seed: and the third likewise. 22 And the seven had her, and left no seed: last of all the woman died also. 23 In the resurrection therefore, when they shall rise, whose wife shall she be of them? for the seven had her to wife. 24 And Jesus answering said unto them, Do ye not therefore err, because ye know not the scriptures, neither the power of God? 25 **For when they shall rise from the dead, they neither marry, nor are given in marriage; but are as the angels which are in heaven.**

Angels are sexless, and therefore cannot have children. They cannot reproduce, but are, in fact, impotent. Lucifer is an angel, and is therefore sexless. Lucifer cannot have a child, being impotent.

So obviously the Allah of Islam is none other than Lucifer—Satan! Allah is the Devil! It is very important to note here that "Allah" does not mean God as the atheist controlled news media wants us to think, but is the **name** of the Muslim's god. I am very much aware that in some perverted translations of the Bible the word "God" is mis-translated as "Allah," but that does not change the truth. Muslims say, "LA (NO) ILAHA (GOD) ILLA (EXCEPT) ALLAH (ALLAH)." "ILAHA" not "Allah" is the Ara-

bic word for God. Allah is the **name** of the Muslims' god.

Muslims and other anti-Semites hate Israelis because their god, Lucifer—the god of hate and death (also known as Molech, Dagon, Baal, Evolution, and Allah)—motivates them to hate Israelis with his insane, unreasonable hatred.

And Allah hates you too.

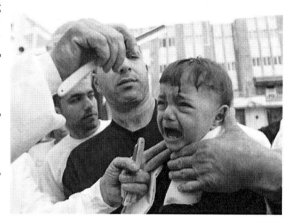

Figure 12.1: *Muslims use razor to slice head of Lebanese boy on Ashoura Day. Only an insane person would think that this is not insane and Satanic. How would you like to have neighbors who do this to their sons each year? Does this indicate that Allah loves children? Is this not sadistic? What kind of God would motivate this behavior toward children?*

Figure 12.2: *This Muslim group, called Laskar Jihad, murdered and raped thousands of Christians in the Maluku islands of Indonesia while Megawati was president. Note that they have masked their faces in shame.*

Chapter 13

Who is the prophet like unto Moses?

There is a very interesting prophesy in the Old Testament, in which JEHOVAH promises to some day raise up a prophet like unto Moses.

> Deuteronomy 18:9 When thou art come into the land which the LORD thy God giveth thee, thou shalt not learn to do after the abominations of those nations. 10 There shall not be found among you any one that maketh his son or his daughter to pass through the fire, or that useth divination, or an observer of times, or an enchanter, or a witch, 11 Or a charmer, or a consulter with familiar spirits, or a wizard, or a necromancer. 12 For all that do these things are an abomination unto the LORD: and because of these abominations the LORD thy God doth drive them out from before thee. 13 Thou shalt be perfect with the LORD thy God. 14 For these nations, which thou shalt possess, hearkened unto observers of times, and unto diviners: but as for thee, the LORD thy God hath not suffered thee so to do. 15 **The LORD thy God will raise up unto thee a Prophet from the midst of thee, of thy brethren, like unto me; unto him ye shall hearken;** 16 According to all that thou desiredst of the LORD thy God in Horeb in the day of the assembly, saying, Let me not hear again the voice of the LORD my God, neither let me see this great fire any more, that I die not. 17 And **the LORD said** unto me, They have well spoken that which they have spoken. 18 **I will raise them up a Prophet from among their brethren, like unto thee, and will put my words in his mouth; and he shall speak unto them all that I shall command him.** 19 And it shall come to pass, that whosoever will not hearken unto my words which he shall speak in my name, I will require it of him. 20 But the prophet, which shall presume to speak a word in my name, which I have not commanded him to speak, or that shall speak in the name of other gods, even that prophet shall die. 21 And if thou say in thine heart, How shall we know the word which the LORD hath not spoken? 22 When a prophet speaketh in the name of the LORD, if the thing follow not, nor come to pass, that is the thing which the LORD hath not spoken, but the prophet hath spoken it presumptuously: thou shalt not be afraid of him.

13.1   What Islam claims

Islam teaches that Muhammad is that Prophet like unto Moses that God said would some day come. Remember the "core issue" (previously discussed in section 3.1 on page 22) is that Muhammad claimed that he got his authority from—and was predicted to come as a prophet in—the Bible. Therefore, if Muhammad can't be found in the Bible, then he is an impostor—a false prophet. So, Muslim scholars have been desperately—but vainly—

searching through the Bible for hundreds of years trying to find him there. Sadly for them, his name is not there, and all the evidence is against them. Muhammad as the Comforter was discussed in chapter 3 on page 21. And Muhammad as the Kidorite was discussed in section 4.5 on page 51. No doubt they were very excited when they found the prophesy concerning the Prophet like unto Moses, but the content and context of the whole Bible dashes their hopes into the ground.

13.2 What the context says

We can easily see that Muhammad could not possibly be the Prophet like unto Moses without even needing to look in the New Testament by simply looking at the content and context of Deuteronomy 18:9–22 (above). Note the following facts:

 ➪ JEHOVAH, not Allah, gave this prophesy. Verse 17 above says, "The LORD said." In the King James Bible, when the word LORD is in all capital letters it refers to JEHOVAH.

 ➪ JEHOVAH, not Allah, would raise up the Prophet. In verse 18, it is the LORD (JEHOVAH) who is speaking and promises to raise up that Prophet.

 ➪ The Prophet would be raised up from among the Israelites. It is easy to see from the context that "thy brethren" (verse 15) is referring to the children of Israel. After all, Moses was an Israelite (read Exodus chapter 2), not an Arab. The Arabs were not his brethren.

 ➪ This Prophet would not consult with familiar spirits. See verses 10–12.

 ➪ The prophecies this Prophet spoke would come to pass. See verses 20–22.

 ➪ The proceeding chapter gives this rule concerning a king: "Neither shall he multiply wives to himself, that his heart turn not away" (Deuteronomy 17:17). It is inconceivable that JEHOVAH would allow this Prophet like unto Moses to have multiple wives plus sex slaves like Muhammad had, that would turn his heart away from God.

13.3 What the New Testament says

But so as to make sure there is no doubt, the New Testament twice tells us point blank that the Prophet like unto Moses is Jesus.

> Acts 3:18 But those things, which **God** before had shewed **by the mouth of all his prophets**, that **Christ should suffer**, he hath so fulfilled. 19 **Repent ye therefore, and be converted, that your sins may be blotted out**, when the times of refreshing shall come from the presence of the Lord; 20 **And he shall send Jesus Christ, which before was preached unto you:** 21 Whom the heaven must receive until the times of restitution of all things, **which God hath spoken by the mouth of all his holy prophets since the world began. 22 For Moses truly said unto the fathers, A prophet shall the Lord your God raise up unto you of your brethren, like unto me; him shall ye hear in all things whatsoever he shall say unto you.** 23 And it shall come to pass, that every soul, which will not hear that prophet, shall be **destroyed** from among the people. 24 Yea, and **all the prophets from Samuel and those that follow after, as many as have spoken, have likewise foretold of these days.** 25 Ye are the children of the prophets, and of the covenant which God made with our fathers, saying unto Abraham, And in thy seed shall all the kindreds of the earth be blessed. 26 Unto you first **God, having raised up his Son Jesus, sent him to bless you, in turning away every one of you from his iniquities.**

Acts 7:37 This is that **Moses**, which said unto the children of Israel, **A prophet shall the Lord your God raise up unto you of your brethren, like unto me; him shall ye hear.** 38 This is he, that was in the church in the wilderness with the angel which spake to him in the mount Sina, and with our fathers: who received the lively oracles to give unto us: 39 To whom our fathers would not obey, but thrust him from them, and in their hearts turned back again into Egypt, 40 Saying unto Aaron, Make us gods to go before us: for as for this Moses, which brought us out of the land of Egypt, we wot not what is become of him. 41 And they made a calf in those days, and offered sacrifice unto the idol, and rejoiced in the works of their own hands. 42 **Then God turned, and gave them up to worship the host of heaven**; as it is written in the book of the prophets, O ye house of Israel, have ye offered to me slain beasts and sacrifices by the space of forty years in the wilderness? 43 Yea, ye took up the tabernacle of Moloch, and the star of your god Remphan, figures which ye made to worship them: and I will carry you away beyond Babylon. 44 Our fathers had the tabernacle of witness in the wilderness, as he had appointed, speaking unto Moses, that he should make it according to the fashion that he had seen. 45 Which also our fathers that came after brought in with Jesus into the possession of the Gentiles, whom God drave out before the face of our fathers, unto the days of David; 46 Who found favour before God, and desired to find a tabernacle for the God of Jacob. 47 But Solomon built him an house. 48 Howbeit the most High dwelleth not in temples made with hands; as saith the prophet, 49 Heaven is my throne, and earth is my footstool: what house will ye build me? saith the Lord: or what is the place of my rest? 50 Hath not my hand made all these things? 51 Ye stiffnecked and uncircumcised in heart and ears, ye do always resist the Holy Ghost: as your fathers did, so do ye. 52 **Which of the prophets have not your fathers persecuted? and they have slain them which shewed before of the coming of the Just One; of whom ye have been now the betrayers and murderers:** 53 Who have received the law by the disposition of angels, and have not kept it. 54 When they heard these things, they were cut to the heart, and they gnashed on him with their teeth. 55 But he, being full of the Holy Ghost, looked up stedfastly into heaven, and saw the glory of God, and **Jesus standing on the right hand of God.** 56 And said, Behold, I see the heavens opened, and the Son of man standing on the right hand of God. 57 Then they cried out with a loud voice, and stopped their ears, and ran upon him with one accord, 58 And cast him out of the city, and stoned him: and the witnesses laid down their clothes at a young man's feet, whose name was Saul. 59 And they stoned Stephen, calling upon God, and saying, Lord Jesus, receive my spirit. 60 And he kneeled down, and cried with a loud voice, **Lord, lay not this sin to their charge.** And when he had said this, he fell asleep.

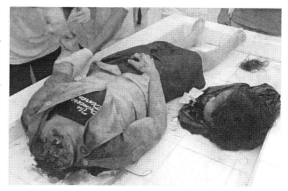

Figure 13.1: *Christian girl beheaded by Muslims. Better martyred than Muslim. Jesus is worth dying for. Every 5 minutes a Christian is murdered for his or her faith—105,000 Christians murdered each year, the vast majority at the hands of Muslims. Muslim reader, in spite of the fact that Muhammad prompts you to hate us, and to try to send us to Hell, we love you with the love of Christ, and want you to go to Heaven. Jesus is the only way.*

Moses	Jesus	Muhammad
An Israeli.	An Israeli.	A Kedarite.
His mother was an Israeli.	His mother was an Israeli.	His mother was an Egyptian.
His mother was a free woman.	His mother was a free woman.	His mother was a bondwoman.
A king mass murdered Israeli first-born boys trying to kill him.	A king mass murdered Israeli first-born boys trying to kill him.	No one tried to kill him when he was a boy.
Was taken to Egypt as a baby to preserve his life.	Was taken to Egypt as a baby to preserve his life.	Never visited Egypt as a baby, if ever.
Went from being royalty to commoner, then back.	Went from being royalty to commoner, then back.	Went from being a commoner to royalty, then back.
Performed miracles.	Performed miracles.	Performed no miracles.
His prophecies were fulfilled.	His prophecies were fulfilled.	His prophecies were not fulfilled.
Fasted 40 days and nights.	Fasted 40 days and nights.	Feasted 30 nights and called it Ramadan.
Delivered people from slavery.	Delivered people from slavery.	Forced people into slavery.
Was willing to die for his people. Ex. 32:31	Died for His people.	Expected his people to die for him.

Chapter *14*

Islam—the largest religion in the world

Many Muslims believe that Islam now being the largest religion in the world proves that it is the true religion from God, but just the opposite is the case. Islam being the largest religion in the world simply proves that it is the widest road to Hell. Jesus said:

> Matthew 7:13 Enter ye in at the strait gate: for **wide is the gate, and broad is the way, that leadeth to destruction**, and **many** there be which go in thereat: 14 Because **strait is the gate, and narrow is the way, which leadeth unto life**, and **few** there be that find it. 15 **Beware of false prophets, which come to you in sheep's clothing, but inwardly they are ravening wolves.**

For hundreds of years the Roman Catholic church had the most followers. That was proof in itself that the Roman Catholic Church was not preaching the truth about how to get to Heaven. Roman Catholicism is idol worship, and teaches salvation by works. The Roman Catholic Church is not now, and never has been, the church that Jesus Christ started in Israel. It is a big mistake to think that Roman Catholicism is Christianity. It is not.

Now Islam has become the widest gate to destruction, also teaching a system of salvation by works. But Islam probably has the lowest standard of works of any false religion. Islam appeals to the depraved nature of man by saying that hatred, robbery, violence, dishonesty, lying, ethnic discrimination, rape, slavery, and murder are righteous as long as it is done in the name of Allah to spread Islam. All those sins are declared by Islam to be good works because Muhammad did them.

14.1 How NOT to get to Heaven

Dear reader, please understand that salvation is not by works, but is a free gift, which through God's great grace, is given to every person who believes in Christ.

> Titus 3:5 **Not by works** of righteousness which we have done, but according to his **mercy** he saved us, by the washing of regeneration, and renewing of the Holy Ghost; 6 Which he shed on us abundantly through Jesus Christ our Saviour; 7 That being **justified by his grace**, we should be made heirs according to the hope of **eternal** life.

> Ephesians 2:8 For **by grace** are ye saved **through faith**; and that not of yourselves: it is the gift of God: 9 **Not of works**, lest any man should boast.

This means that

14.1.1 You can't get to Heaven by keeping the seven sacraments of the Roman Catholic church

Catholic friend, have you perfectly kept the seven sacraments? Most likely not, and what about the Ten Commandments. Definitely not! "For all have sinned and come short of the glory of God" (Romans 3:23).

14.1.2 You can't get to Heaven by keeping the Ten Commandments

The Ten Commandments show the perfect way to live, and should be obeyed by every person on earth. But you don't obey the Ten Commandments, and the penalty for breaking them is to be cast into the Lake of Fire. The purpose of the law has never been to save our souls, but to warn us that we are sinners in need of a Savior.

> Galatians 3:24 Wherefore **the law** was our **schoolmaster** to bring us unto **Christ**, that we might be justified by **faith**.

> 1 Timothy 1:15 This is a faithful saying, and worthy of all acceptation, that **Christ Jesus** came into the world to **save sinners**; of whom I am chief.

14.1.3 You can't get to Heaven by keeping the five pillars of Islam

Muslim friend, have you perfectly kept the five pillars of Islam? Do you pray **five times** a day **every** day? Do you give alms to the poor? If so, do you give enough to actually help, or just enough to put up a good appearance? Do you fast **every** day during Ramadan? Have you made the Hajj pilgrimage to Mecca yet? What if you die before you make the trip? If you are not rich, is it right for you to use up all your children's inheritance on a very expensive trip to Saudi Arabia to kiss a rock? Islam is so cruel on people who ask questions because Islam doesn't have rational answers.

14.2 How TO get to Heaven

The only way to get to Heaven is through faith in the Lord Jesus Christ alone.

> John 14:6 Jesus saith unto him, I am the way, the truth, and the life: no man cometh unto the Father, but by me.

> John 3:16 For God so loved the world, that he gave his only begotten Son, that **whosoever believeth** in him should not perish, but have **everlasting life**.

> Romans 10:9 That if thou shalt confess with thy mouth the Lord Jesus, and shalt believe in thine heart that God hath raised him from the dead, thou shalt be saved. 10 For with the heart man believeth unto righteousness; and with the mouth confession is made unto salvation. 11 For the scripture saith, Whosoever believeth on him shall not be ashamed. 12 For there is no difference between the Jew and the Greek: for the same Lord over all is rich unto all that call upon him. 13 For **whosoever** shall call upon the name of the Lord shall be saved.

Jesus has given me **eternal life** and **the peace that passeth all understanding** which comes from **knowing for sure** that I will go directly to Heaven when I die—completely avoiding Hell. He'll do the same for you provided you trust in Him alone.

Muhammad has already let you know that no matter how good a Muslim you have been you are going to have to go to Hell. What else has Muhammad done for you? Go stick your hand in a fire for a few minutes, and decide how long you are willing to stay in Hell, waiting for Allah to decide to let you out. Then, flee to Jesus to receive eternal salvation now.

Chronological Order of Quranic Surahs

A.1 The Early Meccan Surahs

1 The Clot (96)

2 The Pen (68)

3 The Enshrouded One (73)

4 The Cloaked One (74)

5 The Opening (1)

6 Palm Fibre (111)

7 The Overthrowing (81)

8 The Most High (87)

9 The Night (92)

10 The Dawn (89)

11 The Morning Hours (93)

12 Solace (94)

13 The Declining Day (103)

14 The Coursers (100)

15 Abundance (108)

16 Rivalry in Worldly Increase (102)

17 Small Kindnesses (107)

18 The Disbelievers (109)

19 The Elephant (105)

20 The Daybreak (113)

21 Mankind (114)

22 The Unity (112)

23 The Star (53)

24 He Frowned (80)

25 Power (97)

26 The Sun (91)

27 The Mansions of the Stars (85)

28 The Fig (95)

29 Winter or Qureysh (106)

30 The Calamity (101)

A.2 Middle Meccan Surahs (618-620)

31 The Rising of the Dead (75)

32 The Traducer (104)

33 The Emissaries (77)

34 Oaf (50)

35 The City (90)

36 The Morning Star (86)

37 The Moon (54)

38 Sad (38)

39 The Heights (7)

40 The Jinn (72)

41 Ya Sin (36)

42 Criterion (42)

43 The Angels (35)

44 Mary (19)

45 Ta Ha (20)

46 The Event (56)

47 The Poets (26)

48 The Ant (27)

49 The Story (28)

50 The Children of Israel (17)

51 Jonah (10)

52 Hud (11)

53 Joseph (12)

54 Al-Hijr (15)

55 Cattle (6)

56 Those Who Set the Ranks (37)

57 Luqman (31)

58 Saba (34)

59 The Troops (39)

60 The Believer (40)

A.3 Late Meccan Surahs (620-622)

61 Fusilat (41)

62 Counsel (42)

63 Ornaments of Gold (43)

64 Smoke (44)

65 Crouching (45)

66 The Wind-Curved Sandhills (46)

67 The Winnowing Winds (51)

68 The Overwhelming (88)

69 The Cave (18)

70 The Bee (16)

71 Noah (71)

72 Abraham (14)

73 The Prophets (21)

74 The Believers (23)

75 The Prostration (32)

76 The Mount (52)

77 The Sovereignty (67)

78 The Reality (69)

79 The Ascending Stairways (70)

80 The Tidings (78)

81 Those Who Drag Forth (79)

82 The Cleaving (82)

83 The Sundering (84)

84 The Romans (30)

85 The Spider (29)

86 Defrauding (83)

A.4 The 28 Medina Surahs

87 The Cow (2)

88 Spoils of War (8)

89 The Family of 'Imran (3)

90 The Clans (33)

91 She That is to be Examined (60)

92 The Women (4)

93 The Earthquake (99)

94 Iron (57)

95 Muhammad (47)

96 The Thunder (13)

97 The Beneficent (55)

98 Time or Man (76)

99 Divorce (65)

100 The Clear Proof (98)

101 Exile (59)

102 Light (24)

103 The Pilgrimage (22)

104 The Hypocrites (63)

105 She That Disputeth (58)

106 The Private Apartments (49)

107 Banning (66)

108 Mutual Disillusion (64)

109 The Ranks (61)

110 The Congregation (62)

111 Victory (48)

112 The Table Spread (5)

113 Repentance (9)

114 Succour (110)

Figure A.1: *Muslim woman cuts boy's head with a sword for Ashoura day.*

Figure A.2: *Muslim extremists (above) declaring jihad against Christian extremists. True Christians love Muslims and try to persuade them to believe in Christ who is the only way to Heaven, but true Christians hate Islam because they know that Islam deceives people and sends them to Hell. True Muslims hate both Christianity and Christians, and want to murder Christians to send them to Hell. 1 John 3:15 says, "Whosoever hateth his brother is a murderer: and ye know that no murderer hath eternal life abiding in him."*

CPSIA information can be obtained at www.ICGtesting.com
Printed in the USA
LVOW052233190312

273863LV00001BA/3/P